Suffer the Little Children

Into the Hands of Evil

CHERYLN CADLE

ISBN 978-1-960546-97-5 (paperback)
ISBN 978-1-960546-64-7 (hardcover)
ISBN 978-1-960546-65-4 (digital)

CC Press
cjcadle@hotmail.com
815-549-6439

Printed in the United States of America

SIXTEEN STORIES OF CHILDREN MURDERED BY A PARENT

The most revered gift God has given us is the gift of our children. Out of context, but bone of my bone, flesh of my flesh, I always think of them. We make it our priority to make sure they excel in every area of their lives. We give them the best we have, love them unconditionally, and protect them with our own life if we need to. We would go to extremes to make sure they aren't hurt. Then when their children come along, we are given the privilege to love all over again without the responsibility, but even greater the protective instincts. This is called parenting. No one has to give us a book of instructions (although it would be nice sometimes) or tell us to protect them. This is something we do like it is a reflex.

My precious grandson Dylan was killed in a freaky skateboard accident on May 12, 2021, the darkest day of our family's life. We grieve and miss him so much. At every turn, we think of him and would do anything to have him back. To lose a child/grandchild is the most painful thing someone can go through. So, how is it a person can take the life of their own child? One of the murderers I talk to has also made comments about how much he misses his children. It was during one of the times in my darkest hour that I was praying and felt the calling to write this book and be the voice for children that have been murdered by their parents or guardians. This is the sixteen stories and these sixteen are just a drop in the bucket as to how many children are murdered each year in the United States by their parents or guardians, I can remember as a child always worrying about my mom dying. I loved her so much I could not fathom something happening to her and I would not have her to grow up with. Never even one time did the thought enter my mind that she or my father would take my life. We trust our parents and love them unconditionally.

It has become all too common in many homes that child puts up with abuse or neglect but still does not imagine their parent would kill them. Just in 2020, there were more than 20,000 murders of children 19 and under with 43% of those being murdered by a parent or caregiver. The statistics are mind-blowing as most of us could never even hurt a child let alone kill them. Most of us grandparents would give our own life to save the life of a grandchild. So, what is wrong in our society that we can kill our children? That's a subject for a different book. This book is just to tell the story for those children to have a voice.

As you will notice, a lot of these stories deal with Children and Family services being involved. When I researched the statistics, it was shocking. In 2021, there were more than 400,000 children in Children and Family Services. In 2021, there were a little over 7,000 caseworkers in the United States employed by Children and Family Services. This is a state program, so how is there not more money going toward such an important program? Is there really any program more important? This is the number of children that have been reported. However, there are many more unreported cases.

So, what can we do? We need to appeal to our congressmen and representatives to allot more money in our state budget to help these children. People are very critical when the Department of Children and Family services fails one of these children, but I think these children become just a number. The statistics speak for themselves; there is no way this amount of people can begin to stay on top of this many reported cases. However, when they get into the homes of people and see there is obvious abuse going on, they must remove these children immediately.

The average number of children whose parents have lost their parents' rights is 80,000 per year. There are more than 143,000 children waiting for adoption every year. So, these children are often shuffled from home to home. There is a monetary gain for foster parents, so some of them do it for those reasons, knowing they do not want to give a safe place or love, just for the money. Some of the worse horror stories are about children in foster care.

Each year, about 113,000 children age out of the foster program. These children turn 18 and are no longer able to stay with their foster parents. They have no real education or training, and in many cases, they are just turned out on the street. Research shows these kids still do not have jobs or a dependable way to live at 24 years of age. They live on the street, scrounging meal to meal and there is no one who cares. Often, they get into drugs or alcohol and never really go anywhere. There are exceptions where these kids rise above and get an education and make something good of their lives. One of the stories below is about a foster overcomer, but she still ended up killing her foster daughter.

There has to be someone that will rise up and make these children their cause and help change the system. Until then, things will not get any better. Until then, children will be abused and die at the hands of these people, at the hands of these monsters.

Orphanages are sort of a thing of the past, but if we had orphanages again, these children could be placed in those temporarily for proper placements. In the United States, presently there are no orphanages. In other countries where there are orphanages, they often are really bad stories of neglect. It's very sad how removing them from their abusive homes should ensure their safety. However, a lot of the time, they are being placed into even more abuse.

The sadness grabs me because we are talking about innocent sweet little souls that deserve the same chance as any other child. When they aren't getting the bonding, love, and care in their formative years, the abuse continues sometimes for generations.

It's interesting how many of the child abuse cases reported from foster homes are abused by the mother rather than the father. Again, puzzling since women usually have maternal instincts. Mothers do have the biggest part of the care also.

In the case of the Turpin children who suffered years of abuse from their biological parents are now being removed from their foster parents because of more abuse. There is no doubt some of the children who are foster children may be more challenging when placed in homes. However, it should be no surprise these children would be more challenging to care for on a 24/7 basis, but why does that bring out abuse? This is one of the puzzling things we do not have answers for.

In the case below of Leila Daniels, she was young enough. She had no idea what was happening and I'm sure not understanding why the woman who was her mother figure was mean and abusive to her. Children love and forgive unconditionally, so they do not understand conditional love.

Of the 16 stories in this book, 14 of them I am connected with— the murderer or a family member. Therefore, most of the information I have comes directly from the source. Not that it ensures the truth because coming from the murderer themselves, that is not necessarily the truth.

One of the things I have had to get used to is talking with people who have murdered their family members. To some extent, they are very much alike, having very much the same personality. All of them have someone else to blame for their actions, never wanting to blame themselves.

Many books are written about murderers and I myself like to write about true crime. However, instead of making a celebrity out of the murderer, I'd like to make a celebrity out of the children whose story is in this book. They are the true celebrities as they endured the most heinous of circumstances there could ever be. Maybe, celebrity is the wrong word, but it is to give a voice to those who no longer can be heard—the unsung heroes, the voices that never had a choice to be heard past a very young age. Wouldn't it be interesting if they could give us their voices now? Somehow, I think they would still think highly of their murderer. They would have excuses for them. They would still love them. Endure they must because they are not big or strong enough to stop the person who is killing them. What a betrayal to have the person you love and trust the most take their own hands and kill or torture you until you die. It is the most heart-wrenching way for a child to die. We can only imagine what goes through their minds in the last few moments before they die. We do know one thing: Jesus is with them; they do not die alone.

After my grandson was killed, I joined a couple of groups on Facebook for grieving grandparents. I was horrified to read story after story of people who lost their grandchildren at the hands of an evil person. It is sickening, and I started to feel the pain of each one of these little ones.

So, I am setting out to bring you sixteen stories of children that have been murdered. As awful as it was to lose our Dylan, thank God, we did not lose him to the hands of another. We knew where he was and what happened, and no one else was involved. My heart goes out to those family members who have to endure their loss at the hands of someone else or worse yet wait for weeks or months to find the child's body. In some cases, they never find them.

Sometimes, the best way to get a story told, and get it told truthfully and completely, is by using court documents. So where available, I have court documents for you to read. This is so you can get a total picture of what happened. I find it interesting. I hope you do too.

Join me to be their voice, and please speak up if we ever expect abuse. You never know, you may save a life.

Jesus said, "Let the little children come to me, and do not hinder them, for the Kingdom of Heaven belongs to such as these." Matthew 19:14

CHAPTER 1

Merah, Elias, Nahtahn, Gabriel, and Elaine

THE JONES CHILDREN. (5) children

Murder date: August 29, 2014

Murdered: Merah Gracie, age 8; Elias, age 7; Nahtahn, age 6; Gabriel, age 2; Elaine, age 1

Murdered by their father Timothy Ray Jones Jr. On death row in the Broad River Corrections Institute, Columbia South Carolina.

I was actually writing about their father Timothy Ray Jones Jr. when I decided to write about the children instead of him. He sits on death row today, being sentenced in June of 2019. Timothy and I write back and forth, and I find his mind very interesting. How he thinks is very different than you and I think. What puzzles me is he is gentle, kind, and actually protective of me. It's so hard to believe he was in a normal mind when he killed his children. Timothy says he was in a psychotic episode that fateful night and I'm inclined to believe him. He was going through so much and trying to do it all alone. He was still devastated over his divorce. He told me the worst thing that ever happened to him was his divorce. I find that unreal and don't understand why the worse thing was not the death of his children. At times, he seems to ignore the fact that he killed them, or that they ever existed.

It was August 28, 2014, in Lexington County, South Carolina. A Thursday that seemed to be just a normal day. It started out that way but for the five Jones children, it did not end up that way for this would be the last morning they would ever get up. This would be the last time they would go to school or play with their friends. Who knew? After all, this was their last day.

That weekend was Labor Day, and the children were excited to go see their grandparents for the holiday. They had not seen them for almost nine months because their dad would not speak to his father since Christmas the past year when Timothy became angry with his father for no apparent reason. The grandfather called Tim and apologized even though he had not done anything. He desperately needed to see his grandchildren. Tim and the children lived in West Columbia, South Carolina and they were driving to Mississippi.

There were five of the Jones children. They lived in a rundown trailer and most days, you would not find any food in the fridge or cabinet. Different people said the yard was overgrown and there were toys thrown about. Teachers at the school where the children attended said it was obvious the children did not get fed properly and some of the teachers recalled sharing food they had brought for themselves. The teachers were deeply affected by the children's deaths. My belief is they cared, and they felt a bit of guilt because they did not do more to help them. However, there was nothing more Tim would have let them do. Tim was a proud man who took pride in turning out a good child. He was harsh in discipline and felt to spare the rod was to ruin the child. He did not like that the teachers at school would not physically discipline his children. His beliefs came from an extreme religious conviction he had. He had that belief since coming out of prison before he married and had children of his own. His beliefs were something he pushed onto his wife and demanded they raise a family with these morals and values, so he was hard on his children.

The children's mother did not live in the home any longer. She grew very weary of Tim and the way he treated her and the children, she said. Now, it's unusual that a mother who is afraid of the way her husband is treating her to make the decision to leave home and leave her children with the abuser. However, she said Tim was a good father and she had no means by which to support the children. Therefore, she chose to leave the home and move in with her much younger boyfriend. The boyfriend still lived with his mother, and they lived next door. After the divorce, Amber did get married to him. At the time she left, she was pregnant with their fifth child Louise, who Tim also gained custody of when she was just a very small infant.

Timothy Jones is a brilliant man. He was a software engineer with the Intel corporation. Most people who testified in his trial stated he was one of the smartest individuals they had ever met. Sometimes, there seems to be a fine line between insanity and genius. Tim was not found insane during his trial, but he has told me he is schizophrenic, a mental illness from which his mother suffered and has been hospitalized for years. This story is not about Tim's life, however. I find it worthy to mention his childhood with his mother was extremely abusive mentally and physically. His father who ended up raising him is a very normal and loving father who tried to do everything for Tim to help him turn out normal. Timothy's grandmother also helped in raising Tim. I think the most they can be accused of is spoiling him. I think he was so spoiled he became narcissistic to the point he thought he always had to have his way. He had a grandmother who went way above and beyond in raising a grandchild. So, Tim's only influence was not his mother who left him at a pretty young age though not in his formative years. Yet, schizophrenia is an inherited disease. Although the courts say he is not schizophrenic and I am certainly no professional in knowing the disease, Timothy does say he has the disease and also claims he was in a psychotic episode the evening he murdered his children. He hears voices and those voices tell him horrendous things to do. Usually, when he is in the middle of an episode, he will do whatever the voices tell him to do. He feels that's the only way he can quiet the voices.

Thursday, August 28th, was a hot day in South Carolina. The day was pretty much as normal as any other day. The children went to school hungry and had no lunch with them. Tim Jones Jr. picked up his three oldest children from school at 6:15 p.m. He then drove home and picked up the two younger children. The babysitter said she would feed the children meals when she could because she was afraid they would not be given dinner. Yet, the autopsies showed all of the children died with empty stomachs.

Nahtahn, 6, was seemingly very infatuated with how electricity works. He liked playing with it. Interesting how Tim Jr. made the observation that Nahtahn he thought might have been out to kill him. Would you think your six-year-old son would want to kill you? When asked, he said because Nahtahn wanted to go live with his mother. Nahtahn was Tim's biggest challenge, although, by everyone else, he was considered a very curious but very sweet boy. He was very smart. Therefore, things intrigued him. His teachers found him to be respectful and just an all-around good boy, not a little boy of 6 that had killing on his mind.

Sometime after they had come home from school that Thursday evening, Nahtahn was doing something to four electric sockets in the house. Whatever he did was blow the electric plugs and Tim found out. He became angry with Nahtahn and wanted to know what he had done. Out of fear, Tim said Nahtahn would not tell him what he had done to blow the sockets. After questioning him several times and Nahtahn would not tell him what had happened, he said he "PTd his ass." Meaning, he made him do physical exercises. When asked how long he made him work out, he said about 45 minutes to an hour. He made him do squats and jumping jacks. I'm thinking it was probably more than that. At the end of that hour, Nahtahn still would not tell his dad what he did.

During that time, Nahtahn's mother called as she did each evening at the same time. She testified that Nahtahn was crying so hard he could not talk. She asked him to put his dad on the phone and she asked Tim why he was being so hard on the boy. Tim ended up hanging up on her telling her she always sides with the kids. He said he then smacked Nahtahn on the butt and told him to go to bed, that he didn't want to look at him anymore. My opinion from all I've read is Tim probably hit him, many times. Maybe even shook him hard.

According to Tim Jones, he went to Nahtahn's room about an hour later and he was dead. This set off a string of murders like no other. Tim said he immediately had voices going off in his head

4

saying, "You're fucked now. You need to kill the other four and follow suit." And so, he did. Next, he killed Eli by strangling him with his bare hands, followed by Merah. Then the two little ones he said were too small for him to use his hands, so he strangled them with a belt. First, Gabriel, then Elaine. When asked if they fought back, he replied, "Wouldn't you?" They did fight and Eli was begging him if he would allow him to go with him. When asked what Eli meant, Tim did not know. Merah kept telling her dad she loved him. Old enough to know what he was doing, she realized she was facing death. What a violent and horrible death, again realizing the father she loved so much was snuffing her life away. Their mother testified Nahtahn and Merah wanted to come live with her and that they actually begged to come live with her.

When Timothy's trial was going on, they recorded most of it so you can actually listen to it on YouTube. The authorities promised him they would make sure the children received a good burial. That was supposedly the only thing Tim asked for.

Timothy talks to the authorities when he was arrested like it was just a normal happening when he murdered his children. He said it was nothing unusual for him to PT the children. He said as soon as he realized Nahtahn was dead, the "shit hit the fan" and the voices started going off. As soon as that happened, the voices told him to kill the others. The living room is where he killed the other four children. When he killed the children, he said he just threw those "puppies" in the back of his Cadillac escalade.

There were many things that went off in his head. He sat down and wrote a list of things he was going to do, things such as dissolve, burn, or cut up the bodies. During his interrogation, he would cry one second and then talk normally the next. He had planned to discard the bodies at a sanitation plant. His thought process and the way he talked during his interrogation were definitely not normal, very far from it. You can watch the interrogation on YouTube, it's chilling. It's a brilliant mind gone completely mad.

He went to a Walmart store in West Columbia on 9/3 Wednesday after the murders and purchased a saw, dust mask, goggles, jab saw, muriatic acid, and 5-gallon pale. He then later stopped at a dollar general store and bought trash bags.

5

During this entire time, he had the children in the middle part of his car. From August 28th to Saturday, September 6th, the children were in the car. It was hot and the smell was overwhelming. He covered them with blankets and "a shit load of air fresheners." On September 5th, he was driving down a country road and got stuck. During that time, a police officer came by, and still, the children were in the back. The officer kept going and did not check on what was going on with Tim or if he was up to something,

He would drive home and stay for a couple of days. He drove from South Carolina to Georgia, Alabama, and back. He kept covering more than 700 miles with the children still in between the front and back seats.

While he was home, he still left the kids in the car. He would keep saying he "thinks." He had a hard time remembering everything. I believe due to the trauma. He kept referring to how bad the car smelled. He said they bled out and it was all in the car. He kept saying that Nathan wouldn't tell him why he was playing with the electric sockets because he thinks he was planning on killing him. In Greenville, Alabama, Timothy stopped by another store where he bought ten packages of cigarettes, some zoozoos, and WamWams candy bars. He spent 100.00. That was September 2.

In Camden, Alabama, he went to ATM and pulled out 500.00. He was headed for Las Vegas. This was Saturday evening and he had discarded the children. He put the children in bags and threw them in the grass and weeds. He had driven down a gravel road that was out in the country away from everything, in Alabama, trying to prolong the authorities from finding them. Actually, had he not taken the authorities to where he left them, they may have never found them. Animals had already been eating them.

At some point, he took Nahtahn and tried to cut his leg off but said he just couldn't do it. Two bodies at a time, he took the five children and discarded them. They were all in the same area. It looked just like five bags of garbage he said. Timothy treated them like they were garbage.

He then left for Las Vegas but took a very odd path going there. He went to "Time Warp" and bought "Scooby Snacks." He said when he takes them, it calms the voices in his head. What was interesting is how he kept telling the detectives he needed a doctor. Meaning, a doctor for his mental problems. Timothy did not know what Nahtahn's autopsy was going to show because he said he did not know what killed him. The others he choked. He used his hands with the two older children and a belt around the necks of the little two. Eli asked his dad to take him with him as Timothy killed him. Gabriel said, "I love you, Dad," as Timothy was trying to kill him.

On Wednesday, the school principal and assistant principal drove to Timothy's trailer to check on the children. No one was there, and they commented on what a mess the trailer was. They were concerned even more when there was no answer at the home.

Of course, as Timothy would say, the kids did not go to school on Tuesday. On Thursday, the school called Law Enforcement to do a welfare check on the family. They entered the children into an NCIC, a national crime center.

At 9:00 pm, September 6, 2014, the police were doing a sobriety checkpoint. He was in Mississippi at this time and when they stopped him, they asked him to pull over to the side. They noticed he was acting strange. The police said later when Tim rolled down the window, the car smelled so strongly of death. They knew something was wrong. Remember, the kids were not with him at this point. They called out a detective who said he immediately knew there had been a dead body or bodies in the car. He could smell bleach and there were maggots, blood, children's clothing, and cleaning supplies in the car. They scheduled for a detective to go through the car with a fine toothcomb the next day. Timothy was taken to Smith County Mississippi police station and they called South Carolina. He is arrested for driving under the influence and was also arrested for synthetic cannabinoids. The next day, they questioned him, and he made a full confession. However, his confession was all over the place, sounded very much like a sick man.

That same day, the detective went through the SUV. It was like a horror film. She testified in his trial about what she found. It was beyond something you could ever expect. The smell was horrible, and there was so much blood and body fluid everywhere. The smell mixed with the smell of bleach made it worse. The kids had skin slippage and decomposition was really bad with ten days having passed with them in the car. Also, the temperatures were very hot and when Timothy got out of the car, he did not leave the air-conditioning on.

Timothy led the police to his children. That was awful for the men who found the bodies. They could not readily identify who was who in the bags. It seemed animals had already gotten to the bodies also. He was charged with five counts of murder. However, no matter what, Timothy Jones was responsible for the murder of his beautiful children.

When Timothy Jones killed his children, he knew right from wrong. He had evil in his heart and mind when he killed his children. This is proven by his actions, how he killed his children, how he ran, and how he covered up the murders. He wrote a list of the different ways he could kill his children. He seemed more interested in how he was going to protect himself and how he was going to get out of killing his children. They died at the hands of their father who was in a fit of rage. He did not call for help. They died at the hands of the one they trusted most. A child should be safe in the arms of their father.

Following is a time frame that was written by Fox News. Hopefully, it will be helpful to see the time frame.

Permission given by Lena to use timeline

*A South Carolina man is accused of killing his five children and dumping their bodies along a road in Alabama. Here is a timeline of events leading to the arrest and the discovery of the bodies, according to court records and authorities.

*June 10, 2010: Timothy Ray Jones Jr. begins seeing a therapist after learning his wife was having an affair with a neighbor, according to divorce records. The couple separated, and he ultimately took their five children to live in Mississippi before returning with them to South Carolina. Jones is highly intelligent and a responsible father, a therapist notes.

*October 2013: Jones' divorce is finalized, and he is given primary custody of the children. He's listed as working as an engineer for Intel, making more than $70,000 a year.

*August 29, 2014: Jones picks his children up from school. This is the last day anyone reports seeing him with his children, authorities say.

*August 29-September 3: Jones' ex-wife says he fails to bring his children to stay with her as scheduled. She reports him and the children missing to the Lexington County Sheriff's Department, and the Authorities begin investigating.

*September 6, 2014: Jones is stopped at a drunken driving checkpoint in Mississippi. Deputy spots bleach, blood, and children's clothes in his 2006 Cadillac Escalade. Detectives say they begin to suspect foul play, especially because they could smell death as soon as he rolled down the window.

*September 8, 2014: South Carolina authorities get arrest warrants charging Jones with unlawful conduct toward a child by a legal custodian. State and federal agents travel from South Carolina to Mississippi to speak with Jones.

*September 9, 2014: Jones leads authorities to the children's bodies off a rural Alabama road. Investigators recover five garbage bags filled with human remains, and South Carolina authorities arrange for their return to the state.

*September 10, 2014: Authorities in South Carolina say Jones will face five murder charges when he's returned to the state.

   During the trial, it was very sad how the children had been treated. They suffered from their parent's decision to not stay together, or actually their mother's decision. I write with Tim and he talks about his life as though his children were never in it. End.
   Amber McColley is the children's mother. Timothy met her at work. They lived in a Chicago suburb. They moved to Mississippi to

follow his dad. Amber was going to homeschool their children. Since Timothy killed his children, Amber has had another child with her new husband. Amber testified at his sentencing hearing, asking them to spare his life. His father and grandmother testified also asking for mercy. Timothy did not get on the witness stand and testify for himself. He sat quietly and wiped tears with a handkerchief for a big part of the sentencing hearing. Timothy has told me about each of his children. Somehow, he seems to be able to disassociate. It may be very hard on him, but he does not show that it is. He seems most emotional when it's about himself. However, I know it sounds strange, but I like Timothy.

Timothy was scheduled to die by lethal injection in November of 2019 but was stayed due to the appeal he filed. Timothy told me he is very content in prison. He is on death row, so he is in the cell 23 hours a day. He does not eat or exercise with anyone. He talks to no one. His hope is to win his appeal and receive life instead of death.

His family does not write him or come and see him. They say they cannot handle it any longer. So, I'm not sure, but I might be the only person that has contact with Tim.

Timothy has not heard anything from his appeal just yet. I believe if he does not get the appeal, they schedule his execution to take place within 60 days and 1 week. As much as I hate what he did, and feel he should be put to death, I do not believe I can go to his execution.

Every child is a different flower and all together makes this world a beautiful garden.

–Anonymous

CHAPTER 2

Bella, Cece, and Nico

The Watts Children

August 13, 2018

Three children and their pregnant mother murdered—Bella 4, CeCe 3, Nico an unborn baby boy, and Shanann their mother—by their father Christopher L. Watts.

Since I wrote an entire book on this family, *The Murders of Christopher Watts*, I feel like I have so much information. I spent many hours talking with Christopher between visiting him at the prison and talking to him on the phone, and many letters we wrote back and forth. I've noticed that some of the others I have visited also like to talk about what they did, like a child needing to get something bad off their chests. Christopher has said though that he did not tell anyone in the prison what he did, but there have been several that say he did.

For most of them, their eyes literally turn black when they speak of the murders. This is something that's hard for a lot of people to imagine unless you experience it firsthand. It's something that gives me nightmares because for me it means they would do it again. It is the number one thing that sticks with me. I also have to wonder if their families saw it too but didn't know or understand what they were looking at. It does something to you when you talk with these people. I am forever changed by Christopher Watts. Many people do not believe he committed the murders or that he committed them alone, but I know he did it, and I feel he did it alone. I've seen his face as he told me the things he did. He did not have to go to the trouble of telling me and then writing me about those things if he didn't.

In the case of the Watts family, his little girls thought their dad was their hero and loved and trusted him with everything. By everyone's account, he was a loving and kind father who played with them, cared for their needs, and spent a lot of time with them. He showed a lot of love and cared for his wife also. We have many videos that show Christopher playing with the two girls. With smiles on his face and the girls' face, you can see the love he had for his girls. Something put him in the state of mind to kill his family though.

The day before he killed his family, he told me as they were at a swimming birthday party that he was daydreaming about it.

Bella was four and Cece was 3. Energetic happy little girls, Bella was cautious and a little timid; Cece was brave and liked to explore. They were normal children, seemingly a normal family. What people didn't see is the disturbing mind behind the facade of a killer. The last week before he murdered the children, Christopher told me he thinks the girls could sense what he was planning because their pure and innocent spirits could sense the evil in his spirit and they wouldn't have much to do with him. At the beach, he said they wouldn't play with him. Bella wouldn't even hold his hand.

There were several things that could have contributed to that— his affair that he had been having with a co-worker for almost two months. He told me she was dark and did some very dark things. He said he feels some of that attached itself to him. Maybe it was Shanann's personality; his wife had a strong personality, a very motivated woman who wanted things a certain way and did not hesitate to let Christopher know what she wanted, or the fact that Shanann was pregnant with their third child, a child which Christopher says he did not want. Another baby also made things more difficult for their already mounting debt. He also felt a lot of anger toward Shanann because her and his family were not getting along. His family hated Shanann and did not care who knew it, including her. They did not honor or appreciate her style of parenting and because she was going to do things her way (which she had every right to do), they made things hard on her. They were always running to Christopher with their complaints about his wife. She had finally had enough of their interference and told Christopher they could not spend time with them any longer.

In my opinion, that's something she would not have stuck to. I think once she could let it all settle, she would change her mind. However, there had been a lot of hurt between them. Shanann was an accomplished woman. She knew what she wanted and she had no problem going after what she wanted. She was raising her girls to be confident strong girls too.

Christopher's family seemed jealous that the girls were closer to their maternal grandparents than their paternal grandparents. Christopher's mother had inflicted a lot of hurt from the very beginning of Christopher and Shanann's relationship. To make things even worse, they did not attend their wedding. So, all of this set the stage for his mindset. He said he started planning in his head to kill her and later started planning to kill his girls. He wanted to get rid of the baby because it would interfere with his plan with his mistress. His mistress was pressuring him to leave and divorce his wife and marry her.

Christopher met his family in North Carolina for a vacation. Shannon had gone ahead of him to spend time with family. During that time, there was trouble between Shanann and Christopher's mother. Shanann ended up in tears and had to call her dad to come to get her. Shanann had told his mother that Cece was allergic to nuts.

During that time, there was an open door for Christopher to have his affair. His mistress was a manipulative woman who wanted what Shanann had and was bold enough to go for it.

When Christopher got to North Carolina, he tried to cause Shanann to miscarry by giving her strong doses of Oxycodone. She got very sick and vomited all night, but it did not cause her to lose her baby. He was not treating his family right during this entire week. In his head, all he could think of is how he could rid his life of them.

After a week of vacation, Christopher and Shanann flew back to Colorado. They lived in a beautiful comfortable home. He had a good job, and Shanann was making at least 70k per year. She had a Lexus she drove, provided by her company because her sales were so high. What more could someone want for their life? However, Christopher was not content. He wanted his mistress, and she was playing the game with him. She insisted she wanted them to be together. In his mind, killing his family was the only way. He knew Shanann was not going to make things easy for a divorce. She wanted her family intact and she had every right to fight for it.

After they got home from North Carolina, Shanann had a convention in Arizona for the company she worked for. Christopher stayed home with the girls and Shanann went on her business trip. It was for only three days so she would be home on Sunday, August 12, 2018.

Christopher took this opportunity to plan his evil plot. On the night of August 12, Shanann's plane was supposed to be in around 10:00 p.m., but it was delayed. She ended up not getting home until almost 2:00 a.m.

There are videos on YouTube of her walking up to the door and inside the house. That was the last time anyone saw her. She walked into a death trap and had no idea she was walking into her own death. The man she loved was about to perform the ultimate betrayal. Never would she have thought the kind and gentle man she knew could be capable of destroying his own family.

Once home, she went upstairs and sort of crashed into bed. Christopher was asleep. She cuddled next to him and was rubbing his leg. That woke him and they ended up having sex. Afterward, he went downstairs for a couple of minutes. After that, he went into his 3-year-old daughter's (Cece) bedroom, took her pillow, and smothered her. Next, he went into his 4-year-old's (Bella) bedroom and did the same to her. He then went into his room and slipped into bed. He said an argument between him and Shanann ensued.

According to Christopher, it was like someone took over his body. He said he very quickly choked Shanann to death and she did not fight back. If you are interested in knowing more about this case, I wrote a book *The Murders of Christopher Watts*. I have a very detailed account of everything that happened. I saw him in prison several times and talked to him almost daily on the phone for a year. Also, he wrote me many letters. Those letters are in my book, so you can see his writings and the confessions he told to me.

After he choked Shanann, she relieved herself. He said he knew at that point she was dead. He rolled her in a sheet from their bed. About the time he did that, Bella walked into the room. It really scared him; he was sure he had killed her. She looked like she had really been through something he said. She was crying and asking Christopher what happened to mommy. He told her she was not feeling well. He then dragged her down the steps. He looked and Cece was up now. It was a nightmare for him that he couldn't wake up from. He just found it unreal that she could be up also. What happened here I believe is he just didn't give it enough time and they both woke up. However, he is just so sure they were both dead. He said when he put them to bed that night, he knew it would be the last time he tucked his babies in. He had this planned.

Christopher dragged Shanann into the garage and loaded her body onto the back seat floor of his work truck. He then put both girls in the back seat with their legs just above their mommy. He said they kept asking him about the smell in the truck.

He drove almost an hour to a crude oil field where he worked. He said all the way there, the girls were holding onto each other. Cece was lethargic and not really with it. When he had tried smothering her, I believe it did some sort of brain damage and she was not quite all there.

The oil field where he drove was way out in the middle of nowhere. Nothing else was around. He did not have to worry about anyone seeing him. He just had to get everything done before the guys started showing up for work. He rolled Shanann out of his truck, and the girls sat in the truck while he dug a hole and rolled Shanann in it. As he was putting her in the grave, he noticed she had given birth to their baby boy. Yet he felt nothing for his three children during this time.

He then went to the truck and took the girls and smothered Cece with her blanket. It was easy. She did not fight back, she was already damaged, so it went quickly. He said he took Cece to the first oil battery and put her through the 8" hatch. He says she went in easily.

He then took Bella. She asked him if he was going to do the same thing to her as he did to Cece. He says he did not answer her but put the blanket over her head and smothered her also. It was a violent death. Bella fought back. His timid, soft-spoken baby put up a fight for her life that he did not expect. He said it took much longer for Bella. He put Bella in the next oil battery. Bella did not go in the hatch so easily though. The hole was only 8" in diameter and he had to use his foot to smash her through. He separated them even in death. I asked him why he didn't bury them with their mother. He said he did not want them to wake up again. He also told me he hated Shanann so much that he wanted to put them as far away from her as he could.

He wanted to be free to live his life the way he wanted to without the chains of a family. He had everything most men work for, but to him, divorce was not a choice. He knew there was not enough money for him to walk away. He told me he knew Shanann would keep the girls from him. It makes no sense.

Christopher Watts was a huge pretender, a fake, and a deceiver. He ended up taking a plea deal and confessed to killing his entire family. He was so cowardly that he could not stand trial. He knew he was caught, and he wanted the easiest way out. Christopher Lee Watts received 5 life sentences for the murders of his wife Shanann, daughter Bella, and daughter Cece. He received 40 years for his unborn son. To be served concurrently, his life sentences were without the chance of parole. He did not get a death penalty because his mother-in-law, from the goodness of her heart, did not want to be the reason he would die. Had he only shown that kindness to his family, but then you would have to be a good person to do that.

UPDATE OF CHRISTOPHER WATTS

Regardless of the rumors, Christopher will not be appealing his case. He sent me a message saying everything about his case is the same as it was when I wrote his book. He does not claim anyone helped him kill his family; he did it alone. I don't know how much of the rumors that have gone around are by him at all. I think it's mostly fans that want to say he did not do this alone because some of them do not like Shanann and some of them do not like his mistress. I encourage people to please leave Shanann's family alone and allow these people to grieve for their grandchildren and daughter in peace.

We worry about what a child will become tomorrow, yet we forget that he is someone today.

—Stacia Tauscher

CHAPTER 3

AJ Freund, 5 years old, murdered by mother Joann Cunningham

After looking for AJ Freund for a few days, April 24, 2019 brought the search to a halt when his remains were finally located. The sweet little five-year-old's body was buried in a shallow grave in a wooded area of Illinois. This story hits close to home as AJ lived close to where I live. I've been in contact with his mother Joann since before her sentencing.

So very tragic are the people who have lived in abuse, drugs, and so much dysfunction since they were children themselves. Now his mother, Joann, sits in a prison cell in Lincoln Illinois for thirty years without a chance of parole. Yet in thirty years when Joann gets out of prison, AJ would have been thirty-five years old, the age his mother is now. He would probably be a father, husband, and enjoying life during one of the best chapters in a person's life. He was robbed of a family of his own, choosing his career, or growing old with someone. His life was brutally and viciously taken away from him as if he were an undeserving animal.

Or does the cycle continue after coming up in a dysfunctional home? Would he have followed his parent's footsteps and chosen the only thing he knew—drugs, alcohol, abuse? We will never know, but I think AJ was the one that would have broken the family curse. I believe he would have grown up to escape the brutal and sadistic behavior that dwelt within the home he was being raised in.

AJ was known to be sweet, kind, and caring, always looking out for his little brother, taking the physical abuse at only five years old to spare his younger sibling. Not his mother's favorite, he withstood many beatings and almost constant verbal abuse from the woman he should have been able to run to for refuge. What happens to a small child, almost a baby, when he has no one to run to? How does a child handle that? He's too young to know how to deal with it. However, AJ was smart, and he knew he still loved people regardless of his mother's negative and brutal ways. He clung to life and the positive little boy he was, stayed that way right up until the end. His end was so brutal and he died alone without anyone's hand to hold or comfort from someone who loved him. Dying alone, how must he have felt like he was so alone in the world with no one who loved him? Following is the story of AJ. I feel like I know him. I hope you too will welcome him in your heart and remember his name and him as the little boy who seemed to love and need everyone he met yet protected the woman who brutally killed him. . . because she was his mother.

Here is how the story unfolds. In early June of 2012, the Department of Children and Family (DCFS) had several messages left on their voicemail that Joann Summercamp (Cunningham) was caring for a foster child who was just seven years old and was thought to be neglecting him. She was addicted to prescription drugs and stayed drugged up most of the time. She also has a biological son at that time who was just eleven years old. However, when DCFS did their in-home call, they found nothing to note and closed the complaint.

Just one week later, another call came in from a neighbor alleging there was substance abuse by the mother. The call was handed over to a private agency DCFS had hired to monitor the foster child's care. It's amazing she could have foster children to care for when she had been reported four separate times for neglect of her eleven-year-old biological son.

In June of 2012, the agency that was watching over the foster child found no case, even though Joann was addicted to drugs and was going through a divorce at the time.

In August 2012, Joann had the foster child taken from her because she moved and failed to notify the agency. She just took the foster child and moved into another house in Crystal Lake Illinois with her much older boyfriend, and later, AJ's biological father.

Andrew Freund was an attorney Joann met at the courthouse one day when she was going through her divorce. She looked at him as someone stable who could care for her and her child who she eventually had taken from her and given to her mother to raise. You see, Andrew was really not living any better than Joann. He also was addicted to drugs and alcohol, and this was even better for Joann because she could get her drugs much easier. He was addicted also to cocaine. His name is A.J. Freund Sr.

In October of 2012, DCFS was called by the Crystal Lake Police after they had responded to a domestic dispute between Joann and her live-in boyfriend Andrew. It is totally amazing, but DCFS refuses to investigate.

In December of that year, actually Christmas Eve, Joann's own mother called the DCFS hotline and told them Joann was abusing drugs and her child was being neglected and they were living in squalor. Her mother informed them that she was sure Joann is mentally ill. DCFS said they found nothing credible about the call. The complaint was deemed unfounded.

On October 14, 2013, AJ was born. The beautiful baby boy was born with opiates in his system. So, he fought for his life with his mother's addiction from the very start. When he was just two days old, the hospital called DCFS to inform them of the condition AJ was born into. DCFS investigated this time. They did a drug test on Andrew and Joann and found both of them have heroin in their system. It was certain AJ was being neglected and DCFS removed him from the home.

On October 21, 2013, after the grandmother and mother of Joann petitioned the court for custody of her oldest grandson, stating neglect. The judge ordered permanent custody to go to Joann's mother. Now, Joann had neither of her children.

In November 2013, a court granted temporary custody of AJ to DCFS and they placed him in the home of Joann's cousin. This cousin had no children of her own and quickly fell in love with beautiful AJ loving him as her own.

December 2014. AJ's younger brother was born.

Andrew and Joann were in very bad condition and both of them went into drug rehab in early 2014. They were in drug treatment and were going through random drug screens, counseling, and parenting classes. So, in June 2015, a judge ordered AJ to be given back to Andrew and Joann. Devastated was the cousin that gave him a happy stable home. Joann and Andrew were doing visits and were both compliant with all drug tests.

In September of that year, Andrew was told by the agency that was hired to monitor AJ's foster care to move out of the house because he failed his drug screening. They reported it to DCFS and they logged it as "information only." The failure of this agency boggles one's mind.

February 2016, the judge, in this case, restores guardianship to Andrew Freund and Joann Cunningham (Joann's maiden name).

In April 2016, after 26 scheduled and unannounced visits by DCFS, the case was closed. You have to wonder what they could have seen to turn their eyes toward allowing this child to remain in this home. The social worker notes stated that it was no longer in the best interest of the child for him to remain in a ward of the court and closed the case.

In February 2018, someone called DCFS after they found out that Joann had called the police to her home when she said a roommate was missing and most likely suicidal. This roommate was also a recovering heroin addict. There was never any record of DCFS making a call on Joann after that call.

In March 2018, a social worker at a hospital called DCFS after they had observed some "odd bruising" on A J's face. Because of this bruising, DCFS thought there was neglect after Joann was found in a car asleep by the police. At that time, Joann was completely high on drugs.

DCFS tried unsuccessfully several times to see the children. Finally, she was able to meet with Joann and see the children. Her report stated the boys were clean and she did not find any signs of abuse or neglect.

In May 2018, Joann was confirmed to be in drug treatment. DCFS made a final visit and stated the home was neat, clean, safe, and adequately furnished. The next day, the case was closed finding a lack of credible evidence of abuse or neglect.

In September 2018, the police were called when someone reported there had not been power in the home for weeks. Joann would not allow the police in but one of the officers saw AJ and his little brother and said the children looked happy and healthy. DCFS was contacted by the police, but they declined to make a visit solely on non-working utilities.

In December 2018, Joann called the police to report her former boyfriend stealing her cellphone. The police called DCFS when they noticed a very large bruise on AJ's hip and the house was in total disarray and filthy, with many things needing repair. AJ and Joann both said the bruise was from the family dog pawing at him. However, AJ told a doctor, "Maybe someone hit me with a belt, maybe Mommy didn't mean to hurt me." DCFS allowed the boys to go home with Joann as long as their father was there.

In December 2018, DCFS visits the house unannounced. They found the home clean and in order, much different than the police had described just one day before. Andrew assured them Joann was not on drugs, and there was no corporal punishment used on the boys.

In January 2019, DCFS closes the case once again stating there was no evidence to say there was any form of abuse.

February 2019, police were called to do a well-being check on Joann who was pregnant and had two small children. She had not answered her phone for two days. The police talked to Joann and reported that when they talked to Joann, she said no help was needed. Everything was ok. They did not report anything to DCFS.

The Freund house was sold at a foreclosure auction. However, Andrew and Joann continued to live in the home.

On March 4, 2019, during a search of deleted files on Joann's cell phone, police would later say authorities find a two-minute video from this date that shows a badly injured AJ on a bare, urine-soaked mattress in a crib. The boy is nude except for small bandages on his wrists and circling his hips. Joann, who is recording the video, is heard verbally berating him for wetting the bed. After AJ removes an ice pack from his face, he is seen to have deep red bruising around his eyes and on his neck and clavicle area. AJ had been horribly beaten. Joann had sent the video to Andrew to show him her concerns about their son's behavior, not her behavior toward her five-year-old baby boy, not that she had already beaten him to the point of bad injuries, but his behavior because he had wet the bed.

April 14, 2019, Andrew and Joann forced little 5-year-old AJ to take a twenty-minute cold shower as part of his punishment for lying about soiling his underwear. Andrew suggested this because he wanted Joann to stop punishing AJ so hard. He said to stop with "hard physical beatings" and do a less violent punishment. AJ was put to bed wet, naked, and cold. In speaking with Joann, she told me she just lost it. She was so angry because he wouldn't tell the truth; he was being so defiant. She said she regrets but she just could not stop hitting him. She took the shower head down and tried to spray water directly in his face to make him stop. He was sobbing and that made her angrier. She hit him hard with the shower head and he fell to the bottom of the tub. She screamed for him to get up. She shook him and he looked somewhat lethargic or like he wouldn't look her in the eye. She sent him to bed only to find him a little while later dead in his bed. What a cruel, awful way for a little boy to die.

Later that morning around 3:00 am, Joann googles how to do CPR on a child. If she tried to revive him, it did not work, of course, so she took his body, put it in a tote, carried it to the basement, and left him there. A mother is the person little boys run to for protection, the person who comforts, kisses, and hugs them to help them feel better, the person who forms a loving gentle relationship with their son and helps them to grow and become a man. He was a little boy that in the face of being beaten would still love and seek his mother's approval.

On April 17, Andrew went to Jewel and purchased garbage bags, duct tape, and plastic gloves. Among those items, he had such things as an air freshener and bleach. Andrew put AJ in large plastic garbage bags and put his body in the trunk of his car. He drove AJ to his burial place.

On April 18, 2019, he had a 6:30 a.m. doctor's appointment at the rehabilitation center. When he was finished, around 9:00 am, he called the police to report that AJ was missing.

On April 18, 2019, Andrew called the police to report AJ missing. He told the police that when he got up, he found that Andrew was gone. Andrew and Joann told the police that the last time they saw AJ was around 9:00 pm the night before when they put him to bed. The FBI is called in on the case to help assist in looking for AJ. The police reported the house was in shambles with ripped-up floors, clothes, and garbage everywhere. DCFS investigated and pulled the younger child from the home and put him in foster care under a safety plan. The younger child showed no obvious signs of abuse or neglect.

On April 19, 2019, police felt sure that AJ was not abducted and focused on the family and home. DCFS made public their visits since AJ was born in 2013. I say again, for some reason, she did not like AJ. This is my opinion. Maybe it's because she never bonded with him since she was on drugs when he was born, or whatever the reason, she had no patience, it seems, for him. In talking with her, it was her baby girl that seemed to be her only concern. I never heard any sort of regret or guilt for the way she had treated AJ.

On April 19, 2019, police interviewed AJ's little four-year-old brother. He told the person interviewing him that his mom and dad told him not to talk about AJ. Joann told him that AJ fell down the steps and had a lot of owies. DCFS takes custody of AJ's younger brother.

Joann retains Crystal Lake attorney George Kililis who appears with Joann outside of her home. He tells the public Joann is just worried sick about AJ and she had nothing to do with his disappearance.

On April 20, 2019, Joann and Andrew stopped cooperating with the authorities. The police did take Andrew to the police station for questioning but returned home later in time to attend a vigil with Joann.

On April 21, 2019, Joann was then seven months pregnant, and she answered questions from a Chicago Tribune reporter. In that interview, she described AJ as "Einstein Smart." She also talked about what a great big brother he was. She told the reporter she was staying with a friend because the investigators made her home unable to be lived in and how depressed she was trying to be in the house without her children.

On April 23, 2019, Joann and Andrew appeared in the McHenry County, Illinois court together, for a shelter hearing to determine where the four-year-old son would live. There had been allegations of neglect and abuse

One week after AJ was reported missing, the police and authorities presented the telephone evidence to Andrew and Joann.

April 24, 2019, Andrew confessed his part in the murder and burying of AJ. He took the police to where he had buried AJ. He led them to Com-Ed transmission towers, off Dean Street near Woodstock, Illinois. Police discovered AJ's body wrapped in plastic lying in a shallow grave.

Police removed several items from the house. The evidence they removed was a large tub, several lawn bags, a child's mattress, and a shovel. Animal control removed the family dog, a Boxer named Lucy.

Crowds of neighbors and residents gathered as the news traveled that they had found AJ's body. The people of Woodstock and Crystal Lake wanted to pay their respects. Amongst those people were some that had feared for the children and knew something awful was going on in that house.

Joann Cunningham and Andrew Freund were both charged with five counts of first-degree murder.

On April 29, 2019, Andrew and Joann both agreed to allow DCFS to care for their four-year-old son. Prosecutors attempted to have their parental rights revoked.

On May 10, 2019, Andrew and Joann both pleaded not guilty to all charges against them.

On May 31, 2019, Joann gave birth to a baby girl. She told me she named her Faith. She agreed to keep the child in DCFS custody. However, it was a family member who took the child.

On June 18, 2019, the attorneys are waiting for the result to psychiatric evaluation for both Andrew and Joann.

In August 2019, the judge granted the prosecution's request to see all of AJ's medical records. Then the prosecutors wanted additional records on Joann.

In September 2019, Joann gave a jailhouse interview with CBS. She told the reporter she would kill herself before she would hurt her family.

In November 2019, the city of Crystal Lake was allowed to move forward in having the house that Joann and Andrew lived in to be demolished. This is the house where five-year-old AJ was abused for years and murdered.

December 2019, Joann Cunningham pleaded guilty to the murder of AJ Freund.

March 4, 2020. The house on Dole Avenue, the house of horror where Andrew Freund and Joann Cunningham lived, was demolished. The residents there did not want any reminders of the monsters who lived there. It seemed as though you could hear the screams from the nightmare as the house crumbled, a clear comparison to how AJ lived and lost his life. He was a beautiful little boy who didn't know how to hate but laughed and enjoyed life whenever he had the chance to.

July 17, 2020, Joann Cunningham gave a tearful plea to the judge, stating how much she loved AJ and that she was a good mom to him. No one in the courtroom seemed to have much empathy for the murderer. People cringed when they had to look at pictures or listen to the cellphone recording. At the end of her plea, the judge sentenced her to 35 years in prison, without the chance of parole. Joann will be 72 years old when she is out of prison.

In early August 2020, Joann was transferred to the Logan Correctional Institute in Lincoln, Illinois. This was where I had correspondence with Joann right after her sentencing. Joann was not easy to talk to. She was extremely guarded and not quick to admit any of her mistakes in life. She was a victim, a life victim, having a hard life growing up. She was close to her father, and he died of an overdose of drugs. Her brother committed suicide at an early age. Joann was very close to him, so it was a huge blow for her when he died. She had a bad marriage and bad relationships; she stole, she scammed, and she struggled. Her life was a tragic life, one that no one else wants. Yet I think she could have had potential. Joann is not dumb; she is actually quite smart.

September 18, 2020, Andrew Freund pleaded guilty to aggravated battery of a child, involuntary manslaughter, and concealment of a homicidal death. He was sentenced to 30 years in prison. He will never practice law again, and if he lives to serve out his time, he will be 97 when he gets out of prison.

January 21, 2021, Andrew Freund who was licensed as an attorney in 1984 was disbarred as a result of the convictions.

March 28, 2022, Joann Cunningham files a post-conviction petition pro se, alleging her constitutional rights were violated. She had ineffectual counsel and she was prescribed psychiatric medication while pregnant, leading to hormonal unbalance.

June 1, 2022, McHenry County Judge Robert Wildebrandt dismissed Cunningham's post-conviction petition, saying her constitutional rights were not violated and disputing many of her claims.

During Joann's trial, the prosecuting attorney played some cellphone audio that Joann herself had recorded between her and AJ. There were three in all. You can find this on YouTube under "House of Horrors." They are all very awful, but the third one played is about 15 to 20 minutes in length. I deal with a lot of true crime and I have seen and heard a lot of things, but I have never heard anything as heart-wrenching between a mother and child as this one. It was extremely hard to listen to as Joann berated, yelled, questioned, and cussed at little AJ. You can hear his tiny little voice trying to find the words he thought she wanted to hear. He obviously was afraid of her during the encounter. My opinion was she was poking or pinching him or something during the whole time. It makes you want to cry to hear her call him names and tell him what a liar and horrible little nothing he was. This little boy went through so much abuse, verbal and physical. Actually, I hear it described as torture. After listening to this, you will feel the judge was very kind to her by giving her thirty-five years. Had I been given the decision, I'm afraid I would have given her life. At five years old, life is not even beginning yet. He was sweet, vulnerable, and precious. You can hear it in his voice. I feel God took him to take him from the horrible life he was living.

cvx

During Joann's trial, there were several witnesses for the prosecution. One that stands out to me is the officer who searched the house when they were looking for AJ. They showed several pictures going from room to room. The house was in squalor. The officer testified of the complete filth and the horrible smell throughout the house. He testified how they went through the entire house, going through everything. When they got to AJ's room, there were locks on the outside of his door. When they go into the room, they find there are locks on the outside of the closet. The officer said it shows they probably locked him in the closet. The room I believe had two windows. Both windows had big locks on them, some sort of a device possibly made for that very thing, but they kept the window from being able to go up. I was shocked to see that was the little boy's room. AJ spent by Joann's admission most of his time in that room. What a pitiful existence. One of the officers who was searching the house said as they were going through there, Joann sat out back with a friend, and he testified how she sat with the friend talking and laughing. He said it really had an effect on him.

During the trial, they also played the first interview at the police station Joann gave to the police. She put on lots of drama and tears, acting so worried about AJ and where he could be. She lied so easily and was believable to someone who didn't know she was lying. I couldn't help but wonder as she sat in that courtroom and watched that video how she felt watching herself with the biggest lie of her life. How could anyone ever believe anything she ever says again? Knowing her son was in a plastic bag, laying in a shallow grave, and still acting like she was so upset. At one point, she referred to all the weird people there are out there.

The FBI had more than twenty people come to help look for AJ. They were there for six days working 24/7. They had officers from different police departments who would send officers to help look. In total, about two-hundred people were working 24/7 for six days looking for AJ. All the while, Joann Cunningham and Andrew Freund sat back knowing where AJ was and that he was dead yet said nothing. The State police also came to help and of course, the entire Crystal Lake force.

One of the witnesses was a forensic doctor who was an expert in Forensics. He is the doctor that did the autopsy on AJ. We were not allowed to see the pictures of the autopsy. However, they described the autopsy very well. AJ was beaten with the shower head as the doctor said the marks on AJ matched the shower head. He was struck so hard so many times that it caused his brain to swell to the extent it was crushed. AJ aspirated blood into his lungs, and his brain injury caused his organs to shut down. The blows were extremely painful until he was unconscious. AJ's body was full of bruises. He was beaten from head to toe in a brutal, horrible way. His head had no fewer than a dozen blows, but because of overlapping, there may have been dozens. He had bruises on his face, head, neck, chest, torso, back, stomach, and legs. Joann beat him so badly that in my opinion, she got to some point it didn't matter anymore; there was no turning back. Had she taken him to the hospital, he probably would not have lived. Did AJ walk to his room and crawl up in his bed, or was he carried there? Either way, he lay there and died alone, maybe slipping into unconsciousness first, then dying, maybe just dying. Interesting how through the doctor's testimony, she sat at the table wringing her fingers as if she was very embarrassed.

Right before the sentencing, Joann wanted to say something to the court; she moved to the podium. She talked to the judge about how she loves her children and stated she is a good mom to them. I did not hear her say specifically that she loved or was a good mother to AJ.

I personally cannot understand why there are so many visits from DCFS yet those children were still left to slowly and horribly die in that house under the influence and torture of Joann. AJ was born to someone addicted to heroin and was taken from the home at that time. He was put into a loving and kind home. They pulled him and put him back with his biological mother. When more reports came in and he was being abused again, why was he left to slowly die? In pain . . . alone . . . in fear.

Joann Cunningham appealed her case and lost the appeal. She asked me if I can help her pass laws for women who are having post-partum depression with psychosis. This is her feeling about why she killed A.J. I have to ask if it is possible for a woman to still have post-partum depression when they are 7 months pregnant with another baby.

Children are the hands by which we touch Heaven.

—Henry Ward Beecher

CHAPTER 4

The Vaughn Children

Three children murdered by their father Christopher Vaughn

Abigayle, 12 years old; Cassandra, 11 years old; Blake, 8 years old; mother Kimberley

The Vaughn children were born and lived in Seattle, Washington where their father Christopher Vaughn worked as a forensic computer specialist, and their mother Kimberley was going to school as Forensic Investigator. Seemingly, they had a very good life and family. Being fortunate in most things, they started having money difficulties and Christopher took a job in Oswego, Illinois as a computer analyst.

It was early morning on June 14, 2007, about 5:20 a.m., and the Vaughn family left their home in Oswego, Illinois, a Chicago suburb, traveling to Springfield, Illinois to a water park. The father Christopher woke the children up at about 4:00 a.m. telling them to get up and dressed and that they were going on a day trip to Springfield, Illinois to a water park.

Their trip was to be about four hours long but was cut short after less than an hour on the road when according to Christopher, he pulled off of the I-55 interstate because his wife and mother of the three children Kimberley was feeling sick and felt like she was going to vomit. He pulled just off the interstate, onto a frontage road behind a group of trees. Once there, he pulled out a gun and shot all three of his children in the head, then walked around the passenger side of the vehicle and proceeded to shoot his wife Kimberley in the head, killing all four of his family members. He then shot himself in the leg and wrist then headed toward the main frontage road to flag down help. A man stopped and asked him if he needed help. He told the man he thought his wife had shot him. When the police arrived, they found one of the most gruesome scenes imaginable.

Abigayle who was 12 years old was shot at close range in the chest and then in the face. She was sitting behind the driver's seat and most likely, she was the first one of the children shot. She had a Harry Potter book in her lap and was holding a stuffed animal. Abigayle was a beautiful blonde 12-year-old with a vibrant and fun personality. She was full of life. She loved to dance, read books, and she had just started to notice boys. She was a good student and was wanting to go out for the cheerleading team at school. Her nickname was Abby. She loved her dad and always considered herself a daddy's girl. She was probably awake that frightful morning and for at least a split second must have wondered why her father, a man she trusted with everything in her life, would be shooting her. Horrific is the only word that can describe what happened to her. Had Abigayle lived, she would have been 27 today.

Sitting in the middle seat was Blake who was only 8 years old. Being the youngest in the family, he probably got away with more than the other two. A delightful bouncy boy, he loved sports and playing with his friends. He had started playing soccer and enjoyed the sport, spending a lot of time in his front yard kicking around the ball. As most boys do, he looked up to his father considering him his hero. I believe Blake looked very much like his dad and loved to mimic some of the things he did, always vying for his time.

They believe Blake was the second who was shot. He was holding a blanket when he was shot, possibly asleep. Did he wake up at the sound of the gunshot when his mother was shot? Did he have any idea he was about to be shot? If so, we can only imagine the horror in his little mind.

As human being, how do we look at our child who is part of our flesh and blood, and pull the trigger to take their lives? Blake was also shot in the chest, then the head.

Sitting in the back seat behind her mother was Cassandra, 11 years old. She was a pretty little girl with a personality that would charm anyone. She looked mostly like her mom Kimberley and had a personality a lot like her too. She looked up to her older sister and confided everything in her. She once told a friend she would not live to be an old woman. Was this something she felt or was it just from something she had seen? She loved animals and had a soft heart for people less fortunate than her. She was a good student, her teachers always loved her, and she liked playing volleyball. Unfortunately, she was bullied by some at school. One instance caused her to fall and break her wrist. Kimberley did not appreciate the way the school principal handled things. But Cassandra was resilient. She moved on and the whole incident became a positive thing for her as the other children sided with Cassandra because she was the one hurt. A few years later, when Cassandra would have been a freshman in high school, her maternal grandparents received a birthday card for Cassandra signed by several of her friends. She had not been forgotten. If she could speak today, I have a feeling she would say she has forgiven her dad. Too bad he can't take the responsibility for what he did.

Maybe one of the most emotionless things Christopher did was to take Blake's picture that the police were trying to show him, crumple it up, and throw it. How do we literally "trash" our family?

Christopher was taken to the hospital to have his gunshot wound cared for which was actually more of a superficial wound. About 5 hours after the murders, he was taken to the Lamont police station where he was questioned for 14 hours. During that time, he would not call any of the children by name nor would he look at a picture of any of his family. At one point, he took a picture of his eight-year-old son, crumpled it up, and threw it in the corner of the room, trying once again to discard them. The police officer who was questioning Christopher had more compassion and showed more emotion for Christopher's children than their own father. During the fourteen hours he was being questioned, he sat with his head in his hands or his head on the table the entire time seemingly pretending to not remember what had happened.

I find it interesting that most of the murderers I interview tell the same type of story—they can't remember. I do believe in the case of Christopher Watts that he did not have immediate memory of what had happened, but that was short-term. After the initial trauma, I believe with all my heart, the memory of what they did comes back to them. It is self-induced trauma that may cause temporary memory loss. Plus, the fact right after the incident, they don't want to talk. That changes later though.

I felt compassion watching the two detectives that were at the scene describe the horror of what they saw that day. No matter what experience you had in your job, you are never ready for what that scene offered that day. Talking about it later, it was so horrible and so disturbing that the detectives were still brought to tears talking about it. Aside from how bloody and disgusting the scene was, it was three children, three innocent trusting children.

During the questioning, they found out that Christopher had been going to a dance and strip club where one evening, he tipped one of the women $4600.00. He was continually cheating on his wife, and he seemingly was dealing with some sort of sexual issues. He had an affinity for strippers. One of the women from the dance club testified that he told her he knew his future, referring possibly to killing his family and leaving for Canada. In my research and studies of family annihilators, I have seen a common thread that runs through them all. One of them being they all think they can get away with the crime. Christopher Watts told me he did not even consider they would ever suspect him. Vaughn had made a statement at one point that he was changing and was trying to work on being a family man. It was said that was the reason he planned the water park trip. Personally, I do not feel he ever really planned on going to the water park. The authorities did find out later the trip to the waterpark was not an early morning thought, that it was planned at least a little in advance, maybe the night before, but the children knew when they went to bed the evening before they were planning a trip the next day. That did not work for him. He goes from working on his problems to murdering his family in cold blood. He has told some that his dream was to go to Canada and live in the wilderness. There are things that point to him trying to prepare his life to do this, possibly, why he took his family's life. As with all these sorts of crimes, we have to ask the question "why?"

On November 27, 2012, five years after the murders of his family, a jury of four women and 8 men found him guilty. It did not take them long to see what he had done; it only took them an hour and a half to come back with guilty on all accounts. He was sentenced to four consecutive life sentences. He is spending the rest of his days at a Joliet, Illinois prison.

Just a couple of hours before the funeral, Christopher was arrested for the murders of his family. He asked them why he did not allow him to bury his family. He was told because he had killed them that's why.

Now it seems the family has hired a special investigator that is trying to prove that Christopher did not murder his wife and children. It does not matter how upset Kimberley was about Christopher's lifestyle or how confused she was taking some of the medications she did, I do not believe nor does the evidence the DA presented show she had anything to do with the murders. This unfortunately is another ploy murderers have; to blame their mate. After all, they are dead and cannot testify to the contrary. With Christopher now saying his wife shot him, I feel this is another narcissistic and selfish thing he is doing (This is just my opinion). As far as Abigayle, Cassandra, and Blake, we are their only voice— innocent lives destroyed by their father, a man who seems heartless, a monster. We *will* be their voice! We will help their memories live on and maybe tell their story.

Christopher Vaughn was found guilty on all counts. He is probably one of the coldest and most heartless people you could ever meet. He was sentenced to life without parole. His family does not believe he murdered his family, so they have started digging into some of his claims. He has once again appealed his case. I am told the family has evidence they want to give, again stating Christopher did not kill his family, but it was his wife who shot the children, then turned the gun on himself. A waste of the state's time and money, because of course, he murdered his family.

Children are the living messages we send to a time we will not see.

—John F. Kennedy

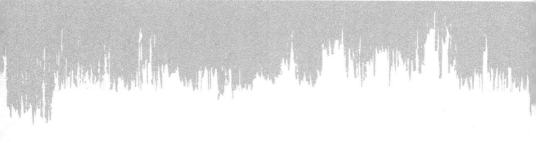

CHAPTER 5

The Coleman Children

Garret 11, Gavin 9, along with mother Sheri 31.

If you are one of the million people who have dug into the Christopher Watts' case, you will find this case intriguing as well. It is so closely similar that it's scary. These two men should compare notes; it's so close to the same. In fact, they can compare notes since they are in the same prison, at the Waupan, Wisconsin Dodge prison.

What is in the hours in the deep darkness of the night that causes these family annihilators to choose this time to murder their family? Do they think it's a time they won't be seen or found out? Does the darkness cover them, or are they part of that darkness? They can hide from the world and do the ugliest deed that could ever be done. However, morning comes and it overtakes the dark, although not the things that are done in the darkness. Yet the light will always reveal what was done in the darkness.

Little boys look up to and trust their fathers. They want to be like them, and if you ask most little boys, they will tell you their dads are their heroes. This question is asked so many times; but how is it a man can put his hands on his children and suck the life out of them?

The story of Christopher Coleman caught my attention when I was writing the Christopher Watts story because they are in the same prison for committing an almost identical crime. They are brother monsters.

Christopher met his future wife when both of them were in the military. Sheri Weiss met Christopher Coleman at a K-9 training seminar at Lackland Air Force Base in San Antonio in May of 1997. Weiss, 21, was an MP in the Air Force Coleman, a Marine, was 22. Christopher and Sheri showed up at his parents' house one day and introduced Sheri to them as a friend he was giving a ride to Chicago. His parents were ministers, and religion and his faith had always been important to him and his brother. It was said the boys even spoke in tongues during some of the church services. Sheri was raised Catholic. Even though she did convert to his religion, his parents never cared much for her. It was said the first time his mother met Sheri, she made a statement she did not really like her.

The next day after, they had been gone from his parents' house for a few hours. He called his dad back and told him they had gotten married, saying they had just gotten caught up in the moment. They dated just a few months before Sheri was pregnant with Garret and that's the reason the two married. Of course, it didn't take his parents long to figure out what had happened. They had Gavin about two years later.

Christopher was hired by televangelist Joyce Meyer to work on her security team. He was promoted quickly and was soon Joyce Meyer's personal bodyguard. It was important to him that he was able to provide very well for his family. Joyce Meyer already knew the family, so it was a good fit for her. Firstly, he was in general security, but when their supervisor quit, they offered Christopher the job as personal security. She paid Christopher $100,000 a year salary, which was double of most people's salary.

Christopher and Sheri bought a home on a beautiful street Robert Drive in Columbia, Illinois, a suburb not far outside of St Louis. Living in a beautiful large two-story home, they were a beautiful family, one friends were envious of. They seemed to have it all. Yet things are never as perfect as they may seem to the outside world.

November is when Christopher said he connected with his girlfriend when she was working as a cocktail waitress at the dog races in St. Petersburg. She testified that he had her flown to Hawaii and Arizona to be with him. In one statement they found on his computer, it said, "November 5th was the day Tara changed my life." He was telling his girlfriend that he was going to divorce Sheri, and probably planned to. However, he started thinking about child support and alimony for Sheri, so it seemed to be better for him to just get rid of them and start a new life, free of any baggage. This seems to be a common thread among these monsters that can take the life of their own children. Why doesn't a father want his children to grow up and experience all the things he experienced, to marry and have their own children, to experience all the things life brings, whether good or bad? Now, do they connect this with anything that would look like God or their religion or belief? What misfires in a brain to even give them the idea to do this? I read someplace that sex between Christopher and Tara was like catnip. That seems like perversion on both parts.

In our society today, it seems like sex has become the foundation for so many crimes. We should be satisfied with what we have and if it just doesn't work, then divorce and do things the right way.

It was in November 2008 that Christopher says his and Sheri's relationship started having problems. People said he shaved his head because he said it made him look tougher, and he had started acting very cocky. He and Sheri did go to some marriage counseling. Christopher traveled a lot, being gone most of the time and even traveling outside of the United States a few times a year. His salary though helped that Sheri did not have to work out of the home and be an at-home mom for her boys, although she did have a small job at their church working a few hours a week. Sheri went to Joyce's son Daniel and told him they were having marital problems. Joyce went to Christopher about it, and she encouraged him to work things out. He told her that Sheri was very controlling and that no matter what he did, she was never happy. He said because of it, they were just not getting along. Joyce asked if he would consider counseling with a pastor they had at the church, and she said Christopher was immediately okay with it. They did in fact go for marriage counseling. Sheri said he would put on a good face for the counselor and then treat her like shit when they got home.

What he left out was he had been involved in an affair with a woman who lived in Florida. She had been best friends with Sheri in high school. Later, Joyce testified she did not know he was having an affair or he most likely would have been fired. Sheri told a friend he had withdrawn from her, was aloof, arrogant, and didn't want sex with her. One night, they did have sex and afterward, he told her not to confuse it with the fact he loved her. Around Christmas time that year is when he asked her for a divorce. She did find out about his girlfriend, but Sheri was not willing to give up on their marriage. She did not want a divorce and she was going to continue to fight for it.

November of 2008, an email came out of the blue to Christopher, Joyce, and her son. It was a nasty threatening email that would have scared anyone. Next year, in January, Christopher received a letter in his mailbox that seemed to be from the same person that had written the mail. It was full of threatening and nasty things. Christopher's neighbor across the street from him was a detective at their local police department so Christopher showed him the letter. He was advised to file a report at the police station. That detective also agreed to install a camera pointed at Christopher's house to catch anyone that may try to cause physical harm to his family. They also patrolled extra at his house for a time, but nothing ever became of it.

During that time, Sheri had told many of her friends that Christopher seemed to have changed. She even confided in one of her good friends that if something happened to her to look at Christopher because he would be the one who would have done it. A little while later, she confided to that friend that around Christmas time, Christopher had asked her for a divorce. She asked her friend to please pray for them. Sheri did not want a divorce; this was on Christopher.

Then in April, another letter threatening the family came again and Christopher took that to the Columbia police department. The letter stated that was his last chance to deny God and his faith publicly and to let it be known that basically, Joyce Meyer was a fraud.

On the morning of May 5, 2009, Christopher set his alarm on his phone to wake up at 5:30 am. According to him, he got up and went to the bathroom, got dressed, and went to the gym for a workout. On his way there, he called Sheri to wake her and said she did not answer. A little while later, he tried again, but still no answer. Then he texted her and asked if everything was ok. He texted again at 6:25 and told her it was time to get the boys up for school. He told her he had 5 more minutes of cardio and he would be on his way back home. He said he was becoming very concerned so he called his neighbor and asked if he would go check on Sheri and the boys, that he would be home in a few minutes he was on his way.

The detective called for another police officer, and they went to the house. They knocked and there was no answer. They found there was a basement window open, so they climbed in. As they were headed up to the bedrooms, they saw writing on the walls in red paint and knew something was very wrong.

When they arrived upstairs and went into the master bedroom, they found Sheri lying in her bed dead. They ran to the boy's room to find both of them dead also. All three of the bodies had ligature marks on their necks which were made by a rope or a cord indicating they had all been strangled. This immediately hit the detective that this could very well be Christopher who did this.

Christopher arrived home just before 7:00 a.m. He was not allowed to go inside. A police officer stood with him. By this time, several officers and detectives had arrived on the scene. The detective and policeman who had initially arrived at the house left and, on their way out, they told Christopher his family was dead. They took Christopher down to the police station for questioning.

When asked, Christopher claimed they were all alive when he had left them that morning. Yet, physical evidence showed they had been dead since about 3 a.m. Physical evidence does not lie. However, Christopher stuck to his story. When asked about their relationship, he said they had been going to marriage counseling and were doing much better, that their main problems were just communication.

The police and others who worked the crime scene said that even though there was no blood, it was the creepiest crime scene they had ever worked.

As the detectives gathered evidence in the case, they found evidence on Christopher's computer that he is actually the person who sent the threatening letters. One of the officers found a receipt in the house for a can of red spray paint. When traced back, it came from a nearby hardware store.

Below is a court document on this case. People of the state of Illinois vs Christopher Coleman.

Below, the document you will read is Christopher's appeal of his verdict. I find it interesting to read these. It allows you to look inside the court and trial somewhat. You will see in this document the judge was very fair, and so were the State lawyers. Christopher represented himself, and of course, that did not help his case, but I feel all concerned was patient with him.

Appellate Court of Illinois, Fifth District

The PEOPLE of the State of Illinois Plaintiff-Appellee, v. Christopher COLEMAN, Defendant -Appellant

Decided: December 31, 2014

1. Defendant Christopher Coleman was charged by information with three counts of first-degree murder after his wife Sheri, and his two sons, Garett and Gavin, were found dead in the family home. After a jury trial in the circuit court of Monroe County, the defendant was convicted and sentenced to three concurrent life sentences. Defendant now appeals raising the following seven issues: (1) whether the trial court erred in allowing the State to present the testimony of an expert linguist on the issue of authorship attribution, (2) whether the trial court erred in allowing the State to present sexually explicit photography and videos of defendant and Tara Lintz, the woman with whom defendant was having an affair, (3) whether the trial court erred in allowing five witnesses to testify to hearsay statements attributed to Sheri Coleman regarding defendant's alleged desire to obtain a divorce and claims that Sheri was ruining his life and whether the trial court erred in denying defendant's motion for a mistrial after one of those witnesses testified that defendant beat Sheri, (4) whether the trial court erred in admitting the expert testimony of Lindell Moore in which he compared spray-

painted writings found at the murder scene to defendant's handwriting, (5)whether the trial court erred in admitting the testimony of Marcus Rogers and Kenneth Wojtowicz, who testified about internet Protocol (IP) addresses, (6) whether the trial court erred in allowing the admission of a hardware store receipt and in allowing a witness to testify to its content, and (7) whether the evidence adduced at trial proved defendant guilty beyond a reasonable doubt. For the following reasons, we affirm:

2. FACTS

3. Pretrial

4. At 6:43 a.m. on May 5, 2009, the defendant, who was employed as director of security for Joyce Meyer Ministries (JMM), an internationally renowned Christian ministry headquartered in Missouri, called his neighbor, Detective Sergeant Justin Barlow of the Columbus Police Department. The defendant told Barlow he had been at the gym and after his workout, he called home to try to wake up his wife, Sheri, but Sheri did not answer. The defendant was concerned something had happened to Sheri. Barlow was aware that defendant had made previous reports to the Columbus police department that he and his family had been threatened due to his employment with JJM. Sergeant Barlow went to the defendant's house to check on the welfare of the defendant's family. Soon, another officer arrived, and after ringing the doorbell and receiving no answer, they went to the back of the house and saw a basement rear window standing open. The police entered the home through the basement window and saw disturbing messages written on the walls in red spray paint. Defendant arrived home and was told to stay outside. The police went up the stairs to the second floor where they found Garett, Gavin, and Sheri dead.

5. When interviewed by the police, the defendant told investigators Sheri was alive when he left the house at 5:45 a.m. to go to the gym. During the interview, police noticed scratches on the defendant's arm. The defendant said he obtained one set of scratches a few days earlier but was unsure how he got them. He said he received another abrasion on his arm after hitting his arm on the gurney in the ambulance in which he was transported after his family was found dead. Initially, the defendant told the police his marriage was good but later revealed that near the end of 2008, he and Sheri had some problems in their marriage, which they worked out through the help of counseling.

6. The police soon discovered the defendant was having an affair with Tara Lintz, a high school friend of Sheri's who was living in Florida. The defendant denied the affair, but after being advised, investigators were talking to Tara. The defendant admitted to the affair but minimized its intensity. As part of the murder investigation, many of the defendant's and Sheri's friends were interviewed. Several friends told the police that Sheri was upset because the defendant wanted a divorce. They said the defendant told Sheri she was ruining his life, but he was afraid he would lose his job with JMM if he divorced her.

7. Investigators went to Florida and interviewed Tara. During the interview, she revealed, inter alia, that the defendant told her he planned to serve divorce papers on Sheri on May 5, 2009, that she and the defendant planned to go on a Caribbean cruise on June 14, 2009, and that they planned a tentative wedding date of January 2010. Tara also told investigators that she had been looking at engagement rings, registering on wedding registration websites, and looking for homes in the St. Louis area for her and the defendant to live in upon their marriage and that they had even discussed baby names.

8. Cybercrime investigators tracked threatening emails received by the defendant pertaining to his job at JMM to the defendant's laptop. In threatening letters addressed to the defendant, the word "opportunities" was consistently misspelled as "oppurtunities." Cybercrime investigators found several documents on the defendant's computer in which the word "opportunities" is misspelled in the same manner as it was in the threatening letters.

9. Medical reports, including the results of the autopsies, showed that Sheri, Garett, and Gavin were all dead before 5 a.m. Police checked the defendant's cellphone records and investigated where the calls were placed by the defendant on the morning of the murders. Based upon the foregoing, the defendant was charged by information on May 20, 2009, with three counts of first-degree murder by strangulation.

10. Prior to the trial, several motions were filed, including a motion in limine or, in the alternative, a motion for a Frye hearing regarding forensic linguistic analysis. The motion set forth that discovery provided by the State indicated the State was going to "attempt to produce evidence that the defendant sent multiple threats to himself, by email and letter, to produce a fictitious suspect who could be blamed for the murder(s)" and was going to "attempt" to produce evidence that the defendant spray-painted graffiti throughout his house when the victims were killed. The motion went on to allege that the State had produced a curriculum vitae and a report from a purported expert in the area of forensic linguistic analysis (FLA) but that "FLA is not an accepted science" and "(t)o allow this FLA testimony under the rubric of expert testimony would be unfairly prejudicial." The defendant sought an order prohibiting any mention of FLA evidence or, in the alternative, "prohibiting the solicitation of expert testimony on the subject of FLA, or grant(ing) the (d)efendant's motion unless the State establishes the validity of the FLA testimony after a Frye Hearing." The defendant

also filed a motion in limine to bar the testimony of the State's alleged FLA expert, Dr. Robert Leonard.

11. The trial court granted the defendant's motion for a Frye hearing. During the hearing, the State presented the testimony of Dr. Leonard, and the defendant presented the testimony of his own expert, Dr. Ronald Butters. After this hearing, the trial court entered the following order:

"The Court, after conducting a Frye hearing, rules that the testimony of a Linguistic Expert may be admitted to the extent of noting similarities between the questioned documents and the known documents without presenting an opinion as to authorship by a specific person and similarities between the questioned documents themselves."

12. The defendant also filed a motion to limine to bar Lindell Moore's testimony. Moore is a forensic scientist with the Illinois State Police whose area of expertise is handwriting analysis. The trial court granted the motion with regard to any reference by Moore to the report of Richard Johnson, another laboratory handwriting analyst at the State Police lab in Springfield. The motion's relevancy objection was taken under advisement and reserved until the time of Moore's trial testimony.

13. The defendant also filed a motion in limine to bar evidence of sexually explicit texts, emails, photographs, and videos exchanged between the defendant and Tara that were seized from computers and cellphones in the defendant's and Tara's possession. An in-camera review of the many items was conducted. The State argued these items were relevant to show the defendant's motive and the intensity of the affair. The trial court permitted three sexually explicit videos, with the caveat that images of breasts, buttocks, and genitalia be blacked out. There was an abundance of intimate photographs, but the State realized all would not be admitted and asked only for a limited amount, which the

trial court allowed, again with the caveat that private parts be blacked out.

14. Both the State and the defense filed pretrial motions and supporting documents with regard to the hearsay testimony of 13 potential witnesses who would purportedly testify to statements made by Sheri regarding the defendant's alleged desire for a divorce and his frustration over the fact that he believed his family was holding him back from realizing his full potential. The State presented 11 of these witnesses during a hearing on these motions. After the hearing, the trial court ruled broadly that the statements were admissible under the code of Criminal Procedure of 1963, which provides a hearsay exception for the intentional murder of a witness. The trial court and the parties then addressed each witness's testimony, after which the trial court ruled that some of the testimony would be admitted under motive and intent exceptions to the hearsay rule, which other parts of the testimony would be excluded. The trial court specifically ruled that Meegan Turnbeaugh's text message from Sheri that the defendant had "beat her" should be excluded, and the state agreed that it would not offer this testimony. In the end, the State presented the testimony of 5 of the original 13 witnesses.

15. II. Trial

16. Jason Donjon, a Columbia police officer, testified that on the morning of May 5, 2009, he was dispatched to the Coleman residence after Detective Sergeant Justin Barlow called the station and advised that he had received a call from the defendant asking the police to check on his residence. When Donjon arrived, Detective Barlow was on the front porch and explained that he rang the doorbell, but no one answered. Donjon then went around the back of the house and noticed an open window with the window screen leaning against a table and patio chairs. A photograph of

the scene was introduced into evidence. Donjon radioed Barlow, who was still in the front of the house, that he found an open window. After identifying themselves as the police and getting no response, they entered the house through the window. They did not find anyone in the basement, so they went up the stairs, where they discovered red spray paint on the walls near the kitchen with disturbing writing, including the word "fuck" and the words "I am always watching." Photographs of the spray paintings found throughout the house were introduced into evidence.

17. Donjon and Barlow heard the garage door open, which turned out to be the defendant arriving home. Barlow told the defendant to remain outside. Another police officer, Officer Patton, arrived on the scene. Patton came into the house to help Donjon and Barlow search. When they failed to find anyone on the first floor, they went upstairs. Donjon testified that when he got to the top of the stairs, he looked into a bedroom to his left and saw a white female, who turned out to be Sheri Coleman, lying naked and face down on the bed. People's Exhibit 10, a picture of how Donjon found Sheri Coleman, was introduced into evidence. Donjon tried to find a pulse but was unable to get one, and he noticed Sheri's "skin was tough or thick." He attempted to roll her over and noticed that "her head, shoulder, arm, all kind of moved as though they were locked into place when (he) lifted her up." He also noticed that Sheri's chest was "kind of reddish-purple deep bruising kind of color." Donjon explained that as a police officer, he has investigated traffic accidents in which people have recently died and in checking for a pulse, he found the skin on the deceased to be soft, "not thick or rigid when (he) moved them, never had that locking thing." He had also never seen a jaundice color or pooling of blood or bruising as he did on Sheri.

18. Donjon then went into Garett's bedroom and found him dead in his bed. People's Exhibit 11, a picture of Garett's deceased body in the bed, was introduced into evidence. Donjon testified there was spray paint in the room, which seemed to be a circle pattern. He also noticed spray paint on Garett's hand and arm. Donjon testified of the skin around Garett's hand and arm. Donjon testified the skin around Garett's eyes and mouth was purple or blue. He noticed that the skin on Garett's neck was thick and tough like it was on Sheri's and that his skin was jaundiced and reddish.

19. Detective Barlow told Donjon that Gavin was also dead. Donjon identified People's Exhibit 12, a picture of the deceased Gavin lying in his bed with the words "Fuck You" spray painted in red on the covers. The officers searched the rest of the home and found no intruders.

20. On cross-examination, Donjon admitted he had no training in determining the time of death. He also admitted that he had not talked to Dr. Nanduri, the pathologist who performed autopsies, or Dr. Baden, an expert who gave an opinion as to the time of death, about how Sheri Coleman looked when he found her body.

21. Officer Patton testified similarly to Officer Donjon. He testified of the spray-painting on the wall leading upstairs, and he specifically remembered "Bitch" being one of the words spray-painted on the wall. He testified the officers heard the defendant downstairs yelling something, so they went down and told the defendant not to come upstairs. The defendant cooperated and was escorted out to the garage through the kitchen. Patton testified that once the defendant was outside, Barlow knelt down, put his hand on the defendant's shoulder, and told the defendant that his family was "gone," and the defendant started to cry. The defendant made no attempt to go back into the house. Patton then used the defendant's garage door opener to shut

the garage door, so the defendant could not go into the house. Patton remembered the defendant saying he needed to call work. Patton heard the defendant using his cellphone to call his father. Patton stayed with the defendant while he talked to his father. At some point, a chaplain arrived and escorted the defendant to the back of an ambulance. The police canvassed the neighborhood but found nothing suspicious. Patton testified the coroner, who has since died, arrived at 10:57 a.m., took pictures of the scene, and took body temperatures of the victims.

22. Patton testified he was at the Coleman residence one other time, January 2, 2009, after the Colemans found a threatening letter in their mailbox. The defendant gave him the letter, which was introduced into evidence. It states: "Fuck You! Deny your God publically or else! No more oppurtunities (sic). Time is running out for you and your family! Have a good time in India MOTHER FUCKER!" Patton pointed out that the word "opportunities" was misspelled in the letter.

23. Gary Hutchinson, a paramedic, testified that he responded to the Coleman house and that the defendant was outside crying when he arrived at about 7:05 a.m. Hutchinson noticed spray paint on the walls. He found the lifeless bodies of Sheri, Garett, and Gavin. He testified that all were cold and stiff, that rigor mortis had set in, and that in his experience, "most bodies that have rigor mortis have been dead for a while." Hutchinson testified that he believed he was sent to the scene "to confirm Barlow's suspicion that (the victims) had been dead for a while." He was only at the house a short time and then transported the defendant to the police station via ambulance. On cross-examination, Hutchinson admitted that he did not put anything in his report about rigor mortis being present.

24. Hutchinson's partner, Jared Huch, testified similarly to Hutchinson. Huch testified that he and Hutchinson checked on Gavin. Huch grabbed Gavin's right arm to see if rigor mortis, a stiffening of the body, had set in. They found rigor mortis present. Hutchinson testified that this is an obvious sign of death, so there is no reason to perform CPR.

25. Deborah Von Nida, a supervisory investigator with the coroner's office, testified she entered the Coleman residence at 11 a.m., and at 11:08 a.m., the ambient temperature in the bedroom where Sheri was found was 76.6 degrees Fahrenheit. She did a liver probe on Sheri at 11:09 a.m. and found Sheri's core temperature to be 90.4. The ambient temperature in Garett's room was 75.2 degrees, and Garett's core temperature at 11:23 a.m. was 91.8. A core temperature of Gavin's body was not established because there were long strands of hair on his body and spray paint, and Von Nida said they wanted to preserve that evidence.

26. Dr. Raj Nanduri, a forensic pathologist, performed autopsies on all three of the victims. She performed an autopsy on Sheri at 3:20 p.m. on May 5, 2009. Dr. Nanduri found a ligature furrow, bruising, and abrasions around Sher's neck. After finding the same type of ligature markings and abrasions on Garett and Gavin, Dr. Nanduri concluded all three died as a result of ligature strangulation. On cross-examination, Dr.Nanduri said she had been asked to give an opinion as to the time of the victims' deaths, but she did not give a time of death, specifically stating, "Time of death is a range." She was not comfortable giving a time of death because she did not have all the findings, and in order to feel comfortable giving a time of death, she would need to know other findings because "the body changes in the post mortem status, you have to have all the finding to at least come to an estimate of time of death." Dr. Nanduri was aware that another pathologist had given an opinion

as to the time of death. She said that in the thousands of autopsies that she had performed, she knew of no other case in which another pathologist was hired to give an opinion as to the time of death. She had not been contacted by the other pathologist to discuss the case.

27. On redirect examination, Dr. Nanduri testified that she gave a range of time of death of six to eight hours prior to 11:04 a.m. based only on Sheri Coleman's body temperature at the time. The formula for deciding the cause of death can be anywhere from one degree per hour of temperature drop to 2.5 degrees per hour. Eight hours would have made the time of death 3 a.m., and six hours would have made it 5 a.m. Dr. Nanduri testified that it would have been helpful to know the responding police officers' observations as far as rigor mortis, liver mortis, and their tactile experience in touching the bodies, but she did not have that information when she performed the autopsies.

28. Dr. Michael Baden, the chief forensic pathologist for the New York State Police who was also the chief forensic pathologist in the late 1970s for the United States Congress Select Committee on Assassinations, looked into the deaths of President Kennedy and Reverend Martin Luther King, testified regarding the time of death. He estimated he has performed over 20,000 autopsies in his 45-year career. He testified there are three cardinal ways to determine the cause of death, including (1) rigor mortis, (2) lividity, which is the color of the body after death caused by the settling of blood, and (3) body temperature. He said the stomach contents can help make a determination, but only if you know when the deceased last ate. He testified a chemical analysis of eye fluid for the purpose of finding potassium can also be of assistance in determining the time of death. The major case squad assigned to the instant case contacted Dr. Baden in May of 2009 for his opinion as to the time of the victims' deaths.

29. Preliminary information provided to Dr. Baden was that there were three victims, said he left the house 1 hour and 15 minutes before the police arrived at the house and found all three dead at around 7:10 a.m. The police said the bodies were cold, rigor mortis was present, and there were changes in the color of the bodies, which sounded like lividity to Dr. Baden. Based upon this preliminary information provided to Dr. Baden, he opined that all three were dead before 5:43 a.m. when the husband left the house. He said it's often difficult to establish a time of death, but in this case, "it wasn't a close call."

30. Given the only real information the police needed was whether or not the victims died before or after 5:43 a.m.

31. The police then provided Dr. Baden with hundreds of crime scene and autopsy photos, police reports, and Dr. Nanduri's autopsy report. Dr. Baden testified that the crime scene photos showed that rigor mortis and lividity were present in Sheri's, Garett's, and Gavin's bodies at 11:00 a.m. He testified with regard to People's Exhibit 16, a picture of Gavin that shows hair that is longer and different color than his on his body. Examinations performed on the hair showed that the longer hair was consistent with Sheri's hair, which indicated to Dr. Baden "that she was strangled first and that the hair was transferred, transfer evidence, probably on the ligature needed to be applied for 'four or five minutes' until the brain is dead. Once the brain is dead, the heart might continue to pump, but there would be a gradual diminution of ability for the heart to beat because the brain is dead."

32. Dr. Baden opined that the same cord was used to strangle all three and that all three deaths occurred around the same time. He believed the murders occurred in sequence, not simultaneously, based on the hair transfer and the fact that "the boys didn't move from the bed." Dr. Baden opined that the deaths "occurred before three AM." He believed "they

were dead many hours before the first responders got to the scene at seven AM."

33. On cross-examination, Dr. Baden admitted that different factors can push the body temperature down, including ambient temperature, skin exposure, nudity, and weight. However, he also stated that the entire total would not cause more "than a degree or two" difference. Dr. Baden explained that the temperature in a body does not drop for the first three or four hours after death. It remains at 98.6 and then starts dropping, so even if Sheri's body was dropping at a rate of 1.5 degrees per hour as was indicated by the two liver probes, the time of death was before 5:43 a.m.

34. Justin Barlow testified that on May 5, 2009, he was a detective for the Columbia police department and lived catty-corner from the Coleman family. Prior to the murders, he never spoke with the defendant. The defendant first approached the Columbia police on November 14, 2008, after he received a threatening email at his work. Barlow did not have any involvement with that. Officer Zach Hopkins took the call, but it was not a crime necessarily occurring in Columbia; however, the Columbia police agreed to provide extra patrols for the Coleman residence. On January 2, 2009, Officer Patton responded to the Coleman house after a threatening letter, previously set forth herein was found in the mailbox. On April 27, 2009, the defendant reported he found another threatening letter in his mailbox. That letter was introduced into evidence as People's Exhibit 25 and warns the defendant "to stop traveling and to stop carrying on with this fake religious life of stealing people's money." It declares, "that is the latest warning" and that "YOUR WORST NIGHTMARE IS ABOUT TO HAPPEN!" The police canvassed the neighborhood and stopped at Barlow's house. Barlow read the letter and thought it sounded more amplified than the first threatening letter, so he called a friend at the Illinois State Police and had a surveillance

camera pointed out of his five-year-old's window toward the Colemans' mailbox. The camera was set up on April 28, 2009, and Barlow testified the defendant was aware of it.

35. On May 5, 2009, defendant called Barlow at 6:43 a.m. and said he was on his way home from Gold's Gym in South County, Missouri. He said he was crossing the Jefferson Barrick's Bridge from Missouri into Illinois and he tried calling his wife several times to get the kids up, but she was not answering the phone and he was concerned. Barlow, who had been asleep, got up, got dressed, called the police department, and asked for a uniformed officer to meet him at the Coleman residence.

36. Videotape from the camera installed in Barlow's residence shows the defendant leaving the house at 5:43 a.m. It also shows Barlow arriving at the defendant's house at 6:56 a.m. It took the defendant 13 minutes to get from the bridge where he told Barlow he was to his home. Barlow testified that the trip normally takes seven minutes.

37. Barlow entered the Colemans' house with Officer Donjon and testified consistently with Donjon about what they saw inside the house, including spray-painted messages and the deceased bodies of Sheri, Garett, and Gavin. Barlow testified there were no signs of forced entry into the home such as broken glass or debris on the floor where the window was opened to the basement. Barlow was aware that he brought moisture into the house with him on his tennis shoes when he entered the basement.

38. After they heard the defendant downstairs asking what was going on, the officers went downstairs and Barlow told the defendant that "they didn't make it." The defendant began to cry. Barlow recalls the defendant asking him what happened, but nothing else. The defendant did not demand to see his family, nor did he try to go upstairs.

The defendant went outside with the officers and sat on the sidewalk and cried, but Barlow testified no one told the defendant what they actually found upstairs. The defendant remained at the scene for approximately 20 to 25 minutes until he was taken by ambulance to the police station, where a 5-hour and 56-minute interview was conducted. A copy of the interview was played for the jury. The jury did not watch the last hour of the interview after it was determined there was nothing of substance in that hour.

39. The defendant did not ask how his family was killed. Approximately four hours into the interview, Trooper Bivens, the other officer conducting the interview besides Barlow, specifically asked the defendant if he knew how his family died. The defendant replied that he did not know. During the interview, the defendant asked for a jacket even though Barlow did not think the interview room was cold. At one point during the interview, officers walked out of the room and the defendant picked up one of the officers' notes and looked at them.

40. On cross-examination, Barlow admitted the defendant provided the police with bodily and handwriting samples. Twenty-five minutes into giving the samples, the defendant said he was tired of writing, so the police agreed he could stop. The defendant also gave the police the clothes he was wearing, his cellphone, and his computer and authorized the police to open his mail and search his house and car. Barlow also admitted that the defendant was being treated as a suspect during the interview.

41. After Barlow's testimony, defense counsel asked the trial court to revisit its ruling regarding the motion in limine concerning sexually explicit photographs and videotapes. Ultimately, the trial court pared down the exhibits even further with one of the three videotapes rather than viewing

it. After hearing arguments from both sides, the trial court specifically stated:

The Court has, I believe, gone back through the items and with that stipulation, believes that the State should be allowed the opportunity to present items that I believe show the intensity of the relationship and yet are not as descriptive as even some of the items that the Court had previously pared down from the larger number of photographs.

So, in other words, I want to record to be certain that the Court has indeed reviewed the prejudice and the probative value of these particular items and found that the probative value does not or is not outweighed by possible prejudice.

Again, I understand the State's frustration. There's a criticism many times voiced toward judges who change their minds. I find more of a criticism with those who won't change their mind.

I believe that the ruling that I have made, although the State may feel that it restricts them, and maybe it does to some extent, but at the same time it accomplishes the purpose of giving the State an adequate opportunity to portray the relationship as they believe the evidence supports; at the same time, it does not unduly point out the relationship to the point that it becomes something that's overbearing and over-focused on the jury.

42. Officer Ken Wojtowicz, an officer with training and experience in computer forensics, including data acquisition, recovering deleted files, data recovery, and analyzing computers, then testified about explicit photographs and videos of the defendant and Tara retrieved from their computers and cellphones.

43. Wojtowicz analyzed the defendant's Blackberry cell phone, Dell laptop computer, a Dell tower, an Apple laptop, and a thumb drive located at the Coleman residence. He also analyzed Tara's Blackberry and laptop. He found

photographs on both Blackberrys and on Tara's laptop, as well as on the thumb drive. Some of the same pictures were found on multiple devices.

44. Wojtowicz testified as to People's Exhibits 30, 31,32,33,34, and 35, which are nonexplicit pictures of the defendant and Tara found on one or both of their cellphones. He also testified about People's Exhibits 36 through 50, which are additional nonexplicit pictures of the defendant and Tara found during his analysis of the different devices. He said there "were several hundred (more) images on their cellular phones." In addition, he found "several hundred" explicit photographs, depicting either the defendant or Tara in various states of nudity. The trial court only allowed four explicit photographs, People's Exhibits 26 through 29. Breasts, buttocks, and genitalia were obscured before the jury was allowed to see them. Wojtowicz testified that he found several videos on the defendant's Dell laptop which depicted the defendant and/or Tara without clothing. People's exhibit 51 was a video of the defendant naked in front of a computer, which the jury was allowed to see, except that the defendant's genitalia were blacked out. People's Exhibit 52 was a video of the defendant masturbating in the shower to a webcam for Tara. The trial court ordered the screen to go black when the defendant actually began masturbating, but the audio was maintained. People's Exhibit 53 was another videotape that included a naked Tara in a hotel room in Hawaii. Tara's breasts, buttocks, and genitalia were blacked out. Per its earlier ruling, however, the trial court did not permit the jury to see any of this video but allowed Wojtowicz to describe the video and play the audio.

45. Wojtowicz identified People's Exhibit 54 as a note he found on the defendant's laptop in the form of an email. The same note was found on the defendant's Blackberry. It lists, inter alia, Tara's birthday, height, eye color, shoe size, ring size, jean size, favorite flowers, and perfume preferences, and her

likes and dislikes regarding food and sports teams. Next to a notation of "Christmas," it states, "promise ring, loves, circle diamond or diamond cross." Another entry on it states, "Our daughter's name: Zoey Lynn Coleman." People's Exhibit 55 is a group exhibit of notes which were found in which Tara updated the defendant's calendar when she got her period, her dog's birthday, and the defendant's birthday.

46. Wojtowicz testified that he was aware of the threatening note found in the defendant's computer and found "several hits of several different files that had the word 'opportunities' misspelled or the word 'opportunity' misspelled the same way with the 'u' replaced or with the 'o' replaced with the 'u.'" People's Exhibits 56, 57, and 58 are the defendant's writings with such misspellings.

47. Tara testified she and Sheri were best friends in high school and stayed in touch thereafter. Tara knew the defendant, but their relationship became more than friends in November 2008 when she saw the defendant, at a JMM conference. Sheri called Tara and told her to go to the conference which was being held in Florida where Tara lived. Thereafter, she and the defendant talked on the phone and texted "constantly." Their relationship became physical in the middle of December 2008 when the defendant dropped off Joyce Meyer in Florida so Meyer could go on a cruise. Tara then met the defendant at a hotel in Orlando.

48. Tara testified she communicated constantly with the defendant between November 2008 and May 2009, during which they profess their love for each other. In addition to meeting at a hotel in Orlando, they also met in Arizona and Hawaii while the defendant was on business for JMM. Tara testified she stayed in the defendant's hotel rooms and had sex with him during these trips. Tara testified she and the defendant planned on getting married after he divorced Sheri. The plan was for Tara to move to Illinois. Tara

testified that she and the defendant got matching promise rings. Tara was wearing hers at trial.

49. The defendant told Tara he talked to an attorney about getting a divorce. The divorce papers were being prepared. He was scheduled to pick up the papers from the lawyer on Monday, May 4, 2009, and he was going to give them to Sheri and ask her for a divorce. The defendant did not give Sheri divorce papers on May 4 as planned, explaining to Tara he was unable to do so because Sheri's name was spelled incorrectly. He said he asked that the attorney correct the typo and the papers and would be ready to be picked up on May 5, 2009. Tara testified that she and the defendant planned to go on a cruise to St. Thomas in June and the tickets had already been purchased with his personal credit card.

50. She testified that she talked to the defendant on her cellphone in the evening but stopped texting about 10:30 p.m. when the defendant told her he was going to bed. She did not have any communication with the defendant on the morning of May 5, 2009. Tara learned about the murders when the defendant's father called her at 10 a.m. and told her that Sheri and the boys had been murdered. Tara testified the defendant texted her while he was being interrogated at the police station and called her later that evening after he left the police station.

51. Two days after the murders, the defendant called her again while she was talking with Illinois detectives who came to Florida to question her. When she told the defendant or the defendant told her that the police were looking for motive, she did not talk to the defendant again.

52. On cross-examination, Tara said she was aware of four threatening letters the defendant received. One was received approximately 18 months prior to the murders.

Tara acknowledged that she received sexually explicit photographs from the defendant's brother, Keith, and that Sheri's brother contacted her via social media and asked her to marry him. She also acknowledged taking a cruise with another male, Jesse, in December 2008, and she said she used the defendant's computers on occasion.

53. Elizabeth McHale MacNeil testified that she lived in Tampa, Florida, that she was friends with Tara in the fall of 2008 and spring of 2009, and that she was aware that the defendant and Tara were a couple. She testified that approximately a week prior to Christmas 2009, the defendant was in Florida and went to the Cheesecake Factory with a group of about 10 people, including Tara and MacNeil.

54. Michael Grist, a crime scene investigator employed by the Illinois State Police, testified he took photographs and collected evidence at the crime scene on the day of the murders after a warrant was obtained to search the home. He collected footwear impressions, latent fingerprints, and samples of red spray paint from writings on the walls. He testified there were no signs of forced entry into the home.

55. Ashley Keller, another crime scene investigator, took video footage of the crime scene which was played for the jury. She also assisted Michael Grist in collecting evidence. She identified People's Exhibits 70 and 71 as pictures she took of the defendant's right arm while he was being interviewed at the police department. On cross-examination, Keller admitted the defendant was cooperative and provided police with all the samples they requested, including hair and handwriting samples.

Christine Cincotta testified that she was good friends with Sheri and was employed at JMM with the defendant. At the time of her testimony, she was still employed by JMM. Christine testified Sheri sent her text messages in late December 2008 in which Sheri informed Christine that the defendant wanted a divorce because the defendant believed Sheri was "messing up" his work life. Christine testified she went out with Sheri in January of 2009 at which time they discussed the defendant's desire for a divorce.

56. Prior to Sheri contacting Christine about the defendant's desire for a divorce, the defendant contacted Christine in approximately mid-December 2008 as part of her job at JMM. Christine handled the ministry's cellphones, and the defendant sent her a message in which he stated that Sheri sent him some provocative pictures on his JMM-issued Blackberry and he wanted to know if those pictures could be seen by others, so she checked with JMM's technical staff and was told that no one at JMM could see the pictures. She so advised the defendant.

57. After Sheri sent her text messages about the defendant's desire for a divorce, Christine got suspicious and told her brother who also works for the ministry about her conversation with the defendant. Her brother then informed Daniel Meyer, Joyce Meyer's son, who also works for the ministry. Daniel told her to check the defendant's phone, which she did. The records revealed that the defendant had made many phone calls and sent many texts to a Florida phone number and that he had received many calls and texts from that same Florida number. It was Christine's understanding that Daniel Meyer was going to follow up with the defendant.

58. Christine testified that JMM's policy regarding employment after adulterous affair is such that "in most circumstances, they probably wouldn't be allowed to work there anymore if they were having an affair." Christine knew of one employee who was terminated for that specific reason. On cross-examination, Christine said she was aware that the defendant and Sheri received counseling with Mike Shepard, a pastor at JMM, and Sheri told her that she and the defendant were

doing better after the counseling. Christine admitted that as far as she knew, the defendant was a good father.

59. Meegan Turnbaugh testified that she had previously worked with Sheri at JMM and the two remained friends after Sheri stopped working there in late 2008 and into 2009. Meegan communicated with Sheri two or three times a week via email, instant message, and direct phone contact. The prosecutor asked Meegan if she could tell him about "one specific occasion as has been allowed by the Court, in November of 2008. Did you have a discussion with her about her relationship with (the defendant)?" Meegan replied that she could, and the prosecution asked if she could "tell us what that was about and approximately when that occurred." Meegan replied, "I received a text message from Sheri that stated Chris had beat her up." Defense counsel immediately objected. At a sidebar, the prosecutor acknowledged Meegan was not supposed to testify in this manner. The trial court sustained the objection and instructed them to disregard the testimony.

60. Meegan then testified that Sheri told her the defendant wanted to leave her and told her that she had ruined his life because he could not leave her due to his position at JMM. Meegan testified it was JMM's policy to terminate any employee who was having an adulterous affair while working for JMM. On cross-examination, Meegan admitted Sheri and the defendant underwent counseling, after which Sheri told her on more than one occasion that things were getting back on track.

61. Defense counsel later moved for a mistrial based upon Meegan's response which included a reference to the defendant beating Sheri. The trial court denied the defendant's motion.

62. Kathy Laplante, a good friend of Sheri's from working at JMM, testified that she communicated daily with Sheri in late 2008 and early 2009. She recalled that in one particular conversation in early 2009, Sheri told her the defendant wanted a divorce because he was tired of her and she and their children were keeping him from his destiny and what God wanted him to do. Kathy was at the Colemans' the Friday before Sheri was murdered at which time the defendant told her he had a working surveillance system in the house. The defendant and Sheri both told her they had a video of an unknown person putting something in their mailbox, but Sheri told Kathy there was really nothing that could be seen on it.

63. Kathy was aware that the defendant looked into some other job opportunities, such as starting a gym and his own security firm, but he stopped looking for other jobs after he received a raise from JMM in January 2008. Kathy was aware that in the fall of 2008, the defendant wanted to take off time from his job in order to renew his wedding vows but was prohibited from doing so by JMM.

64. Jessica Wade, a friend of Sheri's through a St. Louis church they both attended, testified she and Sheri communicated almost daily. On Christmas Eve 2008, Sheri told her the defendant wanted a divorce because she and the boys were in his way, hindering his career.

65. Stephanie Jones, another friend of Sheri's, testified that in late 2008 and early 2009, she was regularly communicating with Sheri via phone, text message, and in person and talked to Sheri multiple times about her marriage. She referred to a series of text messages between her and Sheri on December 27, 2008, during which Sheri specifically asked Jones to pray for her because "Chris wants a divorce." Stephanie said she would indeed pray for Sheri and asked when all of this

happened, to which Sheri replied, "A couple of days ago. He told me and my kids are in the way of his job."

66. Vanessa Riegerix, the Colemans' neighbor, testified that in late 2008, the defendant was at her house and talked about wanting to divorce Sheri because she was spending too much money. He said he was going to wait until after the holidays to seek divorce.

67. Susan Boyd testified that she worked at JMM from June 2004 until January 2008 as a recruiter in the human resources department. She identified People's Exhibit 74 as a script used to interview JMM applicants. Part of the script included asking applicants if they were divorced since being born again and, if they were, attempting to discern the circumstances of the divorce and whether or not there were any Biblical reasons for a divorce. Page seven of the exhibit specifically set forth: "People are reading us, not their Bible. Anything against Biblical principles, such as married people in adultery, or single people living with the opposite sex, would be grounds for termination." Susan testified she specifically knew of a person who was terminated from JMM because of an adulterous relationship. On cross-examination, Susan admitted she was not working at the ministry in 2000 when the defendant was hired and that there were employees who worked at the ministry who were divorced.

68. Joyce Meyer and her son, Daniel, testified via video depositions, People's Exhibit 75 and 76 respectively. The depositions were played for the jury. Joyce testified that the defendant worked for her for approximately 11 years, starting in security and eventually becoming the supervisor of security and her own personal security guard, earning a salary of $100,000 per year. She said the defendant was issued a computer by JMM and she never saw anyone else using that computer other than the defendant. Joyce testified

that when she was initially interviewed by the police on the day of the murders, she was unaware the defendant was having an affair, but by the end of the interview, the police informed her that the defendant admitted he was having an affair.

69. In the fall of 2008, Joyce became aware that the defendant and Sheri were having marital problems. She discussed the situation with the defendant, who told her Sheri was controlling and never happy. Joyce recommended marriage counseling with Mike Shepard, a chaplain with JMM. The defendant and Shepard both reported to Joyce that the counseling was going well.

70. The defendant advised Joyce that he received an email and letters threatening his family if he did not stop working for JMM. Joyce was unaware of any of her 900 other employees ever receiving such threats. Joyce recalled calling the police on May 12, 2009, after her initial interview. She called to report that she remembered that around the middle of April 2009, the defendant did not seem as engaged in his employment as he previously had been. She informed the police that around that same time, she noticed the defendant started using a personal cellphone. Joyce also recalled taking a JMM-sponsored trip to Florida and the defendant asking to stay an extra couple of days to visit with Sheri's friend. At the time, she did not think anything was odd, but in retrospect, she became suspicious.

71. Joyce admitted that if she knew the defendant was having an affair, it could "definitely" have affected his job and further admitted that other employees who had been having adulterous affairs had been fired. She explained that a divorce situation is not necessarily a cause for termination, but it is looked at on a case-by-case basis, and it is not the divorce that necessarily causes termination, but the morality of the situation.

72. Joyce testified that the defendant called her directly on May 4, 2009, told her he was not feeling well, and asked off for the day. She could not recall the defendant ever calling in sick prior to that occasion. She said the defendant was a hard worker and she encouraged him to take time off and spend it with Sheri and his family when he was not traveling with his job. She testified that after the murders, the defendant resigned.

On cross-examination, she admitted that the defendant was an excellent employee who started the security division from the ground up. She said Sheri never contacted her personally about marital problems but contacted her son, who then made her aware of the situation. She recalled that in August of 2008, the defendant asked for time off for his 10th year anniversary, which he was denied due to previously planned JMM out-of-town convention on which he was to accompany her. She said she offered the defendant other dates which he could take off, but the defendant declined. She admitted that to the best of her knowledge, the defendant loved his children and was good to them.

73. Daniel Meyer, Joyce's son and CEO of JMM's United States operation, testified consistently with Joyce about Sheri contacting him about marital troubles and the couple's ensuing counseling. He testified that he became concerned about the defendant's JMM-issued cellphone bill because it was increasing. He had the records pulled from JMM's financial department and found there was a particular phone number in Florida whom the defendant was frequently calling even while traveling internationally. Daniel called the number and a woman answered the phone. Daniel confronted the defendant, who told him that the number was to a friend of Sheri's and he had been calling the friend's husband to seek marital advice. The defendant told Daniel he could check with Sheri. Daniel accepted the defendant's explanation.

74. Daniel was aware the defendant received threatening emails and letters. He testified he offered to have the defendant stop traveling or to have increased security at the defendant's house while the defendant was traveling, but the defendant declined. Daniel agreed there is no policy at JMM that divorce itself is grounds for termination.

75. Shawn Westfall, a police officer, testified that he responded to a call from the Coleman residence on April 27, 2009, about a threatening letter received in the mailbox. He talked to the defendant, who said he found the letter at 6:10 p.m. after checking for the day's mail, not realizing that Sheri had already checked the mailbox at 3:10 p.m. Westfall said that gave a time frame in which the letter was placed in the mailbox. Westfall then canvassed the neighborhood to see if anyone saw any suspicious during that three-hour time period, but no one did. The defendant also advised him that Sheri received a threatening letter on April 6, 2009, while he was traveling with HMM and that Sheri turned that letter over to the police. The defendant told Westfall that the camera system he installed was not working because it did not come with a power source and he was waiting for the power source to arrive in canvassing the neighborhood. Westfall talked to the defendant's neighbor Sergeant Barlow, who arranged to have a camera set up in his house pointed toward the defendant's mailbox.

76. Jonathan Peters, a chaplain for the police department, was called to the scene to inform the defendant's family had been killed. When he arrived on the scene, the defendant was sitting in the driveway. He described the defendant as "stoic" after he broke the news to the defendant that his family had been killed and said the defendant was "absolutely not hysterical. Peters accompanied the defendant in the ambulance. During the drive, the defendant looked down at his right arm and said, "How did that get there?" referring to some marks on his arm. Peters testified he later

saw the defendant strike his right arm on the gurney in the ambulance, but there was no way the marks were caused by the gurney as the marks were there prior to the defendant striking the gurney. Peters recalled the defendant having a similar conversation with Jerry Paul, Columbia's police captain, about the marks on his arm and told Paul he did not know how he got the marks.

77. Jerry Paul testified consistently with Peters that the blow to the gurney would not have caused the marks on the defendant's arm. Paul described the marks as "some scratches and to his arm, the defendant said he did not know, and he 'abruptly' changed the subject and started asking Paul other questions.

78. Four Illinois State Police lab employees testified about evidence collected at the crime scene. Melody Levault, a forensic scientist specializing in microscopy, identified People's Exhibits 77 and 78 as strands of hair recovered from Garett's and Gavin's bodies. She said the hairs were dyed, forcibly removed, and "consistent" with Sheri's hair.

79. Michael Brown, another forensic scientist, testified that he examined fingernail scrapings from the victims and the defendant for DNA finding from the fingernail scrapings of Garett, Gavin, or the defendant.

80. Suzanne Kidd, a forensic scientist, specializing in forensic biology DMA, testified that she performed Y-STR testing, a specialized type of DNA testing that looks only at male DNA on the left-hand fingernail scrapings of Sheri Coleman. She found a partial profile that could not exclude any of the Coleman males as the contributor.

81. Thomas Gamboe, a forensic scientist in the areas of firearm tool mark, footwear, and tire track identification, testified that all the footwear impressions located inside the Coleman

residence he examined were consistent with at least one of the police officers who were at the scene, except for one possible footwear impression found near the basement window of the Coleman residence. Gamboe could not say for sure that it was even a footwear impression, noting that it could have been an impression from a tire on a child's toy or from a hand truck or dolly.

82. Rick Sawdey, a testing lab manager for MI Windows and Doors in Pennsylvania, testified that he does certification testing for all of MI'S windows and doors. The Colemans' basement window was manufactured by MI and contains a forced entry resistance plate on the bottom which means that if someone tries to open the window while that forced entry plate is locked, there would have been damage to it. The Colemans' window showed no damage and showed no signs of being forcibly opened.

83. James Kientz, a network director for AT&T, testified that from reviewing the defendant's cellphone records, he could determine what tower and which side of the tower calls were made from the defendant's phone. Kientz identified People's Exhibit 81 as a map he created to show which rowers had been utilized in making six calls from the defendant's cell phone on the morning of the murder. Calls were made at 5:44 a.m., 6:42 a.m., 6:43 a.m., 6:53 a.m., and 6:58 a.m. The 5:44 a.m. call utilized a tower close to the defendant's residence on the Illinois side of the Mississippi River. The 6:53 a.m. call was made from an area north of a particular tower on the Illinois side of the Mississippi River.

84. Ken Wojtowicz was called again to testify, this time as an expert in the area of IP addresses about the threatening emails sent from a Google Gmail account titled destroychris@ gmail.com. A subpoena was sent to Google, requesting records as far as IP logs and subscriber information for that account. Google then provided the IP addresses that

sent the email threats, and Wojtowicz explained that an IP address "is basically like the address, home address for intern-ology, where that computer is located at, or the modem that's connecting to the internet is located at." The police obtained a search warrant to search Google's records regarding the account destroychris@gmail.com. Google's response to the search warrant showed that eight emails were created under that account and seven of those emails were sent. The eighth was never sent. Wojtowicz testified the account was created at 8:19 p.m. on November 14, 2008, on the defendant's Dell laptop computer which was found at his home. Wojtowiz identified People' Exhibits 59 through 66 the eight threatening emails from the defendant's laptop. The first email, People's Exhibit 59, was sent on Friday November 14, 2008, to a number of different JMM email addresses with the subject line "Fuck Chris's family. They are dead." The body of the email states, "I'm sure this will make it to someone in the company. If you jackasses are like any other company, this will be someone's account. Pass this onto Chris.

"Tell Joyce to stop preaching the bullshit or Chris's family will die. If I can't get to Joyce, then I will get to somebody close to her; and if I can't get to him, then I will kill his wife and kids. I know Joyce's schedule, so then I know Chris's schedule. If Joyce doesn't quit preaching the bullshit, then they will die. Suring the Houston conference, I will kill them all as they sleep. If I don't hit there, then I will kill them during the book tour or the trip to India. I know where he lives, and I know they're alone. Fuck them all and they will die soon. Tell that motherfucker next time to let me talk to Joyce. She needs to hear what I have to say and now she will."

85. People's Exhibits 60, 61, 62, and 63 were much shorter and were also sent on November 14, 2008.

86. People's Exhibit 64 was sent on Saturday, November 15, 2008, to Dan Meyer, D. Meyer, and the defendant's email accounts at JMM and states, inter alia:

    "I know you all got my fucking email. You think I'm full of shit. Just wait. I will shoot their asses with my 40. Kill them all, I'm so sick of bitches like her taking everybody's case so she can fly her jet and pamper her white ass. Fuck you all. Tell Chris I will kill them. He has no idea when, but it will happen."

87. People's Exhibit 65 was also sent on November 15, 2008, to email addresses at JMM while People's Exhibit 66 was created on Sunday, November 16, 2008, but never sent.

88. On cross-examination, Wojtowicz admitted that he does not have a degree in computer science and that most of his training consists of classes taught by law enforcement. He further admitted that he did not search the defendant's laptop for remote access software which would allow a person to run the computer from a different location, nor did he check for malware or viruses.

89. Denis Smith, custodian of records at Google, testified that Google gets requests from law enforcement for records and that there is specific software that is automated that pulls the information. She said that the records are kept in the ordinary course of business for Google. In the instant case, Google received two subpoenas and a search warrant to search a Gmail account and IP addresses for messages and subscriber information on the person who created the Gmail account destroychris@gmail.com. Google provided the information to the police.

90. Marcus Rogers, a professor of computer forensics at Purdue University, testified that he reviewed several images of hard drives given to him by police, including computers from the defendant's house, a JMM computer issued to the

defendant, Tara's computer, and computers owned by the defendant's father and brother, as well as some Blackberry devices and an AT&T USP air card. Rogers described how IP addresses work and the fact that only one computer can be issued an address at a time. The defendant's laptop was able to access the Internet via AT&T, and AT&T issued the defendant the IP address 16612813110. Rogers testified, "(The defendant's) laptop has that address, and no other laptop, no other computer connecting to the internet during the period of time that the laptop has that address can have it. So, this is unique now for that computer for that period of time." Rogers went on to identify destroychris@gmail.com and People's Exhibits 59 through 66 as being produced on the defendant's Dell laptop, which police gave to Rogers to examine, and further testified that the defendant's Dell computer had not been operated remotely but had been turned on and off using a manual switch on the computer during each of the three sessions during which the emails comprising People's Exhibit 59 through 66 had been composed.

91. Rogers testified the antivirus software on the computer was up to date and there was nothing on the computer to indicate that it ever had a virus. Rogers ran antivirus software on the computer system which indicated no viruses. He specifically stated that "the virus companies are pretty good at keeping up to date with what viruses would have been around in 2008, and the fact that no viruses were found by software in 2011 (when he ran the scans) is really good evidence to indicate that there was nothing on there related to that." He also used Windows Registry on the Dell computer, which gave an indication of any virus software or malware software being installed in the computer system.

92. On cross-examination, Rogers admitted the Dell laptop had been used many times since 2008 and there was much more information on the computer than what he analyzed. He

also noted there were six different user accounts on the Dell laptop.

93. Robert Leonard, a linguistics professor with a Ph.D. in linguistics and director of the Institute for Forensic Linguistics Threat Assessment and Strategic Analysis, testified as an expert over the objection of the defendant. He said he had testified as an expert 10 or 11 other times and has testified for both the State and for the defendant, and in the majority of his cases, he has been recruited by the defense. In the instant case, the Columbia police department asked him to analyze threat messages and the known writings of the defendant to see if he could discern similarities or dissimilarities between the writings. He testified that he looks for patterns between two sets of documents, the Q documents (which are the writings in which authorship is questioned) and the K documents (which are writings in which authorship is questioned) and the K documents (which are writings in which the printout of instant messages between the defendant and Tara) in order to determine whether there has been common authorship. The Q documents here were two letters. People's Exhibit 13 and 25, and several emails, beginning with People's Exhibits 59, along with People's Exhibits 7, 8, and 9, pictures of writings found on the walls of the Coleman residence, and People Exhibit 12, a picture of the writing found on Gavin's bed.

94. Leonard first checked to see whether he could establish that the Q documents were consistent and whether there were similarities that would link them together with common authorship. He found approximately five similarities between the messages. First, he found that the messages written on the walls and the emails began with "fuck," "fuck you," and "fuck Chris," which "is pretty much equivalent." He noted that the FI assembled a database called the Communicative Threat Database (C-TAD), which has 4,400 criminally oriented communications, and

of those, only 18 begin with the word "fuck," which makes communications starting with that word rather unique. Second, the documents contain conditional threats. He explained that an unconditional threat would be "I am coming to kill you." For example, the letters he examined contained conditional threats including "Deny your God publicly or else," You had better stop traveling," and "Stop today or else." Third, the documents describe the motivation for the death threats as the defendant's job. Fourth, the gratuitous insults in the writings are limited to "fuck," "motherfucker," "bitch," "son of a bitch," and "SOB." Fifth, the letters contain capitalization in closing.

95. After analyzing the Q documents, Leonard then went on to look for similarities between the Q documents and the K documents and found four similarities. First, Leonard found contraction patterns, such as saying "I'm" instead of "I am" or "don't" instead of "do not." Second, he found fused spellings, which means a word was fused together rather than separated as it should be according to standard writing rules, such as "any time being fused into 'anytime.'" Third, he found apostrophe reversal, including "wont" and "doesn't." Fourth, Leonard found that "you" was not often spelled out but was written simply as "u." Leonard then went on to describe in detail People's Exhibit 84, a document he prepared to show the similarities between the Q and K documents. On cross-examination, Leonard admitted that the FBI refused to give an opinion as to the uniqueness of a variety of phrases that Leonard found to constitute similarities between the documents.

96. Four witnesses testified regarding red spray paint found on the walls of the Coleman residence after the murders. Adrianne Bickel, a forensic scientist for the Illinois State Police, identified People's Exhibits 86 and 87 as paint scrapings from a picture frame inside Coleman residence and a paint scraping taken from one of the walls of the

home. In Bickel's opinion, the scrapings were likely from a Rustoleum brand of paint called Apple Red Bickel then contacted Rustoleum for further analysis. No spray paint cans were located in Coleman's home, and no paint was found on the shoes, socks, or swabs of the defendant's hands.

97. Richard Osterman, a chemist formerly employed by Rustoleum, also examined People's Exhibits 86 and 87 and found they could only have come from Rustoleum spray paint product, either Painter's Touch or American Accents, based upon the unique resins in the samples.

98. Michael Harloff, a former color chemist at Rustoleum who retired the year prior to trial opined, that People's Exhibits 86 and 87 were from "Apple Red" can of Rustoleum, spray paint, based upon his 33 years of experience doing visual comparisons.

99. Karla Heine, a Columbia police detective, testified a Master Card credit card was found lying inside the Coleman residence and the police obtained a subpoena to get the credit card information. She reviewed the Master Card records for the account and found that a can of Apple Red Rustoleum Painter's Touch spray paint was purchased with that credit card on February 9, 2009, at 1:46 p.m. at Handyman True Hardware Store located in St. Louis, Missouri, approximately 7.5 miles from the Coleman home. Heine went to the store and obtained a copy of the receipt, which was signed by "Christopher E. Coleman." People's Exhibit 89, a copy of the receipt, was admitted over the defendant's hearsay objection.

100. Heine also testified that she investigated the alibi of Keith Coleman, who claimed to be in Arkansas the night before and the morning of the murders. She found video footage of him in a Walmart store located in Arkansas at 8:10 p.m. on May 4, 2009. She testified that Walmart is located 313

miles and approximately six hours away from Columbia, Illinois. She also talked to Keith Coleman and his wife, after which it was determined that Keith woke up at approximately 5 a.m. at his home in Arkansas on May 5, 2009, and helped get his stepdaughter ready for school. On cross-examination, Heine admitted that no cans of Apple Red spray paint were seized from the Coleman residence, his car, or any place associated with the defendant.

101. Lindell Moore, a forensic scientist for the Illinois State Police who specializes in document examination and tool marks, was allowed to testify as an expert over the objection of the defense about similarities between writings found on the wall and the defendant's known writing. Moore acknowledged that spray paint writings are "awkward and unnatural," but testified to similarities between six alphabet characters, i, g, c, k, b, and p as well as the suffix "ing" found in the writings on the wall to handwriting samples somewhere between 5 and 20 times, but this was the first time he testified in court regarding spray paint writings. He admitted that he did not know if the spray paintings were written by one person or two or more people. He merely assumed the spray paintings in the instant case were made by the same person. He could not tell from the diaries and the exemplars he was provided whether the writer was right or left-handed. He testified that in addition to the similarities, he looked for differences and admitted there were differences even with the six letters and "ing" in the questioned writings and the known writings. Moore admitted that it is difficult to compare spray-painted writings to handwriting because the distinct body motions used in handwriting while sitting as opposed to spray painting "make it difficult to reproduce habits of a person's writing." Moore agreed he would expect to find similarities and differences between the spray-painted writings and the writings of any person in the world. On redirect examination, Moore explained that

there are inconsistencies in the spray paintings in terms of cursive writing and printing, and the use of small letters and capital letters. Moore found the same inconsistencies within the defendant's journal writings, which indicate a similarity between the writings. Moore pointed out that despite the difficulties in analyzing spray-painted writings and handwriting, he found in both "letters that are constructed in ways that would kind of vary from that of how (he) would expect a person to be taught in school."

102. The State rested and the defendant's motion for a directed verdict was denied. The defense called two witnesses. Steven McKasson, a document examiner who works in the private sector and previously worked for the postal service and the Illinois State Police, testified as an expert about the process of comparing questioned and known writings. He explained that "it's not just picking out things that look the same and counting them up, it's a matter of finding that there are enough habits present in the questioned to say this is a person, this is an individual person, then finding that same set of habits in the known." He testified there are many instances in which an identification cannot be made. He said he was retained by the defense and provided with documents, including photographs of the spray paint on the walls and the known samples of the defendant. He used a powerpoint presentation, the defendant's Exhibit 23, to explain the findings.

103. McKasson testified that the writings on the wall appeared to be disguised because there was a lack of normalness evidenced by the mixing of capital letters and small letters' cursive writing and printing. He said the situation was complicated by the fact that the writings were spray painted, which in itself is awkward and involves moving the whole body as opposed to pen writing which does not. McKasson could not determine how many people were involved in making the writings, nor could he determine

if the writer(s) were right-or left-handed. Because the spray paintings were so disguised, he said "it would be pretty unreliable to draw any conclusion other than inconclusive from that comparison."

104. Ronald Butters, a professor of English and anthropology at Duke University, was called to rebut Robert Leonard's linguistics testimony. Butters pointed out problems in Leonard's analysis such as the frequency of all writers making grammatical errors on occasion and fusing words like "sometime" or "goodtime" rather than "some time" or "good time." As to apostrophe reversal, Butters pointed out that the small quantity of the samples "suggests that it's practically meaningless." He also pointed out that the defendant's use of apostrophes was correct on many occasions and in his opinion, the defendant's incorrect use would be nothing more than a typographical error caused by writing too fast in an informal setting.

105. Butters explained that using "u" for the word "you" in informal writing such as an email or text is quite common today. Butters also believed Leonard was comparing "apples to oranges." He noted that while Leonard put emphasis on the fact her many writings started out with "the F word," the word was actually placed into the heading part of a message, not the actual message. He explained that threats and conditions are commonly intertwined and asserted that Leonard's making that a major category was "not very useful." Butters specifically stated that any similarities in the writings "are linguistically meaningless" and four categories relied upon by Leonard "are useless." Butters agreed with the FBI's conclusion that it could not give an opinion as to the similarities between the writings. He knew of no other instance in Illinois where this evidence had been allowed and said the primary use of authorship identification was for investigative purposes only. He

testified Dr. Leonard should have refused "to testify about this at all because it's not scientifically valid."

106. During deliberations, the jury sent out various notes, including a request to see the window and a request for a magnifying glass. Both were provided to the jury without objection from either party. The jury also sent a request to speak to the judge, and the trial court responded with a note to make all requests in writing. The jury then sent a note in which it requested a definition of "reasonable doubt." The trial court responded with a note which states, "You will receive no instruction defining reasonable doubt. You have received the instructions on the law that you're sworn to follow and the evidence. Continue your deliberation." The jury also sent a note requesting copies of Dr. Baden's and Dr. Nanduri's testimony. While the trial court and attorneys were discussing how to address the request, the jury sent another note, stating, "We are a hung jury." The trial court ceased deliberations. Ultimately, the jury convicted the defendant on all three counts. The trial court sentenced the defendant to three concurrent life sentences. The defendant now appeals.

107. ANALYSIS

108. I. Forensic Linguist

109. The first issue we are asked to address is whether the trial court erred in allowing the State to present testimony of an expert linguist on the issue of authorship attribution. The defendant argues the testimony at the Frye hearing established that the field of authorship attribution is new and more research is needed before it can become a reliable scientific tool and, therefore, the trial court should have barred Dr. Leonard from testifying as to any similarities or patterns within the questioned documents or to any opinions regarding similarities or patterns between

the questioned documents and the known documents. The defendant further contends the trial court erred in allowing the expert testimony because the jurors were capable of comparing the questioned and known documents without the need for expert testimony. The State replies that the Frye hearing was unnecessary because the forensic linguist's testimony was neither scientific nor novel, but even assuming arguendo that Frye applies, the outcome of the hearing was correct. In his reply brief, the defendant contends that the State waived the issues of whether authorship attribution is scientific, or new, or novel by failing to raise them below. However, whether Dr. Leonard's testimony was scientific or new or novel are not issues that can be waived. His testimony was either scientific principle upon which the opinion is based or "sufficiently established to have gained general acceptance in the particular field in which it belongs." This means that an expert's opinion must be based upon a scientific methodology that is reasonably relied upon by experts in the relevant field but need not be accepted by all or even most experts in that particular field. However, a Frye hearing is only necessary "if the scientific principle, technique, or test offered by the expert to support his or her conclusion is 'new' or 'novel.'" Scientific methodology is considered "new" or "novel" only if it is "original or striking" or fails to resemble something previously known or used. A dual standard of review applies with regard to the trial court's admission of expert scientific testimony. Whether an expert scientific witness is qualified to testify in a subject area and whether the proffered testimony is relevant to the case are questions left to the sound discretion of the trial court, but whether the proffered evidence is sound or novel is subject to de novo review.

110. In the instant case, the proffered evidence was similarities between the questioned documents, email and letter threats and the writings on the walls found at the scene

of the murders, and the known documents, emails, and instant messages known to have been written by the defendant. The trial court ordered a Frye hearing "in the interest of safety." After the hearing, the trial court allowed Dr. Leonard to testify about the similarities between the defendant's known writings but did not allow Dr. Leonard to give an opinion regarding authorship by a specific person.

111. First, we agree with the State that evidence of similarities between questioned documents is not scientific. "If an expert's opinion is derived solely from his or her observations and experiences, the opinion is generally not considered scientific evidence." The line that separates scientific and nonscientific evidence is not always clear.

112. The instant case is similar to the United States v Van Wyk, in which an FBI agent qualified as an expert on the subject of forensic stylistics was not allowed to testify as to authorship of unknown writings, but could testify as to similarities between the defendant's known writings and unknown writings. In reaching that conclusion, the Van Wyk court specifically found a lack of scientific reliability, noting that "(t)he reliability of text analysis, much like handwriting analysis, is questionable because, as discussed supra, there is no known rate of error, no recognized standard, no meaningful peer review, and no system of accrediting an individual as an expert in the field." Nevertheless, the FBI agent could testify "as an expert regarding the comparisons of markers between the known writings and questioned writings" because his "expertise in text analysis can be helpful to the jury by facilitating the comparison of the document," making distinctions and sharing his experience as to how common or unique a particular "marker" or pattern is.

113. The same FBI agent, Van Wyk, was allowed to testify 10 years later in United States v Zjac, a pipe-bombing case in which the defendant moved to exclude expert testimony regarding authorship attribution. Even though the FBI agent had since earned a master's degree in linguistics and continued his work in forensic linguistics, he was not allowed to give an ultimate opinion as to whether the two letters were authored by the same person but was allowed to testify as to similarities between the two letters. The court noted that "no clear line exists between scientific knowledge and technical or other specialized knowledge" and noted that "the Rules of Evidence have a liberal thrust, such that there is a strong and undeniable preference for admitting any evidence having some potential for assisting the trier of fact." (Internal quotation marks omitted.) Zajac. That court further noted that rejecting expert testimony is "the exception rather than the rule" and found rather than disallowing the evidence, the better way to proceed is through "(v)igorous cross-examination, presentation of contrary evidence, and careful instruction on the burden of proof."

114. Our review of the record shows threat Dr. Leonard did not apply scientific principles in rendering an opinion. Instead, he relied on his skill and experience-based observations. Moreover, we do not believe that Dr. Leonard's testimony presented anything new or novel. As the state points out, courts have been considering this type of evidence for more than a century.

115. In Throckmorton v Holt, a will contest case, the Supreme Court considered "the opinion of a witness as to the genuineness of the handwriting found in the paper, based in part upon the knowledge of the witness, of the character and style of composition, and the legal and literary attainments of the individual whose handwriting it purports to be." Thockmorton hailed witnesses should

be allowed to testify as to composition and character of style, but should not be allowed to render an opinion as to authorship, as that is a question for the jury. Thockmorton said, clearly, this type of linguistics analysis has been going on for years. While today's experts may be better educated and have garnered more experience, the comparison of documents is not new or novel such that a Frye hearing was even necessary in the instant case.

116. The defendant relies on People v McKown in support of his contention that just because courts have considered forensic linguistic analysis for years does not mean that it is not novel. In McKown I, our supreme court stated, "Given the history of legal challenges to the admissibility of HGN test evidence, and the fact that a Frye hearing has never been held in Illinois on this matter, we conclude that the methodology of HGN testing is novel for purposes of Frey." What the defendant fails to consider is that HGN testing is clearly "scientific" because it is based upon a scientific principle that is not considered common knowledge, i.e., consumption of alcohol causes the nystagmus measured by the HGN test, whereas forensic linguistic analysis does not require scientific analysis. Upon remand, the trial court determined that HGN test results are generally accepted in the relevant scientific fields and that evidence of HGN test results is admissible, and this finding was adopted by our supreme court. Accordingly, the defendant's reliance on McKown I is misplaced.

117. After careful consideration, we find that the trial court correctly allowed Dr. Leonard to testify in the limited manner in which he did. Dr. Leonard was allowed to discuss similarities between the known writings and the questioned writings but was not allowed to give a vigorously cross-examined Dr. Leonard and presented its own expert linguist, Dr. Butters, a professor at Duke University, to rebut Dr. Leonard's testimony. Accordingly, we find no

error in the trial court allowing the State to present the testimony of an expert linguist.

118. II. Sexually Explicit Photographs and Videos

119. The second issue raised by the defendant is whether the trial court erred in allowing the State to present sexually explicit photographs of the defendant and Tara and two videos of the defendant, People's Exhibit 51, a 30-second video of the defendant sitting in front of his computer during which the defendant pops out of his chair to show Tara his erection and masturbating in the shower. In both videos, the defendant's penis is blacked out. The defendant contends the trial court erred in allowing these items into evidence because their probative value on the issue of the intensity of their affair was minimal and was outweighed by the prejudice caused by their admission, specifically a strong likelihood that this evidence would produce intense antagonism and disgust toward the defendant. The State replies that the trial court did not abuse its discretion in allowing the photographs and videos in evidence, especially in light of the fact that substantially fewer pictures were admitted than were available. The two videos were short, and the defendant's genitalia and Tara's breasts and buttocks were obscured. We agree with the State.

120. "Evidence is 'relevant' if it has any tendency to make the existence of a fact that is of consequence to the determination of the action more or less probable than it would be without the evidence." People v Roberson. However, even if the evidence is offered for a permissible purpose, it will not be admitted if its prejudicial effect substantially outweighs its probative value. People v Dabbs. The issue of whether evidence is relevant and admissible is left to the sound discretion of the trial court, and its ruling will not be reversed absent an abuse of discretion. People v Pelo. A trial court abuses its discretion only where its

decision is arbitrary, unreasonable, or fanciful or where no reasonable person would take the view adopted by the trial court.

121. In the instant case, the defendant was employed by an International Christian ministry that strongly disapproved of adultery. The evidence showed that the defendant was at risk of losing his $100,000-per-year job if he was caught having an affair. When the police initially interviewed the defendant, he denied his affair with Tara. When the defendant learned police were in contact with Tara, he admitted to the affair but downplayed its intensity. It was the State's theory that the defendant killed the victims because he wanted out of his marriage to Sheri so he could marry his lover, Tara, and the defendant believed that divorce was not an option. Because the defendant downplayed the intensity of the affair, the photographs were a direct reflection of the defendant's credibility or lack thereof.

122. It is important to point out that after the trial began, the trial court revisited its ruling on the defendant's motion in limine regarding sexually explicit photographs and videotapes and oared down the exhibits even further. Instead of allowing the jury to view three sexually explicit videos, the trial court ordered that the jury be allowed only to hear the audiotape of one of the three videos it originally allowed rather than viewing it. With regard to the video of the defendant masturbating in the shower to a webcam, the trial court ordered the screen to go black but allowed the audio to be maintained. Moreover, Officer Wojtowicz testified there were "several hundred" more sexually explicit photographs he retrieved from the defendant's and Tara's electronic devices which were not introduced into evidence.

123. The trial court specifically noted, "I want the record to be certain that the Court has indeed reviewed the prejudice and the probative value of these particular items, and found that the probative value does not/is not outweighed by the possible prejudice." Under these circumstances, the defendant has failed to convince us he was unduly prejudiced by the minimal amount of photographs (compared to the hundreds available) and two short videos which were allowed into evidence.

124. The defendant further complains about two unredacted photographs on the back of foam core boards containing 8-inch by 10-inch enlargements of some of the photographs which show the defendant's naked torso and his penis and Tara's buttocks and breasts. The defendant admits the "small unredacted photographs on these exhibits were not objected to at trial." Accordingly, this issue is waived and can only be reviewed if the defendant is able to establish plain error.

125. The plain error doctrine allows a court to review forfeited errors if (1) the evidence is so closely balanced that the error threatens to tip the scales of justice against the defendant, or (2) the error is so serious that it affects the fairness of the defendant's trial. People v Chaban. Contrary to the defendant's assertions, we do not believe the evidence was closely balanced. We will discuss the overwhelming circumstantial evidence against defendant when we address the seventh issue raised by the defendant. Here, however, suffice it to say that the evidence established that the victims were all dead before the defendant left the house, there was no evidence that anyone else entered the house, the threatening emails were sent from the defendant's own Dell computer, and the defendant had a clear motive for such heinous crimes. Under these circumstances, we do not believe the presence of two small unredacted photographs

in the jury room was so serious that it affected the fairness of the defendant's trial.

126. III Hearsay Statement of Sheri

127. The third issue raised on appeal is whether the trial court erred in allowing five witnesses to testify to hearsay statements attributed to Sheri regarding the defendant's alleged desire to obtain a divorce and claims that Sheri was ruining his life and whether the trial court erred in denying the defendant's motion for a mistrial after one of those witnesses testified the defendant beat Sheri. The defendant contends the trial court erred in allowing the hearsay testimony and abused its discretion in denying his motion for mistrial after Meegan Turnbeaugh testified she received a text message from Sheri "that Chris had beat her up" because the parties agreed prior to trial that any testimony about the defendant beating Sheri was inadmissible. The State responds that the admission of Sheri's statements to friends regarding concerns about her marriage and the defendant's desire for a divorce was an abuse of discretion and were properly admitted under the statutory hearsay exception for the intentional murder of a witness, under the doctrine of forfeiture by wrongdoing, and to establish the defendant's motive and intent. While the State admits Turnbeaugh's statement regarding the defendant beating Sheri was improper, it asserts that the trial court's denial of the defendant's motion for a mistrial on the basis was not an abuse of discretion. We agree with the State.

128. Section 115-10 6(a) of the Code of Criminal Procedure of 1963 (Code) provides:
    "A statement is not rendered inadmissible by the hearsay rule if it is offered against a party that has killed the declarant in violation of clauses (a)(1) and (a)(2) of Section 9-1 of the Criminal Code of 1961 intending to procure the

unavailability of the declarant as a witness in a criminal or civil proceeding."

The statute requires the circuit court to conduct a pretrial hearing in order to determine the admissibility of any statements offered pursuant to the statute.

129. During the hearing, the proponent of the statement bears the burden of establishing by a preponderance of the evidence (1) that the adverse party murdered the declarant and that the murder was intended to cause that unavailability of the statements to provide "sufficient safeguards of reliability," and (3) that "the interests of justice will best be served by admission of the statement into evidence." The statute provides that it "in no way precludes or changes the application of the existing common law doctrine of forfeiture by wrongdoing."

130. The common law doctrine of forfeiture by wrongdoing provides a hearsay exception for statements made by an unavailable witness where the defendant intentionally made the witness unavailable in order to prevent him or her from testifying People v Hanson. In 1997, the doctrine was codified at the federal level by the Federal Rule of Evidence as an exception to the rule against hearsay. Federal Rule 804(b)(6) provides a hearsay exception for "(a) statement offered against a party that has engaged or acquiesced in wrongdoing that was intended to, and did, procure the unavailability of the declarant as a witness." In 2007, our supreme court expressly adopted the common law doctrine as the law of Illinois. Stechly makes it clear that as applied in Illinois, the doctrine is "coextensive with" Federal Rule 804 (b)(6).

131. In the instant case, the State asked the trial court to conduct a hearing to determine the admissibility of 13 potential witnesses who would testify to statements made by Sheri regarding the defendant's alleged desire for a divorce

and his frustration over the fact he believed his family was holding him back from realizing his full potential. The State presented 11 of these 13 witnesses at a lengthy hearing, after which 5 actually testified at trial over the defendant's numerous objections. The State presented a written proffer, and the trial court gave the defendant the opportunity to present evidence or challenge the proffer, which the defendant failed to do. Based upon the proffer and the defendant's lack of any evidence to the contrary, the trial court found that the State met its burden: the defendant murdered Sheri and the murder was intended to cause her unavailability at a dissolution proceeding. The trial court found the testimony of the witnesses provided sufficient safeguards of reliability and then went through the proposed statements' introduction into evidence.

132. The trial court also determined that the statements were admissible to establish a motive. The trial court allowed limited testimony that the defendant told Sheri she and the boys were holding him back, that the defendant wanted a divorce, and that a divorce might cause his job to be in jeopardy. Prior to these witnesses' testimony, the trial court specifically told the jurors that it was for them "to decide if the statement were made, and if so, what weight, if any, you should give to them." Ultimately, five witnesses, Christine Concetta, Meegan Turnbeaugh, Kathy LaPlante, Jessica Wade, and Vanessa Riegerix, testified about Sheri's statement to them concerning the state of her marriage and the defendant's desire for a divorce. Their testimony is sufficiently set forth in the "Facts" portion of the opinion.

133. The defendant's main point of contention with regard to the statutory exception pursuant to section 115-10.6 of the Code and the doctrine of wrongdoing by a forfeiture is that there was no evidence the defendant actually instituted divorce proceedings. We reject the defendant's contention that the pre-existence of legal proceedings is

a necessity. In People v Peterson, the appellate court held that the hearsay statements of the defendant's second wife that she and the defendant had been discussing a divorce would be admissible under section 115-10.6 of the Code even though dissolution proceedings had not been filed.

134. The defendant contends Peterson is distinguishable because in that case, the defendant killed his second wife with the intent of preventing her testimony at a hearing on the distribution of marital property, and in the instant case, the State was arguing that the defendant killed his wife because he could not seek a divorce for job reasons. We find this a distinction without a difference. The trial court properly followed all the requirements of the statute, and we cannot say the trial court erred in allowing five witnesses to testify in the manner in which they did.

135. Furthermore, the statements were also admissible pursuant to the doctrine of forfeiture by wrongdoing. In support of our findings, we rely on People v Hanson, in which the hearsay testimony by the defendant's sister, Katherine was admitted. Six weeks before the defendant killed Katherine, her husband, and their parents, Katherine told another sister, Jennifer, that the defendant was engaged in a scheme to obtain credit in their parents' name, and the defendant told her that if she told her father, he would kill her. Hanson, 238III.2d. In Hanson, no legal proceedings had been filed by the defendant's parents or anyone else regarding the fraud. In rejecting the defendant's arguments that the trial court erred in admitting Jennifer's testimonial hearsay, and, even if it did, the reliability of the statement must be considered, our supreme court points out that "(h) ad Katherine not been made unavailable by the defendant's wrongdoing, she might have testified as to the threat the defendant made against her." Here, if Sheri had not been killed by the defendant, she could have testified about the

defendant's desire to obtain a divorce but feared losing his job if he did so.

136. We also agree with the trial court that the hearsay testimony presented by the five witnesses was admissible to establish a motive. "Generally, evidence which shows that the accused had a motive to kill the victim is relevant in a homicide case if the evidence establishes the existence of the motive relied upon or alleged." People v Robinson. In the instant case, the defendant told Sheri he wanted a divorce because he believed she and the boys were holding him back from realizing his full potential, but he did not want to jeopardize his job by filing for divorce. Sheri relayed those statements to numerous people. The trial court limited the amount of this hearsay testimony to 5 witnesses out of a potential 13 offered by the State. After careful consideration, we find no error in the admission of this testimony.

137. Nor can we say that the trial court abused its considerable discretion in denying the defendant's motion for a mistrial after Meegan Turnbeaugh improperly testified she received a text message from Sheri that the defendant beat her. In general, a mistrial should only be granted in a case where an error is so grave that it infects the fundamental fairness of the trial so that continuing the proceeding would defeat the ends of justice. People v Bishop. A trial court has broad discretion in determining the propriety of declaring a mistrial. People v Hall. A Court can usually cure an inadmissible statement from a witness by sustaining an objection or instructing the jury to disregard what it has heard.

138. In the instant case, the parties agreed prior to trial that any testimony about the defendant beating Sheri was inadmissible. However, our review of the record clearly shows the State did not elicit this testimony: Turnbeaugh

volunteered it. Defense counsel immediately asked that the statement be stricken, and the trial court so instructed the jury. Overall, we believe Turnbeaugh's inadmissible testimony was of little magnitude in a case with these many witnesses and this much testimony. Any error was sufficiently cured when the trial court sustained the objection and directed the jury to disregard it. Even assuming arguendo, the error caused by the inadmissible statement was not cured, any prejudice flowing therefrom was de minimis in light of the overwhelming circumstantial evidence against the defendant. Accordingly, we find the trial court did not abuse its discretion in denying the defendant's motion for a mistrial.

139. IV Lindell Moore

140. The fourth issue is whether the trial court erred in admitting the testimony of Lindell Moore in which he compared spray-painted writings found at the murder scene to the defendant's handwriting. The defendant contends Moore's opinion as to comparisons between the defendant's handwritten exemplars and the spray-painted writings on the wall was too unreliable and too speculative to have been admitted at trial. The State replies the admission of Moore's expert testimony was not an abuse of discretion. We agree.

141. "Relevant evidence is defined as evidence having any tendency to make the existence of a fact that is of consequence to the determination of the action more or less probable than it would be without the evidence." People v Gonzalez. The determination of whether evidence is relevant and admissible rests within the sound discretion of the trial court, and a reviewing court should not reverse the trial court's ruling absent an abuse of the discretion of the trial court to determine whether expert testimony is admissible. People v Mitchell.

142. Section 8-1501 of the Code of Civil Procedure specifically provides:

    "In all courts of this State, it shall be lawful to prove handwriting by comparison made by the witness or jury with writings properly in the files of records of the case, admitted in evidence or treated as genuine or admired to be genuine, by the party against whom the evidence is offered, or proved to be genuine to the satisfaction of the court.

    This statute permits a witness to compare unknown handwriting samples with the known samples of a party in a case. Thus, we cannot say the trial court abused its discretion in allowing Moore to testify.

143. The defendant admits there are no Illinois cases that specifically address the issue of whether or not testimony comparing known handwriting with spray-painted graffiti should be allowed. He cites cases from foreign jurisdictions, People v Michallow, and Fassi v State, which are not binding on us. The defendant's main concern is with the unreliability and speculative nature of Moore's testimony. While the trial court possessed the discretion to disallow Moore's testimony if it determined its probative value was minimal, the trial court certainly was within its discretion to allow the jury to assess Moore's testimony and assign the weight, if any, it warranted.

144. Moore never identified the defendant as the author of the writings on the wall; he pointed out similarities, which the jury was free to accept or reject based on its own visual inspections of the photographs of the writings on the wall. Defense counsel did an admirable job of pointing out the unreliability of comparing spray-painted writings with handwritten writings, and the defendant's own expert, Steven McKasson, who trained Moore, cast serious doubt on Moore's ability to compare the defendant's handwriting samples with the spray-painted writings on the wall. Therefore, even if it was an error to allow Moore to testify

any error in the admission of his testimony was harmless because Moore's testimony did little to advance the State's case.

145. V. IP Addresses

146. The fifth issue is whether the trial court erred in admitting the testimony of Marcus Rogers and Kenneth Wojtowicz who testified about IP addresses. The defendant contends the trial court erred in admitting their testimony because it violated his right to confrontation, included inadmissible hearsay, and lacked a sufficient foundation. The State responds that assignment of computer IP addresses does not implicate the confrontation clause and that there was sufficient foundation for the testimony regarding the assignment of an IP address to the defendant's computer. We agree with the State.

147. The confrontation clause of the sixth amendment of the United States Constitution, which applies to the states under the fourteenth amendment, provides that "(i)n all criminal prosecutions, the accused shall enjoy the right *** to be confronted with the witnesses against him." U.S. Const., amend, VI. The confrontation clause is violated by the admission unavailable to testify, and the defendant had had a prior opportunity for cross-examination," (Emphasis added) Crawford v Washington. However, hearsay law exempts business records because businesses have a financial incentive to keep reliable records. See Fed. Rule Evid. 804(6). Business records are also generally admitted under the sixth amendment, not because of their reliability under hearsay law, but because they are created for the administration of an entity's affairs, not for the purpose of establishing or proving some fact as a trial. Melende-Dia v Massachusetts.

148. The instant case is similar to United States v Wyss. In that case, the reviewing court found the defendant's sixth amendment right to confrontation was not violated by allowing the government's computer forensic expert to testify based upon examination and comparisons of the defendant's Internet service provider's records, IP addresses, and data assigned to him on certain dates and times, along with data retrieved from an Internet bulletin board's servers which showed the IP addresses and data that corresponded to postings by the defendant's user name. The Wyss court specifically rejected the defendant's contention that a document kept in the regular course of business would become inadmissible if the document was later offered at trial in response to a court order or subpoena. Because the primary purpose of the records was customer billing, Sprint's IP address records were not testimonial in nature and were therefore admissible.

149. Likewise, in the instant case, Google's records were not testimonial in nature. Ken Wojtowicz sent a subpoena to Google in which he requested records pertaining to IP logs and subscriber information for destroychris@gmail. com, Google provided the IP addresses that sent the email threats. Wojtowicz explained that an IP address is basically like a home located. Denise Smith, Google's custodian of records, testified she provided the information in response to the police department's subpoena. She provided the IP addresses for eight specific messages. She testified that the records are kept in the ordinary course of business for Google.

150. Nevertheless, the defendant contends that Wyss is distinguishable from the instant case because in that case, a representative of Sprint, the defendant's Internet provider service, actually testified and was subject to cross-examination, whereas in the instant case, no one following AT&T, the defendant's Internet provider service, testified.

We disagree and point to the following expert testimony of Marcus Rogers which shows that testimony from an AT&T representative was unnecessary:

"So the Google end will verify that this address that was connected, and then in the event log itself, which is on the computer, so it's not even AT&T, it's the event log with the computer, the lap itself collects, that information was in there as well. So, it's on the computer, it would be in the AT&T records, and it would be in Google's records."

Thus, between the testimony of Denise Smith, the Google representative who testified these records were kept in the regular course of business, and the IP addresses found on the computers, there was a sufficient foundation to allow the nontestimonial IP addresses into evidence and allow Rogers and Wojtowicz to testify about them.

151. VI Receipt

152. The next issue is whether the trial court erred in allowing the admission of a hardware store receipt and in allowing a witness to testify to its content. The defendant argues the receipt was hearsay and there was no foundation for its admission. The State replies the receipt was admissible under an exception to the hearsay rule and, thus, there was no further need for extrinsic evidence of authenticity. We agree with the State.

153. The Illinois Rules of Evidence specifically provide an exception to the hearsay rule as follows: "Receipt or Paid Bill. A receipt or paid bill as prima facie evidence of the fat of payment and as prima facie evidence that the charge was reasonable." We disagree with the defendant's argument that this exception only applies to medical bills to show that the bill was reasonable. This exception clearly states that a receipt is an exception to the hearsay rule to show the payment.

154. The admission of evidence is within the sound discretion of the trial court, and a reviewing court will not reverse unless there is a showing of abuse of discretion. People v Becker. Here, Officer Heine testified that after reviewing Master Card statements, she was able to find that a can of spray paint was purchased at a hardware store using the credit card found in the defendant's home. Heine went to the store and obtained a copy of the receipt. The receipt was prima facie evidence that the defendant purchased the spray paint. The defendant was free to rebut that evidence.

155. The defendant virtually admits that the receipt would have been admissible as a business record exception to the hearsay rule. This means the State could have brought in another witness, an employee of the hardware store, to establish that the receipt was kept in the regular course of business. However, we find that the receipt and Officer Heine's testimony were sufficiently trustworthy. Thus, we cannot say the trial court abused its discretion in allowing the credit card receipt into evidence.

156. Even if the trial court erred in overruling the defendant's hearsay objection and allowing the receipt into evidence, we find any error harmless. An evidentiary error may be considered harmless if the properly admitted evidence in the case is so overwhelming that no fair-minded fact finder could reasonably have found the defendant not guilty. People v Miller. Here, the properly admitted and credible evidence overwhelmingly established the defendant's guilt as set forth below.

157. VII Reasonable Doubt

158. The final issue raised by the defendant is whether the evidence adduced at trial proved him guilty beyond a reasonable doubt. The defendant asserts there were many weaknesses in the State's case, such as a lack of DNA

evidence, a confession, or eyewitness testimony. The defendant speculates the jury had many doubts about this case and points to several notes sent by the jury during deliberations in support of this theory. He insists jurors were pushed over the edge by salacious photographs and other inadmissible evidence and that no rational trier of fact could have found him guilty beyond a reasonable doubt. We are unconvinced and rejected the defendant's arguments, finding overwhelming circumstantial evidence against the defendant.

159. When presented with a challenge to the sufficiency of the evidence, a reviewing court's function is not to retry a defendant. People v Givens. Rather, we must consider whether after viewing the evidence in the light most favorable to the prosecution, any rational trier of fact could have found the essential elements of the crime beyond a reasonable doubt. Under this particular standard, a reviewing court must draw all reasonable inferences from the record in the prosecution's favor. A reviewing court should not overturn a defendant's conviction "unless the evidence is so improbable or unsatisfactory that it creates a reasonable doubt of the defendant's guilt."

160. The evidence is unrefuted that the defendant started having an affair with Tara in November 2008. The affair became sexually charged and progressed to the point where the two were discussing marriage and the names for children they planned to have. The defendant was employed as head of security for JMM, earning $100,000 per year. Christine Cincotta, a JMM employee, testified that in most instances, a JMM employee who was caught having an affair probably would not be allowed to work at JMM anymore. She knew of one employee who was specifically fired for that reason. Joyce Meyer testified that if she knew the defendant was having an affair, it could "definitely" have affected his job and admitted that other

JMM employees had been fired for having adulterous affairs.

161. Joyce Meyer further testified that the defendant called her on May 4, 2009, the day before he murdered, and asked for the day off due to illness. Meyer could not recall the defendant ever calling in sick to work in the prior 11 years he worked for JMM. Tara testified that the defendant was going to serve divorce papers for Sheri on May 4, 2009. However, when that day arrived, the defendant told Tara he could not do so because Sheri's name was spelled incorrectly. The defendant explained to her that his lawyer was going to correct the typo, and he would serve Sheri with divorce papers the next day, which turned out to be the day Sheri, Garett, and Gavin were murdered.

162. On November 14, 2008, Joyce Meyer and the defendant received an email from the account destroychris@gmail.com. Minutes later, the defendant received another threatening email. In the ensuing days, more threatening emails were sent to JMM and the defendant. Joyce Meyer testified that to her knowledge, none of her other 900 employees had ever received threatening correspondence. In response to the threatening emails, the defendant contacted his hometown police department and patrols were stepped up in his neighborhood. On January 2, 2009, the defendant called the police to report he found a threatening letter in his mailbox. The police were able to determine the time frame in which the letter was placed in the mailbox. Police then canvassed the neighborhood and talked to neighbors about whether they noticed anything or anyone acting suspiciously during that time frame. No one did.

163. On April 27, 2009, the defendant told the police he received another threatening letter. In response, the defendant's neighbor, Detective Barlow, installed a camera in his home

and pointed directly at the defendant's house. As part of their investigation into the murders, police reviewed film from the camera installed at Barlow's house. It revealed that the defendant left his driveway at 5:43 a.m. on May 5, 2009. The defendant called Barlow at 6:43 a.m. to tell him that he was on his way home from the gym and was concerned because he could not reach Sheri by phone. The film shows Barlow arrived at the defendant's front door at 6:51 a.m., and the defendant arrived home at 6:56 a.m. The film further shows that between 5:43 a.m. and 6:51 a.m., no one went in or out of the defendant's front door.

164. The police investigation revealed no type of tracks or makings to indicate that anyone entered the home from the rear. There were no signs of forced entry into the home. A representative from the manufacturer of the basement window found open by police testified that the Colemans' window contains a forced entry resistance plate on the bottom. This means that if someone tried to open the window while the forced entry plate was locked, there would be damage to it. The Colemans' window did not show any sign of damage.

165. Investigators examined the threatening emails received by the defendant and noticed that the word "opportunities" was misspelled as "oppurtunities." Detective Wojtowicz discovered the defendant made the identical misspelling in his own writings. Wojtowicz subpoenaed Google for information about the destroychris@gmail.com account and learned that the IP address on which the account originated was the IP address on the defendant's laptop, meaning the threatening emails were sent from the defendant's own computer. Professor Marcus Rogers confirmed Wojtowicz's testimony that the threatening emails originated from the defendant's computer.

166. Police officers and paramedics who responded to the scene testified that rigor mortis was present in all the victims. Officer Donjon testified that as he tried to find a pulse on Sheri, he noticed Sheri's "skin was tough or thick." When he attempted to roll her over, "her head, shoulder, arm, and all kind of moved as though they were locked into place when (he) lifted her up." Lividity was also present, as evidenced by the fact that Donjon noticed blood had already pooled in Sheri's chest. Gary Hutchinson, a paramedic, testified that all the victims were cold and stiff when he arrived at 7:05 a.m. and rigor mortis was present. In his experience, "bodies that have rigor mortis have been down for a while."

167. Dr. Raj Nanduri performed autopsies on the victims on the day of the murders. She estimated Sheri died six to eight hours before the autopsy was performed at 11:04 a.m. Accordingly, Sheri was killed between 3 a.m. and 5 a.m. before the defendant ever left the house to go to the gym. Because Dr. Nanduri was uncomfortable with giving a specific time of death, the major case squad contacted Dr. Michael Baden, a world-renowned pathologist. While the defendant would have us believe that Dr. Baden was nothing more than hired gun brought in to make the State's case, the record believes the defendant's assertion. The State was well aware of the high-profile nature of the case. Dr. Baden's testimony in no way conflicts with Dr. Nanduri's testimony. Dr. Baden testified that while it can be difficult to establish a time of death, this case "wasn't a close call" because the only information the police really needed to know was whether the victims died before or after 5:43 a.m. He opined that all the victims were killed before 3 a.m. but definitely before 5 a.m. Dr. Baden also testified that no DMA of anyone outside the immediate family was found on the victim's bodies.

168. The police investigated the graffiti writings on the walls found in the Coleman home and discovered the paint used to make the writings was manufactured by Rustoleum and was "Apple Red" in color. Officer Karla Heine testified that after reviewing the records of the Master Card found inside the Coleman residence, she discovered a can of Apple Red Rustoleum paint was purchased using that Master Card on February 9, 2009, at a hardware store in St. Louis. Heine obtained a copy of the receipt from the hardware store. It was signed by the defendant.

169. Furthermore, the evidence revealed that there were unexplained scratches and bruising on the defendant's right arm as he was taken by ambulance to the police station. People's Exhibits 70 and 71, pictures taken at the police station on the day of the murders, show numerous scratches on the defendant's right arm. Jonathan Peters, a chaplain who accompanied the defendant in the ambulance, testified he noticed the markings on the defendant's arm and later saw the defendant strike his arm on a gurney. Peters was adamant that the injury to the defendant's right arm was present before the defendant struck his arm on the gurney.

170. The defendant, head of security for JMM, told Kathy Lapiante on the Friday before the murders that he had a working surveillance system in his house. Despite all the threats made against the defendant and his family and the defendant's expertise in security, it makes no sense that he would have failed to complete the installation of the security system or failed to lock his basement window.

171. Taken as a whole, we cannot say the evidence is so improbable or unsatisfactory that it creates a reasonable doubt as to the defendant's guilt. On the contrary, the circumstantial evidence against the defendant is overwhelming. Any other potential suspects were ruled out

by the police. The threatening emails were sent directly from the defendant's own computer. The evidence showed the defendant possessed not only a motive to kill his wife and two children but also the opportunity to do so, as all three were dead before 5 a.m., and the defendant did not leave the house until 5:43 a.m. The only reasonable inference that can be drawn from the record before us is that the defendant was still in the home when the victims were killed.

172. Finally, we are unconvinced by the defendant's argument that the jury had major doubts about this case or his argument that the jury was pushed over the edge by salacious photographs or inadmissible testimony. Considering the length of the trial and the amount of deliberations came to a halt until the transcripts of the doctors' testimony could be prepared and provided to the jury as requested, so the jury did not deliberate as long as the defendant asserts. Likewise, as previously discussed, the trial court used extreme caution in paring down these exhibits. We have previously addressed the defendant's arguments regarding inadmissible testimony and have found nothing warranting a new trial.

173. CONCLUSION

174. Our Illinois Supreme Court has noted that a trial cannot be conducted without error and the perfection in trial procedure is virtually unattainable, a defendant in a criminal case is entitled to a fair trial, not necessarily a perfect trial. People v Bull. Accordingly, we believe that no error or combination thereof was so grave that it infected the fundamental fairness of the trial. After careful consideration, evidence for the jury find beyond a reasonable doubt that the defendant killed all three victims.

175. This was an intense, lengthy, and sensational trial with many complicated and hotly contested issues. The record is voluminous. The record also reflects the high quality of representation by the trial attorneys for both sides. The skill and fairness of the trial judge the professionalism by all. The jury upheld the best traditions of our common law jury system of justice. We commend them all.

176. For the foregoing reasons, we hereby affirm the judgment of the circuit court of Monroe County.

177. Affirmed.

CHRISTOPHER COLEMAN WAS CHARGED WITH 3 COUNTS OF 1ST DEGREE MURDER.

HE RECEIVED 3 CONSECUTIVE LIFE SENTENCES FOR THE MURDERS OF SHERI, GARETT, AND GAVIN COLEMAN.

Christopher is serving his time in the Waupun, Wisconsin Dodge Correctional Institution.

> **Don't worry that children never listen to you; worry that they are always watching you.**
>
> — **Robert Fulghum**

CHAPTER 6

Anthony Todt, 46 years old, DOB 9/25/1975; Megan, 42 years old, DOB 01/28/1977; Alek, 13 years old, DOB 09/26/2006; Tyler, 11 years old, DOB 12/30/2008; Zoe, 4 years old, DOB 07/23/2015; dog Breezy.

As I dig into many true crime stories—some I write, about some I don't—I have never found one as bizarre as this story. I will tell you about it and you decide which way to go with what you believe. I don't know how anyone could make this up. If a person has this sort of an imagination, they should write horror stories for a living.

In the fall of 2019, in a very large, very beautiful home in the Celebration subdivision of Disney World, a family was renting a home at 202 Reserve Place, Celebration, Florida. Everyone who knew them said they were a very friendly, very nice family. Tony the father was a physical therapist and had two practices that he and his wife Megan started together in Colchester, Connecticut. Megan was also a physical therapist. Tony and Megan were high-school sweethearts. They were married when Tony got out of college and Megan had two years left.

Megan was diagnosed since her teenage years with Lyme disease. Her family stated she was not debilitated and was energetic, vibrant, and full of life. They told how she was totally about being a mom and her whole world existed around her three children. Alek 13, Tyler 10, and Zoe 4. Her husband Tony testified to a different Megan—a 42-year-old mother who was almost constantly in pain had trouble breathing and a heart condition, even trouble walking at times. He said she was very depressed which is again the opposite of what her family, friends, and neighbors saw in her. Tony said the job of caring for the children and the home was mostly on him because Megan could not function the way she should be able to. When asked why such a difference, he stated because Megan was private and did not want people to know what she dealt with. Since Megan is gone, there really is no way of knowing for positive which is true.

The Todt family purchased a condo at 211 Longview Kissimmee, Florida where they would spend time. After trips to Florida, Megan said the warm weather helped her to feel better so she wanted to move there and have Tony commute between CT and Florida. At some point, they decided the condo was not large enough and signed a lease to rent a very extravagant home in Celebration, Florida which is an extension of Disney, I think on the Disney grounds. The house was in the very upper-class neighborhood where everything looked perfect. It was said at one time the neighborhood resembled Desperate Housewives. Their rent was $4900.00 per month.

The Todts fully furnished the rental house with brand-new furniture, most from Ethan Allen. The house was so large it would be interesting to know what the bill for furnishing it would have been. They moved in and Tony started commuting back and forth. He had office hours Tuesday, Wednesday, Thursday, and was flying Mondays and Fridays. Some of his patients said you could see his lights on some late evenings if you drove by the office. This would be a grueling schedule for anyone to keep. By all accounts, Tony was a loving, doting father and attentive, loving, and caring husband. He referenced Zoe was his little angel. His patients adored him and raved about how good he was. They considered him brilliant as he took many conditions and basically almost healed them through physical therapy. His sisters and mother loved him and had close relationships with him. Megan's family loved him and were very close to him. He even took the family on many vacations, especially her grandparents. Tony was known to be the jokester, life of the party, the funny one. He was class president in high-school and captain of the soccer team. Everyone loved him at school, rare to be that well-liked. His yearbook described him as most likely to succeed. It was described once that he was like a celebrity in the town of Colchester, where most everyone knew him. How, how could someone like this turn so drastically and kill his whole family including the family dog? I easily could write a whole book on this story but I really want to put his children in this book. Maybe at a later date.

According to Tony, in March of 2005, Megan while at Disney Theme Park was bitten by a large bug which caused a large pustule on her leg. This seemed to be the beginning of many health issues he says, setting off a string of emergency room and doctor visits which lead to many different diagnoses. Yet again, the family was not really aware of all of these doctor visits and diagnosis. She had medication-induced hepatitis, a heart condition. And according to Anthony, she had been told by doctors when she was a teenager that she had Lyme disease. He said she dealt with chronic pain and other symptoms that sometimes rendered her unable to function some days. She starts cooking and eating very holistically. She wanted her family to be healthy and enjoy good food that they enjoyed. The family knew she had become very health conscientious. She took lessons in Yoga and became a certified yoga instructor.

According to him, he did most everything in the home. Before she was sick, she had the two boys. Later, she had a third child, a girl. Both Anthony and Meghan were raised Roman Catholic. According to Tony, when she became so sick, she did seek alternative help for her health conditions. She started worshiping as a Hindu. Anthony told the police he was a forced Catholic and didn't necessarily practice.

His patients say right before Thanksgiving Tony had to cancel his appointments. The patients were told it was due to a medical emergency concerning his wife which fit what Anthony had said was going on with Megan's health. However, was this just part of a very carefully laid out plan?

Tony said Megan was saying the end of the world was happening on December 28th and the two of them had made a pack to die as a family, or cross over together. It's interesting that when Tony's sister called the police for a well check on the Todts, she mentioned to police that the last time she talked to her sister-in-law, Megan had mentioned the end of the world coming on December 28th, possibly said as a joke.

Megan was a leader of a Yoga class. The women in that class declined to comment on whether or not she had ever talked about the end of the world coming on December 28, 2019, or whether or not she had talked about her spiritualty, or that she was following the Hindu faith.

In early December, one of the staff members at Tony's practice came to work one morning and the FBI came in and wanted to seize Tony's computers and electronics and files. When Tony came into work that day, he went into another room with the FBI, and they worked with Tony behind closed doors. The office girl said he came out of the room one time and to get something and told her not to worry as it was just a misunderstanding of some sort. Another time, she had to walk into the room where they were and she noticed Tony had a look on his face that said how concerned he was. He made an agreement with the FBI that he was going home for a couple of weeks and he would obtain an attorney and call them for another meeting when he came back. This never happened of course because he never came back.

After Tony went home, he called back later and told the staff to let his patients know the office would be closed until the beginning of January. In early January, a patient said she tried calling the offices and found the phone had been disconnected. Everyone became very concerned. Why would a man who was so respected and loved by so many people just disappear from everyone who knew and loved them? It all seemed more than strange and concerning.

So here is some of what we know:

1. The Todt family was living between two cities—mostly, Anthony; Megan and the kids moved to Celebration, Florida. Anthony would come home on the weekends.
2. It seemed the Todts were living well above their means.
3. Tony was very well-liked by all who knew him.
4. Megan was a mom who was all about her children.
5. Megan was also extremely well-liked.
6. Megan was living a very holistic way of eating and fed her family that way.

7. The Todts owned a condo just two blocks from where they were living in the Celebration rental home.
8. Tony had recently gained a very large amount of weight.
9. By all that everyone could see, they were a perfect family, and Tony and Megan loved each other.
10. Tony had taken out many loans from different loan companies. Some of the loans were for a lot of money. Some hundreds of thousands of dollars.
11. Tony could not pay back the loans and was out of credit line. He owed somewhere close to half million dollars.
12. Tony had state-of-the-art equipment in his practice, even an underwater treadmill.
13. Megan homeschooled the children.
14. The children were all very musically inclined.
15. The Federal Government was after Tony for Medicare Fraud. They were closing in on him. His excuses and avoiding them had run out and there was a warrant for his arrest.

Here are some of what Tony has told in his statements:

1. Megan was in constant chronic pain to the point she could hardly function.
2. Megan was very controlling over Tony.
3. Tony said Megan made a Benadryl pie and fed to the children.
4. Tony did whatever Megan wanted without argument.
5. According to Tony, he loved Megan so much that he would take full responsibility for anything she did.

Megan was estranged from her mother, and her father had committed suicide in November of 2002. It was said she was very close to her dad. She was very close to her grandparents and they took them on trips and spent a lot of time with them. She also had an aunt and uncle she was very close to. In fact, the aunt was more like a mother to Megan. None of these people were aware of there being any health issues to any degree with Megan, other than she had two miscarriages. All they ever saw was an energetic, committed, and loving mother who took great care of her children.

Tony's father had spent decades in prison for hiring someone to shoot Tony's mother. One night, when Tony was four years old, this happened. He remembered being in the hallway and seeing someone shoot her in the face. This did not kill her, and he is close with his mother. To this day, his mother, Loretta, defends Tony's father and says he is not the one who shot her. Tony's father Robert denies it also and had stuck to it all the years he was in prison.

Confession #1. As told to the police by Tony at the first meeting with them:

Anthony Todt was brought into an interrogation room and read his Miranda Rights. He said he understood everything. He sat in handcuffs as he was sworn in to tell the truth. The officer went over the fact that the police picked him up from his home and he was taken to the hospital and treated. Tony told the police that he wanted to be on the other side with his wife and children and very sad that he wasn't. The detective told Tony that he was present at the autopsy the day before.

During the interview, Tony was unshaven, unkept, and had gained a large amount of weight. The police had put him in a white jumpsuit that looked like it barely fit. He looked more like someone in a mental institution. Whether this was intentional or unintentional, who knows.

Tony stated that he and Megan had been watching videos about the afterlife. The more they watched and researched, he said, they realized the end was coming near. And the more they watched, they decided they wanted to go to the other side as a family so they could all be together with no heartache and pain. He says he and Meagan started looking deeper into this and started seriously making some plans. They decided they were going to bring this up to the children and if either of the children did not want to do this, they would spare them. Just before Thanksgiving that year, they sat at the dinner table and talked to the children. They asked them if mommy and daddy were to die, where would they want to go? According to him, they all said they would want to go with their parents. Of course, we do not know how they made this look to the children or how they presented it.

He said they sat down and tried to explain to the children what they were thinking about doing. The children said that if the parents died, they wanted to go with them.

Tony said Megan cooked a pie with sleep-ez and Benadryl in it. However, Tony said nothing happened. Megan started her research in April. They allegedly talked to the kids before Thanksgiving. After research, they decided the easiest thing to do was bleed to death. Again, Tony says he and Megan planned this together.

They wanted the kids to "stick around" until after their school program so it would not bring up any questions. Tony said he was positive the family died before Christmas. The children died first. He and Megan set the alarm at 11:30 at night and got up to kill the children. They went into Zoe's room first. He said he sat there for two to three hours trying to get up the nerve. Megan kept coming in and checking on him to see if he was finished. He wanted to save her soul and said that was a way to do it. First, he had decided to stab them. He said that Zoe rolled over and started screaming so he kind of laid on top of her and held a pillow over her face until she was dead. He did not think he stabbed her at all. He had a small green buck knife but did not use it. He said he sat in the room with her for a while after he killed her to make sure she was gone. When asked by the detective, he said it took about 10 to 15 minutes of him smothering her before she was gone. He said she kicked and fought back a lot.

Then they went to Alek's room. They had decided that Megan would hold his feet down while Tony stabbed him. She is holding his feet and they were just looking at each other. He said he stabbed Alek and he started kicking. Tony reached around and held his mouth and nose until he stopped kicking. There was blood on his bed from where he had stabbed him. He does not know how long it took but he said Alek went fast. They researched how to do the stabbing on Quora.com He tried to look up how to use the knife and how to commit suicide. He started researching that before Halloween. Alek was 13-years-old and the strongest to hold down. Tony said Megan went back to their room and the murder of Alek was completely Tony's responsibility.

They then went downstairs where Tyler, 10-years-old, was sleeping on a pullout couch in the library. They purposely had him sleep there so they wouldn't wake each other up. Megan was outside of the door doing meditation and only him and Tyler were in the room. The detective said that was an awful lot for a human being to go through. But as Tony said, they had the children's salvation in mind, they loved their children, and they just wanted them all to be together. He said he put the knife in Tyler's stomach and he bled out quickly.

Tony and Megan went back upstairs to their bedroom. They decided to take the dog also. He said Megan took the backside of the dog and Tony held his snout and smothered the dog, which Tony said Breezy went quietly and peacefully.

Megan said she wanted to go next; she did not want to be alive without her children. She wanted some wine; she drank her wine, took the knife, and put it into her stomach. Tony said they laid on the bed and he just held her. After about 45 minutes, she said she could feel it but she had not had a lot of bleeding.

Megan told him it was just not working so she asked him to get her some Benadryl. Tony said she took a large bottle of Benadryl and drank it. Then, she laid down and waited for it to take effect. He said at one point, he thought she had passed but then she opened her eyes. Tony told how he got up and went into the bathroom and when he came out, Megan was sitting on the side of the bed and stabbed herself again. He heard a pop. She told him she stabbed herself in the liver. She laid some clean sheets on the bed, so she didn't have to lay on wet sheets from the blood that was already there. Again, she told Tony it did not seem to be working so she asked him to smother her. He said he told her he did not think he could do that. According to him, she said, "If you love me, you will do this. I'm in so much pain, I need you to do this." So, he took a small pillow that was on the bed and smothered her.

After Megan died, Tony said he wanted his family to all be together, so he first brought Zoe, laid her at Megan's feet, and covered her with her favorite blanket. He brought each of the boy's mattresses and put them on the floor at the end of the bed. He said he put a rosary in each of their hands.

Tony said he laid on the bed for twenty-four hours and decided he needed to "get this thing done." According to him, he tried several different ways to kill himself. He tried to hang himself, choke himself, drank large amounts of Benadryl and alcohol, and nothing worked.

One of the most horrible aspects of this whole thing is he stayed in the house with the dead decaying bodies from around December 15 to 18 until January 13th when the authorities picked him up. The bodies were so decomposed they had to be identified through dental records. The odor from decomposed bodies was evident as soon as the police walked into the front door.

Confession #2:

The reason I am calling this confession #2 is because the story he told police is different than this story he told in court the day he testified during his trial. I'm not sure why he changed his story, but the District Attorney did not believe the second story.

This man is narcissistic, arrogant, and used to having his own way. You can tell when he gave his own testimony at his trial. He didn't like it because the attorney for the State was in control, and she called him out on his shit. She didn't believe him, and she didn't let it slide. She could decipher the truth and was hitting the areas he didn't want her to. To me, his second story does not even make sense.

Also, there is the fact that there were very many finite details in his first confession that he gave to the police. I do believe he was drugged up from the Benadryl he took, and he was in a bad state of mind from lying with four dead bodies and a dead dog for almost a month. However, they took him to the hospital first, and I do not believe that he does not remember that day as he says in his trial.

Megan told Anthony the traditional medications were not helping, and that she needed to try something else. She became a certified Yoga instructor. She also wanted to treat herself holistically and spiritually. According to Tony, whenever he was home, he always performed physical therapy on Megan two times a day to help her pain. Allegedly, she still could not hardly function. He stated he sometimes even had to carry her upstairs.

One evening, around December 18, 2019, Tony said he sat down at the dinner table with his family. He was trying to lose weight, so he only had a shake. The children ate their dinner and he got ready to go over to their condo to pick up some things the kids needed and was going to put Zoe's bike together. He said he took their van so he could bring all things back. According to him, after he got to the condo, he went into the back to get his bag of tools, but they were not there, so he walked back to the house to get them. He had told his boys to put them in the van and they had forgotten.

When he got back home, he said the boys were playing basketball and they asked him to play with them. So, he played basketball for a couple of hours, got the bag of tools, and walked back to the condo. He got in the van, he said, just to rest a bit but fell asleep. He said when he woke up, the day was out and it startled him because he should have been home to help Megan by giving her physical therapy.

He drove the van home and said when he walked in the door, Megan was standing at the top of the stairs. She told him she needed to talk with him. He told her he needed to use the bathroom first, so he went into the guest bathroom that was downstairs.

Anthony said Megan was so sick she was about 90 pounds, she couldn't breathe, she had heart issues, and she was in constant pain. Anthony testified that most days, she could hardly climb the stairs.

He testified that Megan sought other means of religious comfort. She was introduced to eastern religion, Hindu-based following. He also testified that before the birth of their oldest son, in November of 2002, her father hung himself. He stated Megan was very close to her father. He also said Megan had miscarriages. After her last miscarriage, he said there were days she didn't get out of bed. He said some days, she felt very helpless. She believed she could go to another life and have a better life and better relationships.

There was a suicide note that Anthony said he found at the computer when he came home that morning. According to him, she told him when he came that morning, that she had killed all the kids. He said there was a blue melted sort of pie sitting on the counter, and some left on each of the kid's plates. He said the house was very quiet, and he felt something was not quite right. Megan had blood on her shirt, so he went to each of the kid's rooms and found them dead.

Let me pause here to say to the outside world, these people seemed highly functional, normal people. Their children were smart and well-rounded, the parents spent a lot of time with them, and even just before their deaths, Tyler had a music recital. We never really know what is going on behind closed doors in someone else's home. Of course, this is coming from Anthony; none of the others have a voice here. Megan's family felt she would be appalled even at the mention of her hurting her children. Yet, there are also many people who feel Anthony could not have been capable of hurting his children or Megan. He always portrayed himself as a devoted husband and loving father. So, what could have happened?

Autopsies:

CHILD FATALITY SUMMARY

County: Osceola
Child's name: Zoe Todt
Child's name: Tyler Todt
Child's name: Aleksander Todt
DOB: 07/21/15 (Date of death for all three children: 01/13/2020)
DOB: 12/30/2008 (This is the day Anthony was arrested so date of death)
DOB: 09/26/2006
(Because they do not know exactly if date of death is 1/13/2020. Most likely, the date of death was around 12/17/2020.)

Circumstances Surrounding Death

On January 13, 2020, the 4, 11, and 13-year-old children, along with their mother, were found deceased in the family home.

According to the Osceola County, Sheriff's Office, the following information was provided:

On December 29, 2019, the Osceola County Sheriff's Office received a request to complete a well-being check on the Todts' home from a family member in Connecticut. The family was concerned because they were told that the Todts had the flu and had not heard from them in weeks. Deputies checked out the home but nothing suspicious was noted. There was no odor or suspicious activity reported by neighbors and the blinds of the home were closed. No one answered the door and the Todt family was known to travel often. Several more attempts to reach out to Anthony Todt were made prior to January 13, 2020.

On January 13, 2020, the Osceola County Sheriff's Office responded to the home to assist federal agents in serving an arrest warrant for the father for crimes out of Connecticut. A safety check of the home was completed, and the three children, their mother, and the family dog were found deceased. This time of death is 9:37 a.m.

The father Anthony Todt was interviewed by Osceola County Sheriff's Office Detectives at Advent Health Hospital and his statement is summarized as follows: "Anthony last consumed Benadryl on January 11, 2020, and was not under the influence of any drugs or alcohol. Anthony disclosed that he and his wife, Megan, had been planning for months to kill their children, and then kill each other in a suicide pact. They all had to die together in order to be with each other in the next life. Anthony admitted to killing his three children, thirteen-year-old Alek Todt, eleven-year-old Tyler Todt, and four-year-old Zoe Todt. At some point right before the murders, Anthony bought at least one knife. It had a large blade on it. Anthony said such a large blade was due to his size, he had to have something large enough for the blade to go deep enough inside him. Anthony used a knife and stabbed the boys in the abdomen, then suffocated them, one at a time in separate bedrooms. He could not remember if he stabbed Zoe but knew he suffocated her on her bed. Once the children were deceased, Megan took grape Tylenol PM and once she was rested, Anthony suffocated Megan until she died.

Anthony waited for all the bodies who were still all in separate rooms to come out of rigor mortis before moving the bodies. Once the bodies were out of rigor mortis, Anthony moved the bodies to the master bedroom so they could all be together as a family. He placed the boys on mattresses next to his bed so they would all be comfortable. He placed his daughter's body wrapped in a sheet at the foot of his bed. Prior to killing Megan, he suffocated the family dog so it could also be with the family in the afterlife. He placed the dog's body in its bed near the boys on the ground. Anthony attempted to take his own life after killing Megan but failed claiming he 'chickened out.' Anthony could not remember exactly when he killed his children but remembered watching college football the following day. Anthony estimated that these events took place on a Friday and possibly before Christmas 2019, but he could not confirm. He claimed sole responsibility for the death of his family and reiterated the premeditation fashion of their murders. He and Megan began planning this suicide pact back in June or July 2019 in an effort for the entire family to be together in the "afterlife." All conversations were recorded and post-Miranda.

The Osceola County Sheriff's Office investigated the deaths of Zoe, Tyler, Aleksander, and Megan Todt (201004290). The detectives believe that the deaths occurred in late December 2019. On January 15, 2019, Anthony Todt was charged with four counts of Premeditated First-Degree Murder and one count of Animal Cruelty. On February 1, 2020, Anthony Todt was charged with four counts of Murder with a Depraved Mind. The father pled not guilty on January 30, 2020, and waived arraignment. The trial is scheduled for April 27, 2020, and the prosecution is ongoing.

On January 14, 2020, District Nine Medical Examiner, Jennifer Nara, M.D., completed an autopsy on Zoe Todt. ME#20-25-0099.

Cause of Death: Homicidal Violence of Unspecified Means in Association with Diphenhydramine Toxicity

Manner of Death: Homicide
Autopsy Findings:

1. Diphenhydramine toxicity
2. No evidence of trauma
3. Early putrefactive decomposition

On January 14, 2020, District Nine Medical Examiner Jennifer Nara, M.D. completed an autopsy of Tyler Todt. ME#20-25-0098.

Cause of Death: Homicidal Violence of Unspecified Means in Association with Diphenhydramine Toxicity

Manner of Death: Homicide
Autopsy Findings:

1. Stab wound of the abdomen:
   a. Injury of large intestine
   b. No hemorrhage
   c. Diphenhydramine toxicity
   d. Early putrefactive decomposition

On January 14, 2020, District Nine Medical Examiner Jennifer Nara, M.D. completed an autopsy of Aleksander Todt. ME#20-25-00097.

Cause of Death: Homicidal Violence of Unspecified Means in Association with Diphenhydramine Toxicity

Manner of Death: Homicide
Autopsy Findings:

1. Stab wound of the abdomen:
   a. Injury of left 8th rib
   b. No injury to small and large intestines
   c. No blood in the abdomen
2. Diphenhydramine toxicity
3. Early putrefactive decomposition

On January 14, 2020, District Nine Medical Examiner Jennifer Nara, M.D. completed an autopsy of Megan Todt. ME#20-25-00096.

Cause of Death: Homicidal Violence of Unspecified Means in Association with Diphenhydramine Toxicity

Manner of Death: Homicide
Autopsy Findings:

1. Stab wounds of the abdomen:
   a. Hemoperitoneum, 100-200 ml
   b. Sharp force injury of mesenteric fat
2. Diphenhydramine toxicity
3. Early putrefactive decomposition

On April 9, 2020, the Department of Children and Families' investigation was closed with:

- Verified Findings of Death and Physical injury to Zoe, Tyler, and Aleksander Todt with Anthony Todt as the caregiver responsible.
- Not Substantiated Findings of Asphyxiation as to Zoe, Tyler, and Aleksander Todt.
- No Indicators of Household Violence Threatens Child to Zoe, Tyler, and Aleksander Todt.

Other Children in the Family:

The family is the only surviving family member and he is incarcerated.

Summary of Current Agency Involvement with Family:

The family did not have any current involvement.

Summary of Prior Agency Involvement with Family

The family does not have any prior abuse history in Florida or Connecticut.

On the day of Anthony's sentencing, Megan's aunt, whom she was very close to came to the podium and said some things to the court. She told the judge how Megan was kind, sweet, caring, and so empathetic to other people. She talked about how her mother, the kids, and Megan would go out for a "girls" day occasionally. She said they would go shopping to buy all the kids' shoes or something, and then they would have lunch. She said at lunch and throughout their shopping day, Anthony would call over and over. Sometimes, every five minutes, he would call again and Megan, after talking to him initially, would not take his calls.

The aunt said he was controlling and had to know what she was doing every moment. She said she talked to Megan about it.

The aunt told how her parents (Megan's grandparents) were so close to the family. She said her mother is 95, and her dad 97. The Todts used to vacation with them, and just do a lot of activities with them. She said her parents loved Megan and the children so much, she didn't know what they were going to do without them. Very touching how she talked about the children as they would go to nursing homes and play music for the elderly residents there and how much the people loved it.

After the aunt talked, the judge asked if anyone else had anything to say. The state did not, the defense said Anthony had something he wanted to say. Anthony stood and went on and on trying to tell the judge the whole story again—how much he loved Megan and the kids and how he didn't do anything to them. He just would not stop talking. His attorney stood 2 to 3 times trying to tell him this was not helping him or doing any good for him. If he had been left to continue talking, who knows how long he would have talked.

The jury found Anthony guilty on all counts. They did not believe the second confession. Anthony was sentenced to:

1. As to premeditated murder in the 1st degree to Tyler Todt, age 11, Guilty; Life without possibility of parole.
2. As to premeditated murder in the 1st degree to Alek Todt, age 13, Guilty; Life without possibility of parole.
3. As to premeditated murder in the 1st degree to Zoe Todt, age 4, Guilty; Life without the possibility of parole.
4. As to premeditated murder in the 1st degree to Megan Todt, Guilty; Life without the possibility of parole.
5. As to cruelty to an animal, the death of family dog Breezy; one year in the county jail.

All sentences to be served concurrently. Time already served: 313 days.

The judge told Anthony he is "a destroyer of worlds." He stated, you destroyed Zoe's world, you destroyed Tyler's world, you destroyed Alek's world. You destroy worlds.

My Conclusion:

I feel bad for the jury, as these things are hard to look at: the pictures and listening to all details. There's no drama that can be added to this story as it is just horrific in itself.

What I have gathered and the people I have talked to about this case are people who were either close to the family or lived by the family. According to all these people, Megan was not a crazy pain-ridden person. She was educated, energetic, and dedicated to her children and to life itself. She wasn't one that would have committed suicide or murdered her own children.

My belief is Anthony planned this whole thing out. Every detail I believe was premeditated. From time to time, you hear things about "the world coming to an end on such and such date." That could have been something he or Megan heard and she referred to it possibly in a joking way. My opinion is Anthony made the pie. I thought he said he did make a Benadryl pie. However, I could be mistaken. I believe he made it and insisted everyone eat theirs because he went to a lot of work to make it. Otherwise, how could he have given them enough to knock them out? I believe he was trying to wait as long as possible for their bodies to decompose so not much could be found.

We never really know people and what they are capable of, yet it seems a little strange both parents who were educated, seemingly well-adjusted people could become that insane.

My opinion was that Anthony was way over his head financially. His overhead had to be huge. He had two underwater treadmills that were state-of-the-art machines, two offices and staff, plus two homes to upkeep. They moved into 2002 Reserve place which is the most upper-class subdivision in the area. The neighborhood is so pristine it would remind you of a neighborhood you would see in a movie or television show. The house was rented for $5,000 per month, plus the payment on the condo. Anthony said he would make a large loan at one loan company to cover another loan company and so on until he owed at least 5 or 6 loan companies, and he ran out of credit. He had cheated by billing the government by the thousands, and I don't know how many accounts. He was flying back and forth every week, working, and according to him taking care of all household chores. Even if he wasn't doing all the household chores (and I don't believe he was), he just was balancing more than any one person could.

Anthony said that a few weeks before he and Megan had a really huge argument, it was bad enough that it took him a while to get back into her good graces (if he ever did). He did know the government wanted to talk to him, and he knew he was in trouble.

So, I think what happened was it had come down to the wire with the government and he knew it. I'm sure he probably downplayed it. However, I think he may have told Megan about what was going on. She probably had no idea and became very angry. My opinion is she didn't know about all the loans or the fraud with the government.

When he left Connecticut after he told the investigators he would meet with them right after the holiday, he knew he would never be back. One of his workers in the office said she didn't believe when he left that day that he would ever be back.

I'm not sure how he did it, but I feel sure he deceived Megan and somehow had her knocked out so he could kill the children. I don't know if he snapped or went crazy with all the pressure and stress he was under. It would be horrible the extreme weight one would have to carry with all of that going on in their life.

Why would he put blame on Megan? I'm not sure other than once he had time to think about things afterward, he didn't want to shoulder all the blame. He wanted her to carry some blame. After all, everything he did was for her and because he loved her so much. According to him, he had her on a pedestal.

Some murderers you can have empathy for are those who realize they made a really bad choice and now they have to pay for it. Anthony is very hard to feel sorry for. He is arrogant, a know it all. He says Megan was the boss in the sense she totally ruled everything in their family. If she was in fact, maybe she had to be.

This is another case—in my opinion, he should get the death penalty. He showed no mercy at all for his entire family including the poor little dog Breezy then wanted to shift the blame to Megan. One of the last things in his sentencing he said to the judge is how he did not do this, that Megan killed the children and then killed herself. I feel no empathy for what he did.

Zoe was a sweet little girl. People said she was smart, loving, and just enjoyed having a good life. She loved her brothers and liked telling them what to do as most little sisters do. She loved princesses and was treated like one herself.

Tyler was a strong, athletic ten-year-old. Good in his studies and in music, he loved making people happy by playing music for them. He had a big heart and really looked up to his dad. He was competitive, loved to play sports, and loved basketball.

Alek was a strong boy, a good size for 13, and also loved sports. He was studious and also loved the piano and violin. He always loved playing for the older people in the nursing homes. People loved his charisma and how smart he was. He was the one who put up the biggest fight, Anthony said. His dad, although much larger than him, had a hard time holding him down.

Anthony said he called Megan so much when she was out because he was worried about her. I believe he called her so much because he was afraid she was going to reveal something that was going on at home, something that might cause her family to say *you need to leave and get out of that house. Take the children and come stay with us.* Who knows, maybe she had threatened that or thought about it. We will never know.

One thing that tugs at my heart is what the friends of the kids and the children in the community were saying, "Will there be a time you will kill me, dad?" The fears it may have put in so many of their heads, a time they will never forget.

So many unanswered questions. I know that readers who are really true crime fans can figure this one out. I look forward to hearing from you and your opinions on this and the other cases.

Children make you want to start life over. Muhammad Ali

CHAPTER 7

Gannon Stauch, 11 years old

January 27, 2020, Colorado Springs, Colorado

Al Stauch, Gannon's father, was away for military training on the week of January 25, 2020.

Stepmother, Letecia, and her daughter Harley were at home with 11-year-old Gannon while his dad was away. On that Sunday morning, Letecia took the kids and went to the mountains for a hike. On Monday morning, Gannon did not go to school. It was posted on social media that he was not feeling well and had a doctor's appointment that afternoon. A neighbor reported that morning they saw Letecia get into a red truck. She backed the truck up to the garage door, got out, and seemed to be loading something into the truck. Someone else got into the truck and they left. There were four hours of Letecia's time unaccounted for. When she came home that day, Gannon was not with her and that was 2:15 in the afternoon. At 6:55 pm, Monday, Letecia called the police to say she wanted to report her stepson as a runaway. Why an 11-year-old child would be considered a runaway, I am very puzzled. If a child of that age is not accounted for, it would always be concerning and a missing child is not immediately a runaway.

She told police that Gannon had gone to play with a friend, and she did not know his name because she did not keep track of his friends. That is what Al is supposed to do. The neighborhood cameras did not pick up the movements of Gannon.

11-year-old Gannon was in the 5th grade. He was the older brother to Laina, 8 years old. He was known as a very loving, kind, and thoughtful little boy. His mother Landon and father Al shared custody of the two children. His mother lived in North Carolina. In 2015, Al married Letecia who had one daughter Harley. In 2020, Al, Letecia, and the three children lived in Colorado Springs, Colorado. Letecia had a hard time holding down a job. She posted online that she was working at a school she never worked at. Later, she would have claimed to work at three different schools that she never worked at. Three weeks before the murder, she applied at a major airline based out of Denver but did not get the job. In January, Al was in Oklahoma for military training. Gannon was reported missing by Letecia. She told police he left home on January 27th, between 3:15-4:00 pm. She told police he was a runaway which was totally unlike Gannon. His mother and stepfather flew in from South Carolina to help in the search for Gannon. People spent a lot of time searching for Gannon and posted posters all through the area. They had hundreds of volunteers helping and looking for Gannon. They had K-9s and anything else they thought could help them. There was blood found inside Gannon's bedroom.

His father Al reported finding a dinner-size pool of blood inside his room. Letecia said he had a bad nosebleed. There were splatters on the wall and blood that had soaked through the carpet. The blood on the walls had 50 blood splatters. There was blood on his mattress. All of it started turning suspicion on Letecia since she was the last person to see him alive. Social media and rumors were flying everywhere. People were very angry about what had happened to this little boy. January 31st, Letecia gave an interview to try and stop the rumors that were going on. She asked the community to stop the things they were doing and left for South Carolina. She says she asked for an attorney during questioning and was denied one. She made an accusation that she had been taking care of him for the past two years because his mother didn't want to take care of him. She said they were getting death threats. She said she will be so glad when they find Gannon and people will apologize for what they have said about her. She gave a message to Gannon that she will be glad when he returns and told people Letecia hasn't done anything. It was all about her, the focus was on how she was being treated, not about Gannon missing. A neighbor found footage from his camera. She left with Gannon that morning and came home at 2:19 in the afternoon without him. When the neighbor took that to Al, he said that Al broke down and cried because he could see she left with him and came home without him. The video showed Gannon moving slowly, getting into the truck. Evidently, she had already beaten him badly.

The community and neighborhood where Gannon lived all put out blue lights to signify giving Gannon a way home. The little boy was known as a child who had so much love.

It's interesting to note Letecia told Law Enforcement she has a Ph.D. that she acquired online from a Christian College. She even referred to herself and signed papers as Dr. Letecia Stauch. However, there is no record of her having her Ph.D. She seemed to live in a narcissistic dream world maybe believing what she said.

Nevertheless, a sad sight to see: Letecia wearing bright lime-green prison attire, shackled at the ankles and wrists as they brought her into the courtroom for a hearing where she was charged with first-degree murder. It's hard to feel sorry for her even with the pitiful look she put on her face. Very interesting for someone who had so much to say, sat quietly as her life and freedom hung in the balance, left to the decision of others. Not so in control anymore.

Letecia wrote a letter to the judge that she was getting death threats in her peanut butter.

When the autopsy report was released, the cause of death was a gunshot wound to the head. A bullet was recovered from his head and his skull had a fracture. The bullet matched a gun found in Letecia Stauch's home and that gun had her DNA on it. There was blunt force trauma to the head as well and 18 sharp, forced wounds over his body. His body was found in the panhandle of Florida in a suitcase under a bridge. There was blood found on a board along highway 105 that ended up being Gannon's. She drove to Florida with her daughter in the car with her, dumped his body, and drove to South Carolina.

There was blood on Letecia's car. She had texted her daughter and asked for her to bring home some cleaning products. Authorities said Gannon died between 2:00 and 5:30 that day.

Letecia was arrested on March 2, in Myrtle Beach South Carolina. It is very telling that everyone is in Colorado looking for her stepson and she is in South Carolina. The behavior does not match that she would be so concerned about Gannon. It's believed that she was in Florida for two days. The small town of Pace, Florida is where Gannon's body was found.

Letecia was also accused of trying to purchase a fake lie detector test.

Some of the things that Letecia had searched on the internet include:

1. I feel like I'm just a nanny not a stepmom.
2. Husband uses me to babysit his kids.
3. I'm just a glorified babysitter.
4. I need to find a new husband.
5. I need to find a guy without kids.
6. One day, someone will wish they had treated you differently.
7. Why should my husband choose me over family.

Some of these things you would think call for intent.

Letecia had a history of problems with Law Enforcement.

Some of the things she told her husband:

The mixture of blood found in Gannon's room is a mixture of her blood and Gannon's blood.

Following is an affidavit that was ready for the judge in this case and then it was leaked and put on social media. However, this was released to the public and in its entirety, it follows:

Attachment "A"

The following Affidavit is submitted to the Court to document the probable cause in support of a request for issuance of an Arrest Warrant for STAUCH, Letecia DOB:8/04/1983.

The offense is fully documented in El Paso County Sheriff's Office Offense Report 20-1382 detailing the offense (s) listed below in Paragraph 2.

With the victim(s) identified as Stauch, Gannon: DOB:09/28/2008; Race: White; Gender: Male.

1. Your Affiant is Jessica Bethel, a duly sworn and state-certified Police Officer and Detective with the El Paso County Sheriff's Office (EPSO), who has been employed as such since 2010. Your Affiant has participated in other law enforcement investigations, including homicide investigations, child abuse, weapons violations, assaults, and other violations of Colorado Revised Statutes. I am familiar with social media networks and electronic methods of communication. I have attended a one-week crime scene analysis training course through the Colorado Bureau of Investigation. I have also relied on other investigators from outside Agencies with more investigative training and experience, including, but not limited to, Federal Bureau of Investigation (FBI) Special Agent Andrew Cohen, and Special Agent David Donati.

2. Your Affiant submits the following facts to demonstrate probable cause to believe that on or about January 27th, 2020, in the county of El Paso, in the state of Colorado, the defendant, Letecia Stauch, also known as (AKA) Letecia Hardin, did commit the following offenses (hereinafter referred to as "The Violations").
   • Murder in the First Degree—Child under twelve—Position of Trust
   • Child Abuse Resulting in Death
   • Tampering with a Deceased Human Body
   • Tampering with Physical Evidence

3. The Affidavit is being submitted to submit the issuance of an arrest warrant for the violation.

4. The facts in this affidavit come from my personal observation, my training, and experience, and information obtained from other agents, law enforcement officials, and witnesses. The contents of this affidavit were derived by reading reports, viewing evidence, and as provided to me by other EPSO Investigators and Special Agents of the FBI.

5. Much of this affidavit was prepared by FBI Special Agent Cohen, but I have reviewed the below facts carefully, and have no reason to doubt any investigator's accuracy or truthfulness in their reports. This affidavit is intended to show merely that there is sufficient probable cause for the requested warrant and does not set forth all my knowledge about this matter.

6. In summary, and as will be set forth below, probable cause exists to issue an arrest warrant for Letecia Stauch for "The Violation." The vast array of investigative techniques in this investigation has produced a voluminous amount of evidence in support of the requested warrant.

7. Investigators have executed physical search warrants and collected evidence from vehicles associated with Letecia, cellular devices she utilized, and her residence. Electronic search warrants have been executed to entities including, but not limited to, Facebook, Apple Inc., Google Inc, AT&T Wireless, Verizon Wireless, ADT Security System, Tile, Life 360, Yahoo, and Ring Doorbell Service. Some of the physical evidences have been examined by a laboratory for DNA profiles.

8. Investigators also recovered a significant amount of exterior video footage from individual, privately owned neighborhood security cameras, businesses around Colorado Springs, Colorado, and cameras in other surrounding areas. Some cameras provided recorded footage of the exterior of the Stauch residence.

9. Historical cellular records and historical cell site details were analyzed (and redacted parts).

10. Some, but not all, of the available photos and other evidence collected from the aforementioned search warrants and other investigative steps are included below and are not meant to represent all the evidence available. Furthermore, there has been no intentional exclusion of photos that could be deemed exculpatory in nature.

11. The information contained in this affidavit can be found in EPSO Case Report.
    Facts in support of a probable cause.
    The Stauch Family and general information.

12. The Stauch Family is a blended family, and all will be discussed at various points below. This representation purposely has little details in order to give an overview of the family structure:
    a. Father—Eugene "Al" Stauch
    b. Stepmother—Letecia Stauch
    c. Daughter—Harley Hunt, minor, 17 years of age (by blood to Letecia, not Al)
    d. Son—Gannon Stauch, minor, 11 years of age (by blood to Al, not Letecia)
    e. Daughter—Laina Stauch, minor, 8 years of age (by blood to Al, not Letecia)

13. The following vehicles will be discussed at various points below:
    a. Red Nissan Frontier—Mr. Stauch's main vehicle
    b. Black Volkswagen Tiguan—Letecia's main vehicle
    c. White Volkswagen Jetta—Harley's main vehicle
    d. Silver Nissan Altima—a rental car obtained and utilized by Letecia's Aunt, Brenda acquired, and utilized by Letecia from January 30 to February 1, 2020, after her Tiguan was seized by ESPO on January 29, 2020

e. White Kia Rio—a rental car obtained and utilized by Letecia on January 28 to 29, 2020

Background of those mentioned in this Affidavit

14. Letecia Stauch, AKA Letecia Hardin, DOB 8/04/1983, is the last person known to investigators to see 11-year-old Gannon Stauch, DOB 09/29/2008, alive. Letecia is Gannon's on adult supervision in the days preceding and on the day of his murder. At the time of Gannon's murder, Letecia was employed by School District 20 as an assistant teacher, although I have also learned that she is no longer employed there.

   a. I was able to locate prior criminal history for Letecia and learned that in North Carolina Robeson County Court Case 2001CRS011193, Letecia was convicted after a trial for communicating threats, a misdemeanor, but I was not able to locate her sentencing information. Letecia was also convicted of unauthorized use of a motor vehicle in Robeson County Court Case 2001CR014645 and was sentenced to 45 days confinement and 18 months of probation.

   b. Although not criminal in nature, I was able to locate a document memorializing the suspension of Letecia's North Carolina teaching certificate #261777 on or about May 11, 2016. As part of that document, it is reported that Letecia had filed unsubstantiated claims of harassment and retaliation, and the North Carolina state board found "that Mrs. Stauch breached her contract by engaging in unprofessional conduct, willfully neglecting her duty, and failing to comply with the provisions of her contract."

   c. Letecia's criminal history is only included by way of background for the court, and because Letecia has been convicted of previous crimes, it is not meant to indicate guilt of the violations or to be considered as the sole basis of probable cause for the requested warrant.

15. Eugene Albert Stauch, AKA Al Stauch, DOB 09/20/1982, is Gannon's biological father and is married to Letecia Stauch. Mr. Stauch was deployed with the National Guard during the days of January 25, 2020, to January 28, 2020. Mr. Stauch spent the night in Denver on January 25, 2020, and departed via commercial airline on January 26, 2020, returning via commercial airline on January 28, 2020. Investigators were able to corroborate this information. Mr. Stauch has cooperated fully in the below investigation.

Summary of Multi-Agency Missing Person Investigation in Colorado:

16. Of note, and in some portions of this affidavit, depending on the date of events being discussed, the investigation may be referred to as a missing person investigation, or a murder investigation. For the purpose of this affidavit, they are indeed one and the same.

17. The subsequent information primarily surrounds the period of Monday, January 27, 2020, to Wednesday, January 29, 2020. Investigators have taken independent steps to corroborate information received throughout the investigation, and in most circumstances, have video footage, cellular communication and location records, security system records, or other records to support the below claims. This summary section is only meant to give the court overview of the investigation, and the facts supporting this summary will be articulated below.

18. On January 27, 2020, at or about 1855 hours, Letecia Stauch reported Gannon missing after calling 9-1-1. During that call, she was instructed to call the El Paso County Non-Emergency line. In summary, Letecia stated Gannon was supposed to be home approximately 1 hour ago, and that she was unable to locate him at his friend's house. Her story dramatically changed multiple times over the following days.

19. As will be discussed below, investigators do not believe Letecia went to any neighboring houses to attempt to locate Gannon, and this was one of her many lies during the investigation. Letecia was unable to provide the actual location of the homes she went to, the names of Gannon's friends he was supposed to be playing with, or the names of the parents of Gannon's friends.

20. Deputies responded to Letecia's residence at 6627 Mandan Dr. Colorado Springs, Colorado and were unable to locate Gannon. Deputies conducted a limited search of the residence and took a report from Letecia. Some of the interactions between the responding Deputies and Letecia were captured on body-worn camera. A missing persons investigation was initiated, and in the coming days, developed into a murder investigation.

21. A tip line was established, and investigators received hundreds of rips and leads from the public by virtue of emails and telephone calls. As part of this tip line, two ransom notes were received by email demanding money (in form of bitcoin) in return for Gannon's return. Investigators took steps to validate these ransom notes, including resolving and geolocating the Internet Protocol (IP) addresses from the email headers, and requesting subscriber information from the Internet Service Providers (ISP) that hosted those IP addresses. One of those ransom notes was sent from a foreign-based email account that is accessible by multiple individuals. Investigators were unable to trace the user of the IP addresses and believed the ransom notes to be fraudulent and strictly designed as a scheme to receive money.

22. Letecia initially claimed that she last saw Gannon on January 27, 2020, when he left their residence to play with his friends somewhere around 1515 hrs. Based on the facts outlined below, and Letecia's statement to an EPSO Dispatcher, Letecia is the last person who ever saw Gannon alive. Letecia

stated she attempted to find him at a neighbor's house and sent her daughter Harley Hunt, DOB 05/01/2002, to look for Gannon at a park.

23. Letecia lied to investigators on multiple occasions, has unexplained, abnormal behavior such as obtaining a rental car, disconnecting her cell phone from the cellular network for an extended period of time, false reporting of an alleged rape, abnormal patterns of travel, a continuously evolving story with material changes in facts and circumstances, and has since left the State of Colorado. These actions, when combined with other facts in this affidavit, support the totality of probable cause for the requested warrant and will be discussed below.

The Murder of Gannon Stauch:

24. The following section will outline what investigators have learned about Letecia's activity on January 27, 2020, and outline the period when Gannon was likely murdered. Some of the information contained in this section will be repeated in other portions of this affidavit or discussed later in more detail. Additionally, there are evidence sources that are mentioned here but not fully defined in other sections.

25. Investigators believe that Gannon was murdered by Letecia Stauch in the afternoon hours (after approximately 1414 hours) of January 27, 2020, at his residence, and more specifically in his bedroom. Physical evidence recovered from the residence and inside Gannon's bedroom support that a violent event occurred in his bedroom, which caused bloodshed, including blood spatter on the walls, and enough blood loss to stain his mattress, soak through the carpet, the carpet pad, and stain the concrete below his bed.

26. Based on evidence recovered from the residence, Gannon's remains were eventually brought through the house, into

the garage, and likely loaded into the back of Letecia's Volkswagen Tiguan. After cleaning the murder scene, Letecia utilized the Tiguan to transport and dump Gannon's remains on the evening of January 28, 2020. Letecia likely disposed of his remains off Hwy 105/S Perry Park Rd in Douglas County, Colorado. Indeed, the Metro Crime Laboratory determined that blood discovered in Gannon's bedroom, the Stauch's garage, and blood on a piece of particleboard located off Hwy 105/S Perry Park Rd. all matched his DNA profile.

27. On Monday, January 27, 2020, Gannon Stauch stayed home from school. Based on text messages from Letecia to Mr. Stauch, Gannon was up most of Sunday evening with a stomach problem. Letecia did tell Gannon's school Grand Mountain Elementary, that Gannon would be absent on Monday. Investigators were able to verify that Gannon was marked as an excused absence that day. Letecia also told Al that "I'm just going to give them an excuse at work and stay with him." Indeed, Letecia did come up with an excuse and told her employer via text message (at or about 043 hours) that her stepdad was killed after being hit by a car and she would not be able to come to work that day.

28. Other electronic evidence, such as time and date-stamped photographs and videos, were recovered from Letecia's cellular telephone that indicate Gannon was likely still alive during the morning of January 27, 2020.

29. As displayed in paragraph 54 below, images were taken on Letecia's cell phone at or about 0813 and 0817 hours on the morning of January 27, 2020, showing Gannon sleeping in his bed. Of particular note, his Nintendo Switch (a small video console) is visible in the photo lying next to him on the bed. Mr. Stauch has said that this gaming system was of high importance to Gannon. To date, investigators have been unable to locate the Nintendo Switch. It should also

be noted that Letecia used her phone the following day, January 28, 2022, at about 1257 hours to conduct a Google search "can Nintendo find my switch." This is also detailed in a list of some of her search history in paragraph 141 and reasonably occurred because she was contemplating how she would dispose of the switch.

30. I conducted a Google search for the term "can Nintendo find my switch" and learned that the Switch does not come with any sort of tracking ability. As such, Letecia likely felt it was safe to dispose of the Switch and use the missing Switch to help deceive law enforcement into searching for Gannon as a possible runaway.

31. Ultimately, investigators located video surveillance from a neighbor's surveillance camera that showed what investigators believe to be Letecia and an individual that appeared to match Gannon's physical description depart their residence in the Nissan Frontier at or above 1016 hours on January 27, 2020.

32. The video camera is several homes away and does not provide images clear enough to make positive identifications of those captured in the recording. The vehicle returned at or about 1419 hours, and Letecia exited the vehicle. After viewing the video, I cannot be sure if another person exited the vehicle or not, but I submit Gannon likely did return home with Letecia that afternoon. These times, corroborated by data collected from an ADT Security System installed in the Stauch's residence, are discussed below in more detail.

33. Based on data returned from Stauch's ADT Security System, the motion detector in the living room or basement did not register any activity from approximately 1012 hours until Letecia and Gannon enter the home until approximately 1422 hours. Investigators confirmed Lania to be at school and confirmed Harley was at work. As such, investigators

believe there was likely nobody else in the residence except Letecia and Gannon.

34. Letecia's historical cell site information, about her IPhone's status, and a text message sent to Harley from Gannon's cell phone, support that Letecia left her cell phone at the Stauch home that morning of January 27, 2020. The fact that Letecia left her phone at home is suspicious on its own, based on her history of extensive use of the phone.

35. I have received forensic search records from Letecia's phone and found she is an active user of social media, including, but not limited to, Facebook and Instagram. A more detailed review of Letecia's iPhone Screen Time log between January 25, 2020, at 0800 hours and January 29, 2020, at 1100 hours revealed that Letecia spent approximately 38,607 seconds on Facebook and Facebook messenger alone which equates to approximately 10.7 hours of cumulative hours over those few days.

36. Letecia's phone was locked at or about 0956 hours on January 27, 2020, and unlocked at 1445 hours on the same day. The timing of the unlocking of the device is significant as compared to her departure to and from the residence and should be noted by the Court. Particularly, Letecia did not open her phone for approximately 30 minutes after returning to the residence.

37. On January 27, 2020, there was a message sent from Gannon's phone to Harley's phone that reads "Tecia left phone at home if you need her text me." This message was sent at or about 1037 hours.

38. Investigators were able to confirm, based on video surveillance footage and purchased receipts, that Letecia traveled to PetCo, located at 5020 N Nevada Ave, Colorado Springs, Colorado. This Petco is approximately 22 miles

from the residence and is an approximately 30-minute drive (based on Google Maps directions). The receipt shows that Letecia completed her purchase at or about 1122 hours. Gannon is not visible on any of the surveillance videos obtained at PetCo.

39. Letecia's whereabouts are unknown between approximately 1122 hours and 1322 hours. At 1322 hours, Letecia was again captured on video surveillance making a second purchase at the same PetCo on N. Nevada Ave. Mr. Stauch sent a text message to Gannon's cell phone at or about 1206 hours that read "Hey buddy." This message was unanswered until 1321 hours. The response was "Can I play Zelda at least." Mr. Stauch replied, "Not today."

40. A significant event occurred on Gannon's phone at or about 1343 hours, which is prior to arriving back at the Stauch residence. There was an internet search for "can my parent find my cell phone if it's off." I submit that this internet search was likely conducted by Letecia on Gannon's phone, and not Gannon himself based on the content of the search, the way the search terms are phrased, and the presence of a "." in between iPhone: and "if". This is very similar to the way Letecia conducted searches on her phone. However, I located other internet searches with a "." in Gannon's search history, which I also reasonably believe were conducted by Letecia. A more detailed explanation of Letecia's search history is included below in paragraph 141.

41. Furthermore, the search term was "parent," singular. I submit it is reasonable that Mr. Stauch, only not Letecia, would be interested in the location of Gannon's phone, and that Letecia was probably deliberating on how, or if, she would dispose of Gannon's phone after she murdered him.

42. I conducted a Google search of "can my parent find my cell phone if it's off" and learned that the first answer returned

in the search engine reads: "The answer to your question depends on what method is being used to track your location…" Gannon's phone was found at the residence. I submit that Letecia did not get rid of Gannon's phone for fear it might be traceable.

43. The Nissan Frontier returned to the Stauch residence at or about 1420 hours. A search warrant, authorized by this court, was executed on the Nissan Frontier and found no indications of blood inside the vehicle.

44. Letecia had been without her cell phone for hours, yet her screen was not unlocked until approximately 1445 hours, which was 25 minutes after arriving back at the residence. During that 25-minute period, there is motion activity both upstairs and downstairs on the ADT records.

45. Letecia returned home from school around 1515 hours. During a recorded forensic interview with investigators, Laina stated that when she returned home, Letecia told her Gannon was asleep in his bed and that she could not see him. Letecia told Laina to go outside and play. I submit that Laina was sent outside because Gannon was likely dead, and Letecia was cleaning up blood from inside the house.

46. At or about 1555 hours, Mr. Stauch sent another message to Gannon's phone, "Hey buddy." This message was not read until 1940 hours. It is likely that Gannon was already murdered by Letecia at the time Mr. Stauch sent the message.

47. Based on exterior video footage, Harley arrived at the residence in her white VW Jetta at or about 1642 hours and picked up Laina.

48. At or about 1652 hours on January 27, 2020, Letecia sent a text message to Harley requesting carpet cleaner, trash bags, and baking soda. Those items were likely used to clean

up the murder scene. Harley purchased these items, and investigators located a receipt documenting the purchase. Harley Hunt has refused to speak with investigators.

49. Investigators do not believe that Harley was present when Gannon was killed. Harley was at work on January 27, 2020, from 0830 hours to 1615 hours, and investigators were able to verify this with her employer.

50. To be clear, investigators have not located any evidence that any person other than Laina and Letecia had access to Gannon between approximately 1000 hours and 1734 hours on January 27, 2020.

Statements and images captured on body camera January 27, 2020:

51. Your affiant has reviewed body-worn camera (BWC) footage and reports obtained from a deputy that responded to 6627 Mandan Dr, the residence of the Stauch family. After responding, Letecia provided verbal consent for Deputies to search the house for Gannon. By the way of a timeline, EPSO Patrol responded at or about 2209 hours, approximately three hours after Letecia initially called 9-1-1.

52. From the BWC, I learned the Volkswagen Tiguan, known to be leased and utilized by Letecia, was backed into the garage when EPSO was at the residence. The position of the Tiguan in the garage is significant, specifically because of the confirmed presence of Gannon's blood in the garage below the area where the rear hatch of the Tiguan would be, and the positive reaction of Blue Star reagent (indicating the likely presence of blood) on the Tiguan's rear bumper.

53. Responding deputies also searched Gannon's basement bedroom, and I have viewed images of Gannon's bedroom taken from the BWC. Below, I have included a BWC image of Gannon's bedroom on the left. On the right, an image

was recovered from Letecia's cell phone, after executing a search warrant that was applied for, and granted by this court. These images both represent the condition of Gannon's bedroom on January 27, 2020, and/or about 0813 hours, and just after 2200 hours.

54. This photo comparison is significant for many reasons and the corner of the bedroom where Gannon's head is visible is the key area discussed in several sections below taken at 0813 hours:

   a. The placement of Gannon's bed is in the immediate location where his blood (based on DNA profile results) was found on the wall, the carpet, and concretes below carpet. These details are discussed below, and a large volume of blood appears to have been in that area.

   b. For the purpose of comparison between the images, it appears that although the sheet may not be the same, the blankets are different, and the pillowcase, if not the whole pillow, is different. I submit that a logical explanation for the missing bedding is that they likely were saturated in blood after Gannon's murder and were removed by Letecia to clean up the murder scene. Furthermore, investigators were unable to locate the bedding in the Stauch residence during any of approximately five searches of the residence.

55. Another photo was recovered from Letecia's cell phone that shows his bed was pushed directly against the wall by the head of the bed. This photo articulates the ability of blood to get onto the walls and floor in the corner of the bedroom. Mr. Stauch stated the position of the bed is unusual, and the bed is usually pushed against the wall.

56. Mr. Stauch spent the night in Denver on January 25, 2020, and flew out of Denver International Airport on January 26, 2020. Investigators were able to corroborate he traveled to Dallas, Texas and ultimately to Oklahoma based on his

flight records. On the morning of January 28, 2020, Letecia rented a 2019 Kia Rio from Avis Rent-A-Car in Colorado Springs. Letecia picked Mr. Stauch up at the Colorado Springs Airport at or about 0850 hours on January 28, 2020, shortly after Letecia rented the vehicle. Letecia and Mr. Stauch drove back to their residence from the airport in the rented Kia.

57. The timing of the rental of the Kia is suspicious, and combined with forensic evidence later obtained from the Tiguan and discussed below, tends to place additional importance on why Letecia felt compelled to rent a vehicle that morning. Investigators located no evidence that the Tiguan was not mechanically functioning or noted any reason why it could not have been physically driven. In fact, the Tiguan remained parked in the Colorado Springs Airport Short Term parking lot until approximately 1900 hours on January 28, 2020.

58. Letecia provided statements to her husband, Albert Stauch, that she was concerned about putting mileage on her Tiguan lease, which justified the vehicle rental. It is noted, however, that during the time of the Kia rental, Letecia only put about 71 miles on the vehicle. During the time period Letecia had the Kia, she would not provide the location of the Tiguan and Mr. Stauch never saw the Tiguan. For example, she told Mr. Stauch that the Tiguan was near French Elementary School.

59. Between investigators and Mr. Stauch, a limited search for the Tiguan was conducted and produced negative results. Investigators later learned she left the vehicle in the short-term parking lot of the Colorado Springs Airport but removed the vehicle at or about January 28, 2020, at 1900 hours. The Kia Rio was returned on the morning of January 29, 2020.

60. I submit Letecia could not pick her husband up in the Volkswagen Tiguan because it likely would have revealed evidence of Gannon's murder, including blood or the actual remains of Gannon himself.

The Kia Rio

61. Investigators applied for, and were granted by this court, a search warrant for the 2019 Kia Rio rented by Letecia Stauch. This vehicle was located at the rental car company at the Colorado Springs Airport and had not been rented to another customer in-between the time Letecia dropped the vehicle off and when investigators seized it.

62. Investigators did take a swab from a stain that was confirmed to be blood in the trunk of the Kia Rio and submitted it to the Metro Crime Laboratory for analysis. A DNA profile was developed and determined it was a mixture of two contributors, one of which was male, and the major male profile did not match Gannon Stauch's DNA.

63. I submit that because the Kia Rio is a rental car, it has likely been utilized by a large number of people, and the blood in the trunk may or may not be related to the investigation, and investigators have not been able to determine the likely age of that blood and have not matched it to any known DNA profiles.

64. Investigators noted the Kia had a significant amount of mud underneath the vehicle, but this did not provide any successful leads in looking for Gannon's remains. Investigators collected the air filters of the vehicle and attempted to identify particles that might be useful to identify where the vehicle might have been driven.

65. Investigators were unable to recover any GPS data or location history for the Kia Rio.

Letecia's Volkswagen Tiguan Is Significant

66. The Volkswagen Tiguan is important to investigators because they believe the Tiguan was used to transport the remains of Gannon from the Stauch residence to a location where Gannon's body was dumped. The definitive location of the Tiguan is unknown to investigators during the time period of approximately 1902 hours on January 28, 2020, to approximately 1200 hours on January 29, 2020. Investigators believe Letecia dumped Gannon's remains on the evening of January 28, 2020, and utilized the Tiguan to do so. The Tiguan was seized from Letecia on January 29, 2020.

67. Letecia had a scheduled interview with investigators on January 29, 2020, at the EPSO, located in downtown Colorado Springs, Colorado. When she arrived at or about 1200 hours, she was driving the Volkswagen Tiguan. Investigators noted that the vehicle was wet and appeared to have been recently cleaned. I submit that Letecia had to clean the vehicle because there was likely visible blood on the rear end, based on the below luminol reactions. Indeed, video footage was recovered that shows a partial view of a car wash located at El Platte Ave/Bonfoy Ave in Colorado Springs, Colorado. This video captured a portion of a black SUV, consistent with the VW Tiguan, at or about 1130 hours on January 29, 2020, at the car cash. The time and location are consistent with raw data obtained from the Tiguan computer system, described in more detail below beginning in paragraph 152.

68. Investigators applied for and were granted a search warrant for the Tiguan, which was seized from Letecia at her interview, and towed to the EPSO Evidence facility. On or about February 1, 2020, the FBI Evidence Response Team (ERT) conducted a search on the Volkswagen Tiguan. In summary, the forensic portion of the search revealed possible

traces of blood on the rear of the vehicle, a rear passenger seat, front passenger seat, and an area near the glovebox based on luminol Forensic latent bloodstain reagent tests. Swabs from the trunk area were sent to the Metro Crime Laboratory for further analysis. These results revealed that a DNA profile could not be developed and that the swab from the trunk was negative for the presumptive presence of blood.

69. To be clear, luminol is a chemical used to detect trace amounts of blood at crime scenes, and although I do not have a chemical or biology background, I have learned that luminol reacts with iron in hemoglobin, found in the blood. When applied, luminol emits a blue glow when a reaction occurs. I am also aware that there are things other than blood that could cause a reaction, such as other chemicals, and I do not submit that just because luminol reacted with a substance, the substance must be blood, and only that there is a strong probability of suspected blood. The positive reaction to luminol is meant to be combined with other facts in this affidavit in support of a probable cause.

70. Several areas of the Tiguan reacted to luminol as mentioned in paragraph 68. Specifically, the search team found evidence of suspected blood on the rear bumper, and step plate of the rear bumper. The location of the blood is significant because this vehicle was backed into the garage at Letecia's residence on the day of Gannon's murder. The search of the residence is discussed below, but it is noted that evidence of Gannon's blood (based on the DNA profile) was also located on the floor of the garage, consisting of where the rear end of the Tiguan would have been.

71. A photo is included below to demonstrate the reaction of the luminal reagent to the likely presence of blood. Particularly, the position of the reaction leads investigators to believe that blood was likely in contact with the rear bumper of

the Tiguan, and most reasonably while loading Gannon's remains in the trunk. Swabs from the exterior bumper have also been submitted to the Metro Crime Laboratory, but those results have not yet been returned. However, The Metro Crime Laboratory did return a result from the trunk of the Tiguan that was negative for the presumptive presence of blood.

Luminal reaction on the rear bumper of the Tiguan

72. Within the Tiguan, a receipt from a Dollar store was located, time stamped January 27, 2020, at 1714 hours, and documented the purchase of trash bags, baking soda, vinegar, and the items listed in paragraph 74.

73. Investigators believe that Harley purchased those items at the direction of Letecia, based on the following text message, sent from Letecia's cell phone to Harley's cell phone on January 27, 2020, at or about 1652 hours.

Letecia's reaction on the rear bumper of the Tiguan

74. Also included in this Dollar store purchase were baby oil, baby lotion, cotton rounds, and bubble gum. Investigators do not believe these items were involved in the cleaning of the murder scene, and likely have no investigative value at this point.

75. I know from personal experience that baking soda and vinegar are common household items that can be used to clean blood. Additionally, I conducted open-source internet searches that revealed vinegar is one of the most common items used to clean blood stains, and that when baking soda is applied to blood stains prior to vinegar, it has an efficient effect in removing blood stains.

76. While the purchase of items such as vinegar and baking soda are common, and in no sense illegal on their own, the timing of the purchase of these items and Gannon's suspected murder are beyond coincidental.

77. Also located was a parking receipt for the Colorado Springs Airport that documented the Tiguan was brought into the Airport's short-term parking lot at or about 0830 hours and left the lot at about 1902 hours both on January 28, 2020.

78. On January 29, 2020, Letecia returned the rented Kia at approximately 0900 hours, and she was picked up by someone driving the white Jetta. Investigators were unable to confirm that Harley was driving the Jetta.

79. Investigators were able to download telematics and stored electronic data from the Tiguan. A more in-depth exploitation of the Tiguan's electronic systems, more specifically its historical location, was developed and will be discussed below in more detail beginning in paragraph 152. Investigators were able to determine some of the locations of the Tiguan on the evening of January 28, 2020, including its location in the area of Hwy 105/S Perry Park Road in Douglas County, Colorado.

80. Investigators also served a search warrant to AT&T related to an International Mobile Subscriber Identity (IMSI) designated to Tiguan's Carnet feature. AT&T responded to this search warrant and provided Network Event Location System (NELOS) data that would give an estimated location of the Tiguan was generally in the greater northwest portion of Colorado Springs and likely also in an area North of the Air Force Academy and southern Douglas County. I submit that during this time period, investigators believe that Letecia disposed of Gannon's remains.

81. Of note, during the time period of approximately 2030 and 2220 hours on January 28, 2020, Harley's cell phone is connected to a tower that would service the Stauch residence, over approximately 30 miles from Letecia's supposed location. There was activity on Harley's telephone during the time, and investigators do not believe that Harley was with Letecia when she disposed of the body. However, at approximately 2226 hours, Harley's cell phone leaves the Stauch residence and goes to the area of Powers and Carefree where investigators believe she picked Letecia up.

The January 29, 2020 interview and the report of alleged rape of Letecia Stauch

82. As mentioned above, Letecia voluntarily came to the EPSO for an interview with investigators, but only after she was evasive and avoided speaking with investigators one-on-one. Her interview was audio and video recorded, and the below information includes her own statements, as well as an investigation geared toward corroborating those statements. In general, her statements are reasonably categorized as untruthful, incomplete, and misleading.

83. Letecia was supposed to arrive at 10 am on January 29, 2020, but did not arrive until noon. Although she spoke with investigators on the phone several times, she did not want investigators to come to her home and was difficult at best to track down. Investigators provided food and water to Letecia during the interview.

84. Of interest, Letecia brought several pieces of notebook paper with her that contained notes she had written down. During the interview, she referred to these pieces of paper and asked investigators if she could just read her notes. Investigators were not able to seize these documents. I have conducted hundreds of interviews with subjects, victims,

SUFFER THE LITTLE CHILDREN

and witnesses. It is extremely rare for an individual to bring notes to an interview.

85. Letecia drastically departed from her initial statements given to ESPO Deputies regarding the report of Gannon's disappearance. In summary, Letecia said she had been held at gunpoint and raped by a Hispanic male she knew as "Eguardo" and that Gannon was abducted by that male after he finished raping her. The interviewing detectives believed her statements were false based on prior experience investigating sexual assault cases.

86. Letecia said she arrived home around 1430 hours on January 27, 2020, disarmed her security system, and then went into the basement. She said that "Eguardo" was in the basement, attacked her, and pointed a gun at her. She said that after "Eguardo" held her at gunpoint, he allowed her to go upstairs to greet her stepdaughter, Laina Stauch, DOB 01/23/2012, who had just arrived home from school. Letecia said she sent her outside to ride her bike, then returned to the basement where "Eguardo" vaginally penetrated her against her will between 1530 and 1630 hours. During this period, she believed that she had hit her head and may have blacked out. Investigators noted no injuries on Letecia's head during their contact with her.

87. Letecia also said that during the attack, Gannon jumped on Eguardo's back and that "Eguardo" was able to throw Gannon off his back and across the room. After "Eguardo" had finished, he had the gun held to Gannon and demanded a suitcase. Letecia provided him with a brown suitcase and a cardboard box. "Eguardo" attempted to sexually assault her again, but she hit her head and blacked out again.

88. Letecia stated that she tried to fight "Eguardo" off but was unsuccessful. I know from training and experience that if an individual holds another person at gunpoint,

he or she would likely not allow the person to have an opportunity for escape as Letecia described being allowed to greet her stepdaughter upstairs before returning to the basement. Most crucially, if Letecia's story were accurate, any reasonable person would have immediately called 9-1-1 and reported the home invasion, rape, and kidnapping of their child. Letecia called law enforcement hours later and did not report the alleged rape until approximately two days later.

89. Of even more significance, Letecia said she cleaned up the area where this alleged attack had happened. She straightened up signs of disturbances in Gannon's room and cleaned up the utility room. Investigators recovered cleaning supplies, such as carpet brushes, which contain suspected carpet fibers. I submit that Letecia did in fact clean something up, but it was the murder scene of Gannon, not a sexual assault.

90. Investigators took steps to corroborate Letecia's statements before dismissing them as false and misleading. For example, investigators reviewed video footage from a neighborhood security camera that captured the exterior of the Stauch residence from the day of Gannon's murder and did not observe a Hispanic male entering the house. Investigators did observe Laina arrive home on the school bus at or about 1511 hours, observed her enter the residence, and observed her riding her bike at or about 1530 hours.

91. Furthermore, Letecia was offered the opportunity to have a Sexual Assault Nurse Examiner (SANE) conduct a forensic examination at a local hospital. Ultimately, Letecia did not want to have the exam completed. When given the opportunity to provide investigators with evidence that would possibly identify "Eguardo," Letecia refused to cooperate.

92. Letecia stated that she met "Eguardo" on January 26, 2020, the day prior to Gannon's murder. She generally described a Hispanic male with brown hair and brown eyes but could not provide any specific identifying information. In summary, she told investigators that Gannon had knocked over a candle on Sunday causing the carpet to burn. After that incident, she drove around the neighborhood where residential construction was taking place. She met "Eguardo" who was working on a house and asked if he would repair the carpet in her home. "Eguardo" agreed and Letecia provided him the garage door code and they agreed he would repair the carpet while she was shopping the next day.

93. To the extent Letecia spoke about Laina, investigators were able to corroborate those statements but never observed "Eguardo" or anyone else arriving or leaving the residence during that time period based on exterior neighborhood video footage of the front of the Stauch residence. Specifically, exterior video footage revealed that Laina was riding her bike outside between approximately 1530 and 1542 hours. Furthermore, the front door of the residence opened and closed at 1528 hours, based on data from ADT Security System, discussed more below.

94. I know from training and experience that when individuals concoct lies, most reasonably to conceal the truth, they oftentimes leave portions of truths within those lines. I submit that the statements Letecia made in reference to Laina, and that the time period Laina was at the residence, are likely true based on video evidence. Her other statements, however, are blatant lies designed to mislead investigators.

95. Investigators also reviewed Letecia's phone records during the time period of the alleged rape, of 1530 to 1630 hours on January 27, 2020. During this time period of the alleged rape, of 1530 to 1630 hours, Letecia had phone activity

including an outgoing phone call, and numerous iMessages (Text Messages using an iPhone) to Mr. Stauch and Harley, namely, to discuss purchasing a new set of headphones for Albert. These text messages occurred at the following times: 1541, 1542, 1543, 1544, 1545, 1611, 1619, and 1620.

96. Investigators also were granted a search warrant by this court that was served to ADT Home Security, which requested data stored on the ADT servers related to The Stauch residence. The Stauch residence was equipped with basement and living room motion detectors and contact detectors on the front and rear doors. ADT was in possession of logs that documented the time, date, and type of event that generated a log. For example, when either the motion detector was activated, or the front or rear door opened or closed, there is a record of that event.

97. Letecia claimed that she was raped in the basement between 1430 and 1530 hours. During that time, the back door of the residence, located on the main level, was opened and closed ten times. If indeed Letecia was being raped in the basement, it would be impossible for her to open the upstairs' back door of the residence at the same time. I submit that Letecia's claims of being raped in the basement are false, based on her cell phone activity, and the stored ADT data.

98. The logs from ADT indicate significant activity in the basement of the residence where evidence suggests Gannon was murdered. For example, between January 23, 2020 and January 26, 2020, and the hours of 1500 to 1700, the average number of basement motion events was 3.5. On January 27, 2020. The average number of basement motion events was 10.3. A possible scenario for the increase in activity is that Letecia was going upstairs and downstairs in order to get cleaning supplies and clean the murder scene.

99. Toward the end of the interview, Letecia said she wanted to leave. Investigators seized her telephone and detained her while they applied for a search warrant to obtain DNA collection. Letecia began stuffing tissues in her pants and said she was having chest pain and shortness of breath. Investigators immediately requested medical assistance, and paramedics from the Colorado Springs Fire Department arrived. Letecia had appropriate responses to the paramedic's questions.

100. I am aware that Letecia has made statements regarding Gannon's disappearance to individuals other than law enforcement, including but not limited to, her friend, her husband, and the media. Indeed, some of those conversations have been captured and memorialized in recorded phone conversations and email messages. Letecia's stories have continued to evolve and material facts continue to change, including but not limited to, the identity of her attacker, the location of Gannon's abduction, and details of the alleged rape.

101. During her statements, Letecia did deny killing Gannon and provided explanations as to why there was blood in her Tiguan, blood in Gannon's bedroom, and why she was in the area of Palmer Lake, Colorado.

Letecia is transported to a local hospital in Colorado Springs on January 29, 2020

102. Letecia was transported to the hospital via ambulance from the EPSO for further medical attention. Letecia was accompanied by Detectives during the ride to the hospital. Unlike questions at the ESPO by paramedics, during the ambulance ride, Letecia was unresponsive to questions by medical personnel and seemed to have a miraculous recovery when they arrived at the hospital. The ambulance ride was audio-recorded.

103. Letecia received medical care at the hospital, and the details of that care are not included in this affidavit for medical privacy reasons. Letecia did not have any life-threatening issues and signed herself out prior to all her exams being completed.

104. Letecia continued evasive behavior at the hospital, particularly after investigators told her they were going to detain her pending the issuance of a search warrant to collect her DNA. Ultimately, the search warrant for the collection of non-testimonial evidence was signed and executed. A second warrant for the compelled SANE exam was initially authorized by this court but then was quashed by the court. To be clear, Letecia did not allow a SANE exam to be completed.

105. Letecia was not in custody after the warrant was executed at the hospital and left the hospital. There was physical surveillance being conducted by law enforcement in the area, and investigators learned Letecia was picked up by an unknown person at the hospital and was reunited with her daughter several miles from the hospital.

106. Although her behavior was not illegal, submit that as pressure continued to increase from investigators, Letecia became more and more desperate to leave the hospital, likely because she feared being caught in her lies. Furthermore, Letecia did not want to pursue collecting evidence that might assist law enforcement in identifying and finding her supposed rapist.

Searches of Letecia's residence and the discovery of confirmed blood in Gannon's bedroom

107. Investigators searched the Stauch's residence several times over several weeks after applying for, and being granted, search warrants from this court. The purpose of these

searches was to collect evidence, including biological evidence, in support of the captioned investigation. The forensic searches were conducted by the Colorado Springs Metro Crime Lab. To avoid confusion, the January 28, 2020 initial search was authorized by Mr. Stauch, and he provided consent to search the residence. Not all evidence recovered is included below. However, the forensic testing results of several items, including a pair of size 8.5 Nike Shoes, are discussed in paragraph 126.

108. Gannon's remaining family members were living in the residence during the period of these searches, and investigators did not initially seal the residence off. Crime scene analysts from the Colorado Springs Metro Crime Lab responded to the residence and found traces of blood throughout the residence based on Blue Star Forensic latent blood stain reagent tests. There was visible blood in Gannon's room, in the garage, and in other portions of the house.

109. Blue Star Forensic stain has similar limitations to luminol, which has been described and discussed above.

110. By way of background, the residence located at 6627 Mandan Dr. Colorado Springs, Colorado is a ranch-style single-family home, approximately 2500 square feet with a two-car attached garage. There are four bedrooms and three bathrooms in the residence. Two of those bedrooms are in the basement, including Gannon's. Next to Gannon's room, there is an unfinished utility room, and on the other side of the basement, another bedroom and a bathroom, and the garage is accessible from the inside of the residence.

111. The Blue Star reagent was applied to Gannon's bedroom, the hallway leading to the utility room from his bedroom, the utility room itself, the staircase and landing upstairs from the utility room, the pathway to the garage from the stairs,

and the garage area itself. In all those areas, investigators found positive results for the likely presence of blood.

112. Specifically in Gannon's bedroom, in a corner of the room, investigators located an area where suspected blood had seeped through the carpet, through the pad, and stained the concrete. Furthermore, there was also bloodstain and projected blood splatter located on the walls in this area. Indeed, over 50 droplets of suspected blood were found on the wall near Gannon's bed. Crime Scene investigators also suspected someone attempted to clean the walls based on the way the Blue Star reagent reacted on the wall.

113. Gannon's mattress was also seized and contained a red stain consistent with blood in the same area as the stain on the carpet, and the blood cast off on the walls. The stains on the mattress were swabbed but were not tested with Blue Star reagent. The laboratory results have not yet been returned, but because other blood in the area was determined to be Gannon's blood, investigators suspect the blood on the mattress is also Gannon's blood.

114. I have included several crime scene photographs that include the wall next to Gannon's bed, and the carpet and carpet pad that was removed by the investigators to expose the concrete below. Based on the orientation of Gannon's bed, the vast majority of the blood would be in line with the position of his head and torso and consistent with the stain of the mattress displayed above.

115. I submit that the blood located in Gannon's room appears to have been cleaned up, based on residual blood residue on the baseboards, an electrical outlet cover, and the blood that soaked through the carpet. DNA laboratory testing has confirmed it was indeed Gannon's body that has not been found, reasonably indicating this was likely the scene of Gannon's murder.

116. Investigators have requested, but have not yet received, a report from Tom Griffin, who is an International Association for Identification (IAI) Certified Senior Crime Scene Analyst (CSCSA). Mr. Griffin examined the blood splatter on Gannon's walls. Mr. Griffin preliminarily reported that the stains on the walls are consistent with one or more blood-spatter-producing events, which could include gunshot, blunt force, or a stabbing. Mr. Griffin did not believe the blood stains were aspirated blood, primarily due to the lack of air bubbles in the stains. Furthermore, the shape of the stains was affected by the surface texture of the drywall itself. The final report from Mr. Griffin has not yet been received and is pending peer review.

117. Trace evidence swabs of suspected blood were obtained from the electrical socket next to Gannon's bed. These swabs revealed the blood was indeed Gannon's blood, based on DNA profile testing. The electrical socket also has evidence of streak marks, which are reasonably suspected to be from Letecia's attempted cleaning. When investigates removed the outlet cover, a visible red stain was present outlining its edges. The presence of this stain tends to support that there was enough blood around the outlet cover to seep around its edges, leaving a visible outline.

118. I have also included a photograph of the suspected blood stain in the concrete, located in the corner of the bedroom where Gannon's bed was positioned (this stain is also visible in the photo depicting the suspected blood spatter on the walls). The carpet above this stain in the concrete was clean, and investigators suspect Letecia cleaned the area based on carpet fibers on scrub brushes, the acquisition of carpet cleaning supplies, vinegar, and baking soda. 6627 Mandan Dr. was a newly constructed building, and the Stauch family was the only family to reside in this residence.

119. On January 29, 2020, investigators recovered a piece of carpet from the utility room with possible blood stains. The recovery of this carpet tends to further support the positive alerts from the Blue Star reagent in the utility room. The Metro Crime Lab reported the substance tested presumptively positive for the presence of blood but was unable to develop a DNA profile.

120. On January 29, 2020, investigators found in the dishwasher multiple carpet brushes with suspected carpet fibers on them, and the dishwasher appeared to have been run. Investigators believe these brushes were used to clean up the murder scene. To be clear, no formal testing was completed to confirm the fibers on the brushes were carpet.

121. Investigators also located an empty gallon size container of vinegar within the residence. Mr. Stauch believed there was approximately 1/2 of the container left before he left for Oklahoma on January 25, 2020. As mentioned above, additional vinegar was purchased on January 27, 2020.

122. EPDO Deputies that responded to the Stauch home on January 27, 2020 did not notice the blood stains in Gannon's bedroom and it should be noted the initial report was that Gannon had left the home and had not returned. As additional information was developed, more forensic searches of Gannon's room were conducted, which revealed the aforementioned evidence. There were small traces of blood found in the depressions of the drywall and paint texture that Letecia failed to remove when she cleaned the murder scene.

123. I have received and reviewed Metro Crime Laboratory Report Lab Case #20MCL00267, completed by Serologist Sherrie Holmes /6622. Although I have discussed results related to the DNA testing in other portions of this affidavit, the intention of this section is to provide clarity and

eliminate the ambiguity of which sample were submitted to the laboratory, and which samples were or were not attributable to Gannon Stauch's DNA. Additionally, there is an unknown contributor in some of the DNA profiles that were developed. As mentioned elsewhere in this affidavit, I do not have a biology background, but I am aware that a DNA profile is very accurate.

124. Investigators submitted swabs from Gannon Stauch's toothbrush bristles, toothbrush head, and from a tooth retainer that Mr. Stauch said belonged to Gannon. DNA Buccal swabs were also taken from Gannon's biological father, mother, and Letecia Stauch. From these samples, DNA profiles for these individuals were developed and used as a comparison for another testing.

125. In summary, Gannon's DNA profile was found from blood samples taken in the garage, on the outside of size 8.5 Nike shoes, and in Gannon's bedroom. Letecia's DNA was recovered from the interior of the size 8.5 Nike shoes. I submit to the court that the lab results tend to corroborate the theory that Gannon was indeed murdered in his bedroom, brought into the garage, and his remains loaded in the Volkswagen Tiguan, subsequently to be disposed of in an unknown location.

126. To be more specific, a serology study was conducted by the Metro Crime Laboratory, and the following samples tested positive for the presence of blood. These samples were also analyzed and compared to known DNA profiles of Gannon Stauch, Letecia Stauch, and Albert Stauch.
   a. 4269 S-01A.01 (taken from a piece of carpet found inside a carpet roll in the utility room)—Found to be a mixture of three contributors, at least one of which is male. A DNA profile was not suitable for comparison due to the number of contributors and the complexity of the mixture.

b. 4269 S-14.01.01 (taken from the garage of the Stauch residence, directly under where the rear hatch of the Tiguan when reversed into the garage)—This DNA profile from the blood is a mixture of two contributors, one of which is male. The major profile matches Gannon Stauch.

c. 4269-S-14.02.01 (taken from the garage of the Stauch residence, directly under where the rear hatch of the Tiguan when reversed into the garage)—This DNA profile from the blood is a mixture of two contributors, one of which is male. The major profile matches Gannon Stauch.

d. 4269S-14.03.01 (taken from the garage of the Stauch residence, directly under where the rear hatch of the Tiguan when reversed into the garage)—This DNA profile from the blood matches Gannon Stauch.

e. 6839 SWI-1.01 (taken from the carpet at the base of the garage stairs)—A DNA profile could not be developed but tested presumptively positive for the presence of blood.

f. 6839 SW2-01.01.01 (taken from the blood-stained carpet fibers in Gannon's bedroom)—A DNA profile was obtained from the blood and matches the DNA profile of Gannon Stauch.

g. 6839 SW2-01.01 (taken from the corner of Gannon's bedroom on the carpet pad by his bed)—A DNA profile from the blood stain is a mixture of two individuals, at least one of which was a male. The major profile matches the DNA profile of Gannon Stauch.

h. 6839 SW2-02.01 (taken from the electrical outlet cover in Gannon's bedroom by his bed)—A DNA profile from the blood stain is a mixture of two individuals, at least one of which was male. The major profile matches the DNA profile of Gannon Stauch.

i. 6839 SW2-03.01.01 (taken from the electrical socket in Gannon's bedroom near his bed)—A DNA profile was obtained from the blood and matches the DNA profile of Gannon Stauch.

j. 6839 SW2-04.01.01 (taken from the back side of the carpet in Gannon's bedroom, near his bed)—A DNA profile was obtained from the blood and matches the DNA profile of Gannon Stauch.

k. 6839 SW2-04.02.01 (taken from the blood stain on top of the foam from the carpet in Gannon's bedroom)—A DNA profile was obtained from the blood and matches the DNA profile of Gannon Stauch.

l. 1153998 (taken from the trunk area of the Volkswagen Tiguan)—Was found to be negative for the presumptive presence of blood.

m. 4269 S-08 (taken from a teal couch pillow in the basement of the Stauch residence)—Was found to be presumptive positive for the presence of blood, but no DNA profile was able to be developed.

n. 4269 S-01.02.01 (taken from the outsole of the right Nike shoe)—A DNA profile was obtained after swabbing a confirmed bloodstain on the outsole of the right size 8.5 Nike shoe and was found to match the DNA profile of Gannon Stauch. Furthermore, a DNA profile was obtained from a swab of the inside of the shoe, which matched the DNA profile for Letecia Stauch.

Historical cell site location for related cellular telephones

127. Investigators applied for and were granted search warrants by this court to obtain historical call detail records to include cell site locations of cellular devices known to be utilized by Letecia and Harley. Your Affidavit has reviewed information from this analysis, and in summary, learned the following information.

128. Historical cell site analysis helps to determine the location of a cellular telephone based on cell tower antenna locations and orientation. Locations are determined by the activity of

the cellular telephone, and represent an approximate area, not an exact location. Different cellular carriers report this information in different formats and fashions.

129. The historical cell site analysis identified unusual activity for Letecia, including potentially disconnecting her cell phone from the cellular network for several hours. I submit that by disconnecting the phone, Letecia intended to prevent law enforcement from being able to determine her location. Specifically, this occurred on January 28, 2020, during the evening she disposed of Gannon's remains.

130. Investigators applied for and were granted a search warrant for Letecia's cellular telephone. A physical download was conducted and investigators were able to remove data inclusive of text messages, call records, the specific times her cell phone was unlocked, battery levels, and other information. In summary, investigators learned that Letecia lied to her employer, her husband, her friends, her daughter, and the children's babysitter. I will not include each and every text message or lie.

131. Additionally, there are messages that would otherwise tend to corroborate her statements about Gannon's whereabouts on the afternoon of January 27, 2020, if in fact, he did go to play with his friends. As discussed in other portions of the affidavit, Letecia's story was false and misleading, and these messages were likely sent by her as part of a larger plan to support her initial lies about his disappearance.

132. For example, on January 24, 2020, at approximately 0512 hours, Letecia had a conversation with Stephanie, the children's babysitter (saved in the phone as "Stephanie Sitter"). There is no indication that Gannon ever went to a doctor, and Letecia never brought that up with investigators. Some but not all of their conversation is below.

From: Letecia To: Stephanie Sitter 01/28/2020 5:14 "This happened at 3:30"

From: Letecia To: Stephanie 01/28/2020 5:14 "We talked to him and told him to be home by 6pm"

From: Stephanie To: Letecia 01/28/2020 5:14 "Someone posted he didn't go to school today."

From: Letecia To: Stephanie 01/28/2020 5:15 "He had to go to the doctor for his stomach."

From Letecia To: Stephanie 01/28/2020 5:15 "But he was home in the afternoon"

From: Stephanie To: Letecia 01/28/2020 5:15 "Where did he say he was at"

From: Letecia To: Stephanie 01/28/2020 5:16 "Honestly, I do not keep up with friends."

133. Letecia made statements to investigators via text messages that could be considered exculpatory in nature related to the presence of blood in the basement of their residence, as seen in the below text message. I have talked with investigators that were in the Stauch residence on January 27, 28, and 29. There was no odor or smoke, and no evidence of smoke. In fact, one detective noted the basement smelled like coconut and was very pleasant. Furthermore, I know that burns oftentimes do not produce wounds that bleed profusely,

134. The below message appears to contain instructions from Letecia to Harley to purchase carpet powder, baking soda, and trash bags, on or about January 27, 2020, 4:52pm. These messages are important because investigators believe the purpose of these items was to clean up blood from the murder of Gannon. This text message was also referenced above in paragraphs 72 to 76.

From Letecia to Harley: Carpet powder 2 things, baking soda, trash bags

135. Investigators also recovered limited GPS and location data from Letecia's phone. There are crucial time periods, such as the evening on January 28, 2020, when investigators were not able to recover location history because Letecia disconnected her phone from the cellular network or turned the phone off.

136. Letecia stored several written notes within her iPhone. The majority of those notes contained what appeared to be usernames, passwords, or insurance information. There were several notes that appeared to reference her unhappiness in the relationship and shed some light on potential household instability.

Letecia's internet activity between January 25 to 29, 2022

137. I was able to review some, but possibly not all, of the stored internet search history and the websites visited, recovered from the forensic physical download and search of Letecia's iPhone.

138. Between the dates of January 25 to 28, 2020, Letecia viewed websites associated with searching for a job in states other than Colorado, such as Los Angeles, CA, Orlando, Fl, Pensacola Beach, Fl, and Fort Lauderdale, Fl. Letecia also viewed apartments and 2-bedroom rental properties in Florida. Additionally, she visited a moving cost calculator website.

139. Letecia's internet activity also captured a search for a rental car and visited the website Priceline.com on January 28, 2020, at or about 0817 hours. I submit this timing is consistent with the acquisition of the Kia Ria, mentioned in this affidavit.

140. Letecia appeared to use Google, a popular online search engine. I have included some of her queries to Google, along with the date and approximate time of the search. Not all of her Google searches are included below. I submit that Letecia's search history is important because the history suggests she might have been struggling as a stepparent and additionally suggests she was not happily married to Mr. Stauch (see items, 1, 10, 12, 13, 14). While her search history alone does not provide a motive for the murder of Gannon, it does shed light on her inquisitive thoughts about her position with the family, memorialized in Google's search engine.

141. I also direct the Court's attention to the way Letecia's search terms are sometimes entered. Letecia hits the "." key instead of the space key multiple times while searching the internet (in approximately 44% of the searches listed below). This will be significant during the discussion of a search conducted on Gannon's phone, as was discussed above in paragraph 40, and will be further discussed below. There are other searches on Letecia's phone that use a "." and additional search history over a longer time span does exist that is not listed below.

Good Search Test String

a. find real military singles
b. parenting should be 4 people not one
c. I'm over doing everything for my step kids and their mother doesn't help
d. mom advice from step mom
e. if you aren't involved in your kids life you are shitty
f. my husband's ex-wife does nothing for her kids
g. I wonder if my husband's ex-wife is sending me a valentine's card since I raise her kids
h. someday some people will wish they treated you differently
i. why should my husband chose me over family
j. find me a rich guy who wants me to take care of his kids

k. find me a guy who wants me to take care of his kids and get paid

l. parents are those who put their kids before their nails

m. parents are those who put their kids before their nails

n. my son burned the carpet how do I fix it

o. will humidifier help if exposed to smoke

p. smoke affects will humidifier help

q. Colorado law for kid staying home

r. school is out is it ok for my kid to stay home alone

s. son is sick but I have to go to work

t. son sick can he stay home

u. suede repair for sofa

v. el paso sherriff office number

w. what is the process for my runaway child

x. police steps for our runaway

y. police steps for our missing child

z. today's flight okc

    aa. can Nintendo find my switch

    bb. car not Volkswagen

    cc. they are asking for our sons toothbrush but says nothing is wrong

142. Investigators were also able to recover internet search history that was deleted from Letecia's phone. No time and date association were located with the date and I can only ascertain that the searches were conducted prior to the EPSO seizing Letecia's cell phone, on January 28, 2020. Some, but not all, of the search history is included below. Some of the other deleted search terms included travel planning, shopping, job searches, and other seemingly innocent activity. I have not purposely left out any particular search that would be exculpatory in nature, and I am not intending to portray that all of Letecia's deleted searches were nefarious in nature. More of Letecia's searches on Google

- find me a new husband book
- I feel like I'm just a nanny not a step mom
- husband uses me to babysit his kids

- are there any free money to move away from bad situations
- my husband never post about me but does everything else
- my husband only cleans up for the army not me
- I'm just a glorified babysitter
- find a new husband
- sent my husband sexual messages and he ignores them
- make my husband want me more
- I feel like my husband uses me to babysit his kid
- find a guy without kids

Some deleted internet search terms located on Letecia's iPhone no-date information was available.

Letecia Stauch's consciousness of guilt

143. During the first 24 to 48 hours surrounding the disappearance of a child, it is reasonable that an assumingly innocent parent or stepparent would be contributing to search efforts, and fully participating in the effort to recover the child.

144. In the 24 to 48 hours surrounding Gannon's disappearance, Letecia rented a vehicle, turned her cell phone off for approximately four hours on the evening of January 28, 2020, washed her Tiguan immediately prior to coming to the EPSO for an interview, evaded law enforcement's attempt to conduct a more in-depth interview, and did not participate in the search for Gannon.

145. On Tuesday, January 28, 2020, between 0848 and 0854, Letecia instructed Harley to "Pull your car in the garage" via text message, presumably to temporarily cover up any potential evidence left behind. To be clear, Harley has her own vehicle that was mentioned above in paragraph 13, specifically a Volkswagen Jetta.

146. On January 28, 2020, at approximately 1604-1617 hours, investigators asked Letecia for Gannon's toothbrush to recover his DNA. At or about 1619 hours, Letecia did a search in her internet browser of "they are asking for our son's toothbrush but said nothing is wrong". At or about 1631 to 1633 hours, Letecia has a text conversation with Mr. Stauch.
Letecia: "Something isn't right I think they are hiding something"
Mr. Stauch: "Who", "the police?"
Letecia: "Yes", "They asked for tooth brushes"
Mr. Stauch: "hmm", "what do u think they are hiding?"

147. Also on January 29, 2020, at or about 2245 hours, Letecia made a statement to investigators via text message. At the time of this statement, Gannon had been missing for approximately 27 hours, and Letecia believed she was a subject in his disappearance without any prior prompting from law enforcement, or notification of such:
Letecia: "What do you want from me? Because I have nothing. One of your very own leaked to me what you guys are doing. I did nothing and/or am being set up. I'm not really even sure other that being told that by another blue with El Paso. I was told I couldn't go home to sleep and on top of that, men were sent to a home with a minor female and she was forced to stay there not to even leave for food. Every conversation that said even at this moment I can hear inside. What do you want from me?"
Detective Bethel: "Come in to talk to me. I would just like information to find Gannon."

148. After ESPO investigators seized Letecia's Volkswagen Tiguan on January 29, 2020, she obtained a 2020 Nissan Altima. Investigators applied for and were granted a warrant by this court to install a GPS tracker on the vehicle. Investigators monitored this tracking device, which provided particularly

useful information on January 31, 2020. A map with some of this data is included below. This information will be discussed below and relates to the area north of Palmer Lake and along Highway 105/S Perry Park Road in Douglas County Colorado.

149. In summary, investigators believe Letecia utilized the rented Nissan Altima to return to the area in which she disposed of Gannon's body. Indeed, investigators recovered a piece of particle board from this area.

150. The fact Letecia came back to this area on January 31, 2020 is significant, and investigators have not uncovered any evidence that Letecia has family or friends that live in the area or any legitimate reason for her presence in the area other than to dispose of incriminating evidence.

151. I submit a reasonable theory for the fact Letecia returned to this area, based on the information presented in this affidavit as follows. Letecia disposed of Gannon's remains at nighttime and likely was nervous about the location she chose, and may not have even remembered where she dumped Gannon's remains. Investigators believe that on January 31, 2020, she went back to the area to review the area while the sunlight was available, to ensure no evidence was viewable from the road, to ensure his remains were adequately covered to prevent detection, and to see if any law enforcement was in the area.

The explanation of the Volkswagen Tiguan data

152. Investigators were able to remove a computer chip from Letecia's Volkswagen Tiguan, which was examined by the FBI. The FBI was able to recover data (hereinafter "raw data"), which included, but is not limited to, the estimated location of the vehicle specifically related to the evening of January 28, 2020, and the morning of January 29, 2020.

153. The raw data has not been scientifically evaluated, and the raw data that was provided was not portrayed to be an exact representation of the vehicle's activities. Additionally, I have been told that the raw data has particular limitations, including the inability to show the exact location of the vehicle. For example, if the Tiguan was taken off the road, the raw data may not show that and display the estimated location on the nearest road. Furthermore, the estimated location may have some degree of fluctuation in accuracy, estimated to be approximately 50 to 100 meters.

154. FBI Agents, including Special Agent (SA) Donati, took steps to verify and corroborate the data recovered from the Tiguan. In summary, SA Donati was able to take some of the raw data, including location and time stamp, and compare it to other evidence. As with other forensic evidence discussed in this affidavit, investigators believe it to be reliable.

155. For Example, the Tiguan raw data placed Tiguan leaving the Colorado Springs Airport just after 1900 hours on January 28, 2020. This information matched the time stamp of the January 28, 2020 Colorado Springs Airport parking receipt to the Tiguan data. The Tiguan raw data indicated the Tiguan stopped near a King Soopers' parking lot for approximately 10 minutes after leaving the Airport, between 2008 hours to 2018 hours. SA Donati was able to review surveillance footage from that King Soopers which indeed showed a dark SUV matching the description of the Tiguan sitting in the parking lot during that same time period. Other footage, including video footage from a Wendy's restaurant in a separate location, helped to further corroborate the raw data.

156. Of significant importance, the raw data showed the Tiguan in the area of Hwy 105/S Perry Park Road between 2115 hours and 2130 hours on January 28, 2020, and I have included a map depicting that data. The raw data also indicated the

Tiguan stopped for approximately five minutes, in an area approximate to the recovery of Gannon's blood on February 15, 2020. This is the same area Letecia likely drove to in her Nissan Altima rental vehicle on January 31, 2020. The recovery of Gannon's blood is in this area.

157. Investigators were also able to compare Letecia's historical cell site information, including NELOS data, against the Tiguan raw data, and found no reason to believe that Letecia was not the driver of the Tiguan on January 28, 2020.

158. Investigators contacted several consensually monitored telephone calls with Mr. Stauch. Specifically, Mr. Stauch, at the direction of law enforcement, communicated with Letecia via telephone and email. These communications have been recorded and memorialized and consisted of hours of recorded conversations. I will not provide a transcription of these calls but will summarize the importance of particular changes in Letecia's story, and will also include exculpatory information related to Letecia's statements. Letecia never admitted to killing Gannon.

159. For the purposes of refreshing the court, here is a summary of some of Letecia's statements whether to law enforcement, directly through the media, and/or to Mr. Stauch in recorded email and voice communications
    • On January 27, 2020, Letecia stated—Gannon left to play at a friend's house and did not come home at 1800 hours like he was supposed to.
    • On January 29, 2020, Letecia stated—She was held at gunpoint, raped, and Gannon was abducted by her rapist.

160. Within Letecia's falsehoods, there were details corroborated by physical evidence that would be near impossible to know without being intimately involved in the murder. Letecia has made statements to explain the blood on the walls in

Gannon's bedroom, blood on the rear bumper of the Tiguan, and blood in the garage of the Stauch's residence. Details of the location were not previously disclosed to investigators. Her statements continue to evolve in a dramatic way to ESPO.

161. The majority of the conversations between Letecia and Albert Stauch began around February 13, 2020. Over several days, Letecia's story continued to change. During a phone call on February 13, 2020, Letecia stated that Gannon was burned by a candle to the point that his skin bubbled, and that Gannon peeled the burns off and wiped the blood on his bedroom wall. Mr. Stauch did not ask about the blood on the walls of his room during this call. The fact she provided information about blood on the wall likely indicates her knowledge of the murder scene.

162. On February 14, 2020, Letecia had an additional conversation with Mr. Stauch and provided four additional versions of Gannon's disappearance.

Story #1: When ESPO came to their house on January 27, 2020, the abductor was still in her residence, and that she tried to signal to EPSO Deputies that there was somebody in the residence. It should be noted that, EPSO Deputies checked the entirety of the house and no additional person was located during that search.

Story #2: She was raped by Quincy Brown at her residence, and Brown abducted Gannon. She knew Brown's identity because she saw a paper and his identification card fell out of his pocket that had his name on it. Letecia sent a photograph of Quincy Brown to Mr. Stauch via text message (it is noted this photographed mirrored image online wherein Quincy Brown was listed as a Most Wanted suspect, discussed below).

Story #3: Quincy Brown followed her from Petco, and at some point, was laying in the middle of the road in front of her car. When Letecia stopped to avoid running the man over, he jumped into her car and made her take him home, then raped her.

Story #4: Letecia and Gannon were near County Line Rd/Hwy 105 in northern El Paso County on January 27, 2020. Gannon was riding a bicycle in that area and fell off, hit his head, and was then abducted by Quincy Brown. In this version of events, Quincy Brown was driven by a man named Terence.

163. The story #4 has several interesting considerations. During the period of February 12 to 14, 2020, it was public knowledge by the virtue of media coverage that investigators were searching for Gannon in the area of 105/S Perry Park Road in southern Douglas County near the El Paso County line. Letecia brought this location up on her own, without prompt during a conversation, and provided an alibi for why she was in that area. Letecia was adamant that investigator's efforts to search for Gannon in that area would be futile. This area turned out to be significant based on the Tiguan's location on January 28, 2020, and that Gannon's blood was found in this area, discussed below in more detail.

164. Furthermore, as mentioned above, Letecia drove through the same area in her Nissan Altima rental vehicle on January 31, 2020.

165. I submit that based on raw data retrieved from the Tiguan, Letecia was likely in the area of Highway 105/S Perry Park Road on the evening of January 28, 2020, and Gannon's remains were dumped in the vicinity of that area. Letecia's story lays the foundation for a reason why investigators may locate Gannon's body with head trauma.

166. On February 15, 2020, Letecia provided additional conflicting stories to Mr. Stauch, including that the story she told Albert Stauch about Gannon falling off the bike was a lie because it was what she believed he wanted to hear.

167. Letecia stated the blood in the corner of Gannon's room was a combination of hers and Gannon's. In this explanation, she stated that the abductor anally penetrated both her and Gannon with an object. Additionally, she was tied up and some point in the abduction, and the abductor was still present during the EPSO visit that night.

Quincy Brown

168. Quincy Brown, age 37, was listed on El Paso County's Most Wanted List in February 16, 2020. I was able to locate Brown's photo on KKTV New, website, where they describe Brown as a black male (it is noted that during one of Letecia's stories, she described her rapist as a Hispanic male). The photo on the website appeared to be the same photo Letecia sent to Mr. Stauch. Brown has outstanding arrest warrants for failure to register as a sex offender and failure to appear. These warrants appear to have been open since 2018.

169. I was able to find a criminal history for Quincy Brown, date of birth 10/21/1981, which included but was not limited to a 2001 arrest for 1st Degree Kidnapping in El Paso County Court Case 2001CR4383, which was pled to Felony Menacing. Investigators have uncovered no evidence to support that Quincy Brown was involved in Gannon's disappearance.

Gannon's blood is located in Douglas County, Colorado on February 15, 2020

170. As mentioned above, investigators began to focus a search effort for Gannon's remains in the area of Hwy 105/S Perry Park Road in Douglas County, Colorado on February 12, 2020. There is not an exact address to reference due to the rural nature of the area. This particular location was deemed important base on raw data from the Tiguan on January

28, 2020, and the location data from her rental vehicle on January 31, 2020.

171. On February 15, 2020, searchers located a piece of particleboard during that search. The particleboard had a stain that appeared to be consistent with blood and is pictured below. I have added a red circle to indicate the location of the blood stain. The particleboard was collected by the FBI Evidence Response Team, and transported to the Metro Crime Lab, also on February 15, 2020. An initial test revealed a positive presumptive result for the presence of human or high primate blood. Further testing was conducted, and a DNA profile was developed and compared to Gannon's on February 16, 2020. That profile matched the DNA profile of Gannon Stauch and is documented in Metro Crime Laboratory Report 20MCL00267.

172. The reasonable explanation for the discovery of this particleboard, with Gannon's blood on it, is that Letecia used this particleboard during the disposal of Gannon's remains.

173. The area in which the particleboard was found is rural in nature it is likely populated by wildlife including predators such as bear, coyotes, and mountain lions. Gannon's remains have not been located, and while investigators will continue to search the area, it is possible those remains have since been scattered since January 28, 2020.

174. The below map depicts the area where the particleboard was recovered, compared with raw data from the Tiguan's location (while idling for approximately five minutes) on January 28, 2020, and then GPS tracker data from the Nissan Altima on January 31, 2020. As noted above, the raw data of the Tiguan has an estimated 50 to 100-meter variance.

175. Additionally, investigators were granted a pen register/trap and trace device order, global positioning system (GPS) pings, and cell site sector information. Investigators monitored Letecia's telephone, and recorded hours of communication between Stauch and others. Each and every communication intercepted is mot included within this affidavit.

176. As during other portions of the investigation, Letecia continued to provide different stories to different people about Gannon's disappearance. Letecia provided false information to her sister, and other family members during which Letecia provided multiple different stories for what happened to Gannon. Several of these stories were discussed above.

177. On a February 16, 2020 call at or about 1928 hours, Letecia told a female, believed to be Teela Cummings, that she had been giving Al numerous false stories because she knows he will not believe anything she says.

178. On February 17, 2020 call at or about 1353 hours, Letecia told a female, believed to be associated with Laura Abernathy, that she was thinking about flying out to Colorado to take a lie detector test to prove her innocence. During that call, she stated, "They think I'm still in Colorado."

179. On another February 17, 2020 call at or about 1611 hours, Letecia told an unknown female that she is going to take a lie detector test, but that the test is not admissible in court, and no law enforcement would be present.

180. On February 17, 2020 call at or about 1014 hours, Letecia called 321-247-6876. I conducted research on that phone number and learned it was associated with "fakepolgraph. com." During that call, Letecia stated she never got a confirmation for a test day she paid for. Letecia provided the spelling of her name, and before disconnecting the call,

the unknown male stated he would resend her results to her email.

181. I viewed the website "fakepolgraph.com" and found the following information:

FAKE POLYGRAPH TEST

Get a Fully Verified Fake Polygraph Test, Certificate, providing you have taken a real Polygraph test. You choose the "Questions, Location, and Results." We send you a fully verified Report within 1 business hour. The Fake Polygraph Results are emailed from a local and real Polygraph Company. If your partner calls the authentic company, our team will confirm the test details. We are sure they will believe us. We have nationwide "real" polygraph companies in the following countries: UK, Ireland, Australia, USA, and Canada.

Our Polygraph Reports are 3 to 4 pages long and replicate a real report. The local Polygraph Company branding and Contact Details are the fake Polygraph Test Report. The Polygraph test results are mailed from a real Polygraph Test Company.

Screenshot taken on 02/19/2020 from fakepolygraph.com

182. Also on February 18, 2020, at or about 1116 hours, Letecia again called 321-247-6876. During this call, Letecia inquired about an email she received. The unknown male stated that his report was blocked by management based on the content of the questions and stated that with any illegal activities, they reserve the right to not send the report. Leticia's response was the following:
Letecia: "What do you do now, just delete it and go on about life and keep the money?"
Male at FakePolyGraph.com: "Yes, we do indeed"
Letecia: "Ok, I gotcha, thank you, goodbye"

183. Investigators contacted Luke Devlin utilizing the phone number 321-247-4876 that Letecia called. Mr. Devlin

provided information to investigators, including the questions and answers that Letecia had provided.

184. Letecia provided the following questions and the answers that were supposed to be truthful to "fakepolygraph.com."
    a. Do you intend to answer these questions regarding your stepson truthfully? YES
    b. Is your birthday August 4, 1983? YES
    c. Did you participate in any way in causing harm to your stepson? NO
    d. Did your stepson return with you to your home? YES
    e. Did you participate in any way causing the death of your stepson? NO

185. I submit to the court that if Letecia had nothing to hide, she would not have to pay for fake polygraph results.

Conclusions

186. Based on data collected by the FBI and reported in the Journal of Forensic Sciences, I learned that in over 71% of homicide cases that involve false reporting, the reporting party is responsible for the murder. To be clear, this statistic is not being provided as sole probable cause for the requested warrant but as an additional fact to be combined with others listed in this affidavit.

187. Based on Leticia's internet history, it is reasonable to believe that she was unhappily married to Mr. Stauch and had some degree of resentment toward the family as a stepparent. Furthermore, the day before Gannon's murder, Letecia appeared to be researching a move to another state to a two-bedroom apartment.

188. Letecia has not provided a fully truthful statement to investigators at any point during this investigation, particularly regarding the circumstances of Gannon's

disappearance. This would reasonably be suspected activity of an individual that committed the crime under investigation, namely murder. Within approximately 24 hours of Gannon being reported missing, and without external prompt, Letecia made claims to law enforcement that she was being set up.

189. Initially, Letecia and Gannon were playing with neighborhood friend between approximately 1515 hours and 1600 hours and was expected home 1800 hours. Within a few days, Letecia changed her story to label herself as a victim of rape, felony menacing with a weapon, and assault, resulting in Gannon's abduction by her rapist. Her stories continued to evolve to include a new location of Gannon's disappearance over 30 miles away, several completely different sets of circumstances and unprompted explanations for why Gannon's blood would be found by investigators in key locations.

190. Letecia was unable to provide a logical reason why she rented another vehicle while she still had access to the Tiguan. Based on the aforementioned facts, it was likely because it contained the remains of, or evidence of Gannon's remains, based on positive reactions to luminol in the Tiguan on the bumper, indicating the likely presence of blood on the rear tailgate. A suspected blood sample from the interior of the trunk area returned a negative result for the presumptive presence of blood.

191. Gannon's mattress has a large red stain on it that is consistent with blood. Based on the orientation of the mattress in the room, it appears that is where Gannon's head and upper torso would have been. Below that same area, a substance that was confirmed as blood by the Metro Crime Laboratory soaked through the carpet, the pad, and stained the concrete. This blood matches the DNA profile for Gannon Stauch. In this same area, blood samples taken from the wall, namely as

electrical outlet, were also confirmed to match Gannon's DMA profile.

192. Gannon's blood, again matched to his DNA profile, was also found on a piece of particleboard in the area of Hwy 105/s Perry Park Road in Douglas County, Colorado. This particular area is consistent with Letecia's travels on January 28, 2020 and January 31, 2020 based on GPS tracker locations of her Nissan Altima rental vehicle and raw data from the Tiguan.

193. During her stories to Mr. Stauch, without prompt, Letecia provided explanations for why blood would be found on Gannon's bedroom wall. Other than Letecia being present for Gannon's murder and being present for the cleaning of the murder scene, there is no reasonable explanation how Letecia would know there was blood on Gannon's wall, as that evidence had not been released to the media. Again, without prompt, Letecia provided an alibi for why she was in the area where the particleboard was recovered.

194. By combining cell tower data, reviewing video surveillance, and checking security system logistics, investigators believe based on the evidence the only three individuals with access to Gannon on the afternoon of January 27, 2020, were Letecia, Harley, and eight-year-old Laina. With the exception of Laina, who is not considered a suspect, it appears nobody other than Letecia was with Gannon at the Stauch residence between the hours of approximately 1416 and 1734 hours on January 27, 2020, when investigators suspect Letecia murdered Gannon.

195. Gannon has been missing for approximately four weeks, and there has been national news attention on major networks related to his disappearance. Local efforts, including posters, news coverage, search teams, and social media postings have also failed to locate Gannon, comprising thousands of man-

hours in several different locations. Additionally, although the EPSO has received hundreds of tips, nobody has provided information that has led to Gannon's location. His family and friends have not heard from him, and Gannon is only 11 years old with no financial resources.

196. Letecia Stauch was the last person to see Gannon alive. Investigators have not located Gannon's remains at this point in time, although the search continues. As additional time increases without locating Gannon, the more likely it is that Gannon is not alive.

197. Based on the facts set forth above, I submit probable cause exists to believe that, on or about January 27, 2020, within the state of Colorado, and within El Paso County, Letecia Stauch committed the offenses, in violation of Colorado Revised Statues to include: Murder on the First Degree-Child Under Twelve—Position of Trust, 18-3102 (1Xf), Child Abuse Resulting in Death, 18-6-401 (lXa), Tampering with a Deceased Human Body, 18-8-610.5, and Tampering with Physical Evidence, 18-8-510 (1Xa).

198. Therefore, your affidavit respectfully requests the issuance of an arrest warrant charging the same. Signed the 28th day of February.

Letecia Stauch was arrested on March 2, 2020 for the murder of Gannon Stauch, 11. She was arrested in Myrtle Beach, South Carolina. The authorities found Gannon's body in Pace, Florida March 18, 2020. She has been held in the El Paso County Jail where she faces more than 12 counts including first-degree murder. She now has been in the jail for more than 2 years. She is a protected prisoner, not being allowed to mix with the general population of the jail. She is in her cell for 23 hours a day.

In February of 2022, she announced her plea to not guilty by reason of insanity. Her defense lawyers filed a motion to waive a jury trial. When she changed her plea to insanity, it requires the state to conduct yet another mental health evaluation. The judge said he will not rule on waiving a trial without a jury until they get the mental evaluation.

In April 2022, the judge said doctors from the state hospital needed more records that Stauch told them about, records that were in South Carolina where she used to live. The original plan was to have the report done by the end of May. Her attorney flew to South Carolina to get the records. The results of her mental evaluation were scheduled for June 9. However, on June 9, the court said it had not received any reports and was unable to move forward. The next hearing date was scheduled for July 28, 2022 in hopes a trial could be set the beginning of 2023.

It's reported the evaluation is finally in the judge's hand and a hearing has been set for August 25, 2022. It is everyone's hope that this case can finally move forward at that time.

Preliminary hearing testimony reveals Gannon Stauch was shot and stabbed.

After being arrested for Gannon Stauch's murder, Letecia Stauch waives the right for an attorney and made the decision to represent herself. She was adamant to represent herself stating she believed experts in the legal system held no value in her case. In her Arguello Advisement, she said she has 23 hours a day to work on her case, and besides, she has an "ace in the hole," insinuating she was innocent. She said she was confident in two pieces of evidence, that no science can discredit, and it will clear her name.

Below is a letter Letecia wrote to the judge.

Judge Werner,

On 2/19/2021, I was unable to talk with Judge Bain about my conflicts with my defense team due to:

1) The actual privacy of the booth and the transport over.

I explained in detail to him expressing my concerns of privacy.

2) I had a very difficult morning mentally because I am not mentally well. One of the main issues with my attorney is their lack of ability to gather evidence. Due to this, I find little value in the term "expert." First, they were unable to obtain my mental health records from Charleston, S.C. when I finally paid a firm in S.C. to obtain them. In 2016, I was diagnosed with and received treatment before work for over 28 hours of care. The school district even provided extra services and later let me medically resign due to the ongoing reality breaks. In 2018, I was hospitalized in Canada (crossing the border) for 2 days and completed more OP treatment when I returned. I tell you this because it sets the stage for why I cannot work with my attorneys. I signed release forms for them to get all this information so they would have a better understanding of why I'm all over the place. Some days, I asked them to use the info from a non-biased doctor (who worked with me more than 2 hours) but instead, they sent a lady who was clearly an actress and friends with the D.A. She spoke about him in an unprofessional manner, their history, and his election. Now I'm sure all this was true, but I thought she worked for the court, not one particular side. My attorney did this to make me look like a perjurious individual. Instead, it was malfeasances on their part. I have included several reasons to support my claim as I kept a timeline of these conflicts.

Communication is broken beyond repair. I explained these issues to Judge Bain including the lack of access and visitations in great detail.

Inconsiderate of evidence—Since March of 2020, I asked my attorneys to preserve the Gamestop footage, to locate the Texas Police officer whom I spoke with, and to get the Cruise passenger list. Instead, they spent months contacting my family for mitigation. When asked certain things, they kept saying they will let the investigators know. 1 year later, same answer.

My evidence—I haven't physically seen any while being held at CJC for 1 year. Yes Covid, but inmates were still being held as our constitutional rights were adjusted.

Overlooking Statue and Evidence—They overlooked the competency statue about video recording. Human error? Okay, but this happens often with evidence in which I (the non-expert) has to provide corrections to evidence.

Sharing info—They were texting my family and giving them info that they should not have causing several disputes.

My judge—They filed that motion (knowing this county would not grant me new attorneys) to sabotage any chances of a trial by judge. They knew I wanted to present evidence to him w/o exposing any on my son's father. However, they created incorrect conflicts instead of addressing the real issues. They could have filed the Pro Se only instead of talking about my defense to sabotage my trial by judge.

Defenses—Indeed, I am innocent but I will not put myself or others in danger running the defense against my biological son when the system is letting two men run free who are involved. One is a prominent member of an independent business. They used NFRI to get a hearing, knowing that I'm not guilty to cover up their lack of presentation. Although, "I had bouts of insanity" and still do, I did not murder or abuse anyone nor would that be a defense because it's my understanding that you actually did do it. However, I will protect my bio son and I will protect the drugs and violence documented from my stepson.

The truth is the court is holding the wrong person and for the wrong crimes. This whole process has been nefarious from denying me an attorney, threatening me in the bathroom away from cameras to confess, taking advantage of me being delusional, threatening my other kids' freedom or else, etc. I am going to keep making it known, Sir, just how much the state has done in this wrongful incarceration. I will continue to be an advocate for myself because I am not a murderer and the level that the prosecution goes through to promote a wrongful conviction is absurd. Truth is they could see a video from someone else and they would dismiss that person as a lunatic. They have far too much invested in this wrongful incarnation to admit they are wrong. For these reasons and because my defense team is in cahoots with them, I am left with no other choice but to represent myself. Denying me my rights under the constitution has happened throughout this process from the detectives, the jail, and now my legal team. Every day, I am getting worse mentally due to inadequate representation and being held hostage for a crime I did not commit. These are my conflict issues and my reason for asking to go Pro Se. As always, thank you for your time. Signed by Letecia Stauch.

At the end of Letecia's March. 12 hearing, the letter was discussed. In that letter, she tells the judge her access to her attorneys were hindered by the jail. The judge asked her if that was not the case, would she still want to represent herself. She replied, "I wish to represent myself, Sir." The Judge ordered that the letter from Letecia be unsealed and remind her it is of public record.

On the first page of her letter, Letecia stated the doctor who conducted her second competency evaluation was clearly "an actress" and friends with the D.A. She also says she deals with "bouts of insanity" but maintains her innocence throughout the letter. She placed the Judge in a difficult situation. She has brought up reasons why it's difficult for her to represent herself. There is always the opportunity to enter a plea of incompetent to proceed, even though in Letecia's case her competency has been evaluated twice. She can't say, on one hand, that "I don't trust anybody else in the system and therefore I'm going to represent myself. But by the way, I don't know that I'm doing a very good job of it, either."

Her attorney Stephen Longo's initial concerns was that of the competency issue. Yet it's already been determined by the court that she is mentally fit to stand trial. Lango stated that "Attempting to be manipulative type thing, where she's really trying to convince the judge that she knows she's probably competent to stand trial but wants people to think she's not competent to stand trial."

Her preliminary hearing was moved to May 20, 2020, to give her time to review evidence while in jail.

Records show that on May 3, 2020, Letecia requested state attorney be assigned to her case after having waived her right to counsel and deciding to represent herself. Letecia Stauch I believe felt she is so intelligent she could represent herself. Did she come to the conclusion maybe she isn't that smart?

The records show that on May 7, 2020, an attorney, Josh Tolini was appointed to her case. Her preliminary hearing was then scheduled for September 9, 2020.

After months of delays, Letecia Stauch, the woman accused of murdering her 11-year-old stepson, Gannon Stauch, was back in court for a preliminary hearing on September 9, 2021.

It is believed she killed Gannon in her home in Lorson Ranch on January 27, 2020.

At this hearing, prosecutors must produce enough evidence and convince the court to take this case to trial. The judge told them he would rule on the evidence on September 23, 2020. Letecia would not attend the hearing and the prosecutor said she does not have the right to not appear, but the judge disagreed with him.

The first witness called in the hearing was Sargent Jason Yoder from Santa Rosa, Florida Sheriff's office. He testified that he was called to check out a body that was found in a suitcase along the Escambia, River Bridge in 2020. When he opened the suitcase, there was a body wrapped in blankets. He described seeing injuries to the body described as a fractured skull, a gunshot wound to the lower jaw, and eighteen sharp force wounds, and what appeared to be defensive wounds on the hands. He testified he later learned the identity of the boy as Gannon Stauch after a match was made using DNA analysis.

He testified the coroner who handled the autopsy, said the cause of death is listed as a gunshot wound with blunt-force trauma to the head.

Kevin Clark, formerly of the Colorado Springs Police Department, said he presented data collected from vehicles and Stauch's phone to track her whereabouts the day after investigators believe Gannon was killed. The trips include random trips in southeastern Colorado Springs, Falcon and into Douglas County. This shows why investigators spent time in all those areas conducting searches before Gannon's body was found in Florida.

District Attorney said that information recovered from a budget rental van on February 1, 2020, showed Stauch traveling from Colorado to Florida and then South Carolina. He said Letecia made stops in Pensacola, Florida, just after midnight on February 4. They had data to back this up. He said she also made a reservation at a Candlewood Suites in Pensacola using her cell phone and that around 4:15 a.m. on February 4th, her phone pinged about three miles from where Gannon's remains were found.

Sgt. Rosario Hubble with the El Paso County Sheriff's Office testified that she gained access to Letecia's phone that showed Gannon in bed. He was alive and uninjured at that point. The bedding in the picture appeared to be the same bedding that was found in the suitcase. After Gannon was reported missing, there are pictures of his bed with different bedding, which does show the bedding was changed sometime between January 27th when the first pictures were taken and in February when the second picture was taken.

There is also a picture of Gannon's bedroom with the bed removed from the room. The carpet had been ripped up in the corner that was under his bed. Underneath, there was a stain that tested positive for being Gannon's blood. The stain soaked through the carpet and the padding and went straight through to the cement floor. Before the carpet was pulled up, there was no visible blood on the carpet. Letecia had spent time cleaning and scrubbing the carpet. Sgt. Hubble also testified there was a 9mm gun found in the bedroom of Letecia Stauch. Tests in Florida showed that Gannon was killed with a 9 mm gun.

Special Agent Andrew Cohen of the FBI testified that the Stauch home had a security system that there was no evidence of anyone coming into the Stauch home during the time Gannon was being killed. DNA showed the major profile on the 9 mm gun was that of Letecia. He also testified the day which Letecia killed Gannon can be pinpointed.

> **Children begin by loving their parents; as they grow older, they judge them; sometimes they forgive them.**
>
> **—Oscar Wilde**

CHAPTER 8

**Foster Parents kills 2-year-old girl Leila Daniel,
DOB 07/18/2013**

The Atlanta Journal headline read . . . Warrant: Henry commission
candidate beat, starved foster child.

I guess that title sums it up. However, the story inside of that is
even more disturbing than even the title of the article. I will try and
lay out as best as possible what happened. There is a lot of players to
this story, and a lot happened.

We will start with the biological mother, Tessa Daniel, a young
mother addicted to meth. So sad because she really wanted to kick
the addiction. I can't imagine myself, but I think we are all addicted
to something, whether it's coffee, sugar, food, exercise, or drugs. The
thing with meth is it's designed to make you an addict. After one use,
the person wants more and more. I've been told it's the hardest thing
there is to fight. Tessa wanted to and she even tried, in many ways,
but the addiction was just too strong. And I surmise, she had people
in her life that made it easier to give in than to fight it. One thing I
could tell by listening to her testify in the trial is she loved her girls.
She loved them so much, and she never abused them. She wanted
custody of them, but she also knew she was not good for them when
she was doing drugs. She showed gratitude for someone that would
take them and love them when she couldn't. She was incarcerated at
the time the girls were in foster homes. They were many. At the time

of the murder, there was Millie P., 4 years-old, and Laila Daniel, 2 years-old—beautiful, trusting, sweet little girls with a zest for life. Millie the four-year old was positive and upbeat even with all she had gone through in her short life. Years ahead of her age, she could reason, talk, and remember anything.

Then there was the great grandmother; she loved the girls so much. However, although she could keep Millie, Laila was a little too young for a woman her age and she couldn't keep up with Laila. She tried but was not physically able. She had a very special bond with Millie and she loved spending time with her, and Millie loved spending time with her great-grandmother. Therefore, she was thankful when the Rosenbaums came along and offered to give the girls a forever home, love, and care for them both. After all, part of their care-plan was to keep them together. The girls wanted that too. Millie loved her little sister and tried her best to help her. Besides, the Rosenbaums offered to allow her to continue to see the girls.

Jennifer and Joseph Rosenbaum, 27 years of age. Jennifer was in her third year of law-school and Joseph was a corrections officer. By all appearances, they looked like the perfect match for the girls—well educated, seemingly well adjusted, have their own home, and able to afford for the girls to have a good life. A lot of love to give from a couple that could not have a child of their own. Jennifer was doing an internship at the district attorney's office and came across the children's case. She found out their biological mother was in the same foster home she was in as a teenager. What better mom than one who understands what a child goes through being a foster child? Again, just a perfect match. She was able to use her influences to get DCFS to consider her and Joseph to be foster parents and finally adopt.

Thus, the foster program started. They took whatever courses that were needed and then started with supervised visitation. Then it turned into unsupervised visitation, then overnights, then weekends. At that time, the girls were happy in another family's home. That foster mother became concerned when the girls would come back from overnights with bumps and bruises. She didn't necessarily think right away there was abuse, but maybe Jennifer and Joseph weren't watching them close enough. She reported this to DCFS and once even took them to the Emergency Room, then by the DCFS office to document everything. She did not want anyone to think she had done something to the girls. She loved them, and even though she had children of her own, she made sure they ate well and all needs were being met. She knew they were temporary foster children.

DCFS decided it was safe to allow Jennifer and Joseph to have the girls anyway. In July of 2015, the girls were given to the Rosenbaums fulltime.

It was going to be a busy schedule as Jennifer was going to school, doing her internship, and Joseph was working two jobs. He was to care for the girls while Jennifer was gone during the day, and she would care for them in the evening. However, things did not go exactly as they had planned for them to go.

It wasn't long before the small amount of abuse became a large amount of abuse. The girls were pulled up and down the stairs by one arm. They had their arms twisted and both of them suffered arm fractures without being given any medical care. Imagine the pain of that. Jennifer would punch them in the stomach with her fist. Authorities are not sure if she used something other than her fist or not. They were kicked in the stomach and back. They were hit with unknown objects, and they were hit many times in the head, neck, ears, back, and legs with belt buckles and again, authorities don't know what else was used on them.

Jennifer was careful though not to put too many bruises where others could see them. She lied to people, telling them the girls were in daycare and gymnastics. Millie was in gymnastics for a while, but Laila never was. Yet, she told everyone that when Laila got a very bad break in her leg that it was from gymnastics. She would tell Millie if anyone asked her what happened to tell them it was from gymnastics. We know Jennifer broke Leila's leg and injured the other leg, but we just don't know how. The doctors testified in court about that break being a difficult bone for children to break and they usually only saw kids with those breaks that had been in serious accidents. However, Jennifer managed somehow to break that bone, the upper part of the shin bone. The doctors testified a very painful break. Jennifer did not seek help for several days. When she did, the doctor immediately suspected possible abuse. He referred her to a clinic to have it set and even called and let them know it was a possible abuse situation. Jennifer did not take Laila to that doctor as she had promised to do. Instead, she waited several more days and took her to a different doctor to see Laila and set the broken bone. Heartbreaking to think how painful that break was and what Laila went through. As a mom myself, I imagine a little girl going to sleep at night in so much pain that she fell asleep out of exhaustion. Mothers are meant to comfort, hug, and take their pain away, not cause their pain.

The abuse was constant and not easy. Those gentle little girls loved Jennifer unconditionally, even to the point of telling others what she told them to say.

By testimony of several people, Laila loved to eat. They would all say she was a junk food eater, and she loved her food. She would eat hers and anyone else's she could get a hold of. Not with Jennifer though. Food was withheld from her until it affected her looks and health. She stopped eating almost altogether and this was all caused by Jennifer. I suggest she used that as punishment, or because she got aggravated that she loved food so much that she was going to show her. Cruel to withhold food from an already abused child. I believe Laila was starved more than Millie, yet Millie was smart enough to know her sister was not being fed like she should have been. I think possibly the reason she was crueler to Laila than Mille was partially because Millie was so smart and she might tell on her.

There was one incident that Millie told about where they were having dinner and was forced to eat mashed potatoes. She couldn't eat them all and was forced to finish. She vomited because of it. Jennifer then forced her to eat the vomit. These are the things we know. How much worse was it really?

This abuse went on from July until November 17, 2019. It was around 5:45 pm, dinner time. According to Millie, they were sitting at the table when she said Laila started shaking. Jennifer described it as choking and maybe a seizure. She said she grabbed her out of the highchair, held her over the kitchen sink, and "patted" her on the back to try and dislodge the particle of food. Nothing came out, so she says she laid her on the floor and called 911. She was instructed by the dispatcher to give CPR. Jennifer said she didn't know how to give

CPR. So, the dispatcher very patiently gave her detailed instructions step by step in giving CPR.

The EMTs arrived and took over, saying Jennifer was on the floor next to Laila when they got there. One EMT who testified said immediately when he saw Laila, he knew it was child abuse. He was set back at how many bruises she had. A paramedic who testified said as he looked down at her laying on the floor, he thought how she had escaped a very bad situation and she was now free. These men had a heart for what was going on and they didn't want to give up on her. They said she was already dead but they went above and beyond because they didn't want to give up on her. One of the paramedics testified that when they laid her on the stretcher in the ambulance and he looked at her little body so full of abuse, he just couldn't believe how bad it was. Even her vaginal and diaper area was abused, it made him sick.

The ambulance rushed to the hospital as fast as they could get her there. Once inside the hospital, the nurses and doctors took over. She was already dead, but they continued to perform CPR on her. She was flatlined and they could not get her back at all, so she was finally called. The staff knew immediately they were dealing with abuse.

Later that evening, the police already had a warrant to search the Rosenbaums' house. They wasted no time following all leads and anything Jennifer told them, they sought to verify. The trial was amazing, almost three weeks long, mostly the prosecutor's case. They called person after person, relying on their expertise in some cases to verify evidence. The closing arguments by the prosecution was amazing by itself. Some of the witnesses were Laila's family members, some of them doctors. The medical examiner and the coroner both testified. They were detailed and very specific and broke things down so laymen could understand.

One of the amazing testimonies was from the Medical Examiner. She was the one who did the autopsy. She took a lot of the bruises Laila had and looked at them from the inside, examining how bad they were and at what stage of healing they were in. She took each injury, each break, and helped us to understand it. One of the saddest parts she testified about was Laila's liver and pancreas. Her pancreas was split in two pieces because of the blow or blows it took. There was a large laceration in the liver that caused Laila to bleed out into her stomach, which was actually her cause of death. Laila did not choke on chicken. There were never any signs of chicken found and there was no chicken in her stomach. She was a little girl who was tortured to death, and had it not happened, Millie was right behind her.

No one could save Laila, not her mother, not her great-grandmother, not the doctors or paramedics. She was brutally treated worse than an animal, and her small body could not sustain any more pain or torture.

During the course of the few months that both girls lived in the Rosenbaums' home, both girls were severely abused. DFCS who is responsible for the girl's well-being while they are in foster care and being placed in foster care neglected to do their jobs.

Tessa and Leila's biological father sued the Georgia Department of Children and Family Services. I believe in Georgia the acronym is DFSC. However, they were sued. There are many areas where the DFSC let the girls down, and had they done their job correctly, Leila would still be here today. I should not say the agency didn't do their jobs, but a couple of the caseworkers did not do their jobs. They since have been fired, but that does not bring Leila back.

From the very beginning when Jennifer asked for the girls, had the caseworker done her job, and sent the background check on Jennifer, she would have seen that Jennifer was an abused foster child herself. In that case, she should never by law have been given the privilege of fostering a child. Children who were foster children are not allowed to be a foster parent.

Several people told the case worker Ms. White they felt the girls were suffering some abuse. When the caseworker went to the Rosenbaums to check on the girls, she did not remove their clothing and do a full body check. Had she done that, she would have seen in fact their was abuse.

She failed to report anything she did see to her superiors. She passed off bruises and scratches to no big deal. She may have been able to prevent the broken bones even. Had she looked further into the bruises she did see, she most definitely would have been able to see she was being abused.

The judge did not award any money to Leila's parents, which I defiantly think was the right decision, but the agency had already fired the two women responsible for the neglect of duties.

Millie testified that if they fell asleep in the car, they would get spanked when they got home by Jennifer. Evidently, this happened more than once.

Millie testified that Joseph spanked her and Laila once, but he was in the room and watched many other times. Millie says she heard him and Jennifer arguing one time and she heard Joseph yell, "Kill Laila." I think what he was saying is if you continue to beat Laila like you are doing, you are going to kill her.

Yet nothing that was said was going to stop Jennifer. I don't know if her being a foster child had anything to do with what she did, but you would think it would have the opposite effect on her. Since she did not testify in her own trial, we do not know of any abuse she went through as a child.

A beautiful life was lost and so much damage this case has done. Jennifer and Joseph lost their lives to the prison system. Jennifer got life sentence plus 40 years. Joseph got 30 years plus 20 years supervision for turning his head to the abuse instead of reporting his wife before it was too late.

I want to be a voice for Laila. She does not have one for herself and really never did. She wasn't able to say help me. The closest she came was with her great-grandmother once. She was putting her in the car seat when Jennifer came for them, and she said Laila grabbed her neck and had this look in her eyes of help me, please! I think it haunted the grandmother because of course she didn't know what was going on. Let's all take the moment that if we think for any reason a child is being abused that we take the time to report them. If we are wrong, there is no harm done, but you just might save a life.

Millie is a survivor; she will grow up and be ok. I'm sure she has things that will stay with her, but she is an overcomer. Something so sad is what her psychologist testified to in the trial. She said Millie told her she was afraid. When the psychologist asked her what she's afraid of, Millie answered, "I know there are good people and there are bad people, but what scares me is I don't know the difference." This is so wise and mature of a seven-year-old to say.

The one good thing that came out of this is Millie found a forever home. She now lives with her new mother and her two younger biological sisters. Her biological mother, the same mother Laila had, gave birth to two more daughters since the trial. She lost her parental rights and the unselfish woman who adopted them has given them a loving and stable home. In court when Millie was asked who she lives with, her answer was "Mommy."

Jennifer and Joseph Rosenbaum faced a combined 49 counts—from aggravated battery, child cruelty, to murder. A jury handed back guilty verdicts on most of those counts.

Here is the breakdown of the guilty verdict (Jennifer and Joseph were charged jointly on some of the counts.):

Jennifer Rosenbaum

Count 1
Malice Murder—Not Guilty
County 2
Felony Murder—Not Guilty
Count 3
Aggravated Assault—Guilty
Count 4
Felony Murder—Not Guilty
Count 5
First Degree Cruelty to Children—Guilty
Count 6
Felony Murder—Guilty
Count 7
Aggravated Battery—Guilty
Count 10
Aggravated Assault—Guilty
Count 11
First Degree Cruelty—Guilty
Count 12
Aggravated Assault—Guilty

Count 13 First Degree Cruelty to Children—Guilty
Count 14
Aggravated assault—Guilty
Count 15
First Degree Cruelty to Children—Guilty
Count 16
Aggravated Assault—Guilty
Count 17
First Degree Cruelty to Children—Guilty
Count 18
Aggravated Assault—Guilty
Count 19
First Degree Cruelty—Guilty
Count 20
Aggravated Assault—Guilty
Count 21
First Degree Cruelty to Children—Guilty
Count 22
First Degree Cruelty to Children—Guilty
Count 23
First Degree Cruelty to Children—Guilty
Count 24
Aggravated Assault—Guilty
Count 25
First Degree Cruelty to Children—Guilty
Count 26
Aggravated Assault—Guilty
Count 27
First Degree Cruelty to Children—Guilty
Count 28
Aggravated Assault—Guilty
Count 29
First Degree Cruelty to Children—Guilty
Count 30
Aggravated Assault—Guilty
Count 31
First Degree Cruelty to Children—Guilty

Count 32
Aggravated Assault—Guilty
Count 33
First Degree Cruelty to Children—Guilty
Count 34
First Degree Cruelty to Children—Guilty
Count 35
Aggravated Battery—Guilty
Count 36
Aggravated Assault—Guilty
Count 37
First Degree Cruelty to Children—Guilty
Count 38
First Degree Cruelty to Children—Guilty
Count 39
Aggravated Battery—Guilty
Count 40
First Degree Cruelty to Children—Guilty
Count 41
Aggravated Battery—Guilty
Count 42
First Degree Cruelty to Children—Guilty
Count 43
Aggravated Battery—Guilty
Count 44
Aggravated Assault—Guilty
Count 45
First Degree Child Cruelty—Guilty
Count 46
Aggravated Assault—Guilty
Count 47
First Degree Child Cruelty—Guilty
Count 48
Second Degree Child Cruelty—Guilty
Second Degree Child Cruelty—Guilty
Joseph Michael Rosenbaum
Count 8

Second Degree Murder—Guilty
Count 9
Second Degree Cruelty to Children—Guilty
Count 12
Aggravated Assault—Guilty
Count 13
First Degree Cruelty to Children—Guilty
Count 14
Aggravated Assault—Guilty
Count 15
First Degree Cruelty to Children—Guilty
Count 18
Aggravated Assault—Guilty
Count 19
First Degree Cruelty to Children—Guilty
Count 22
First Degree Cruelty to Children—Guilty
Count 23
First Degree Cruelty to Children—Guilty
Count 26
Aggravated Assault—Guilty
Count 27
First Degree Cruelty to Children—Guilty
Count 30
Aggravated Assault—Guilty
Count 31
First Degree Cruelty to Children—Guilty
Count 32
First Degree Cruelty to Children—Not Guilty
Count 34
First Degree Cruelty to Children—Not Guilty
Count 35
Aggravated Battery—Not Guilty
Count 36
Aggravated Assault—Not Guilty
Count 37
First Degree Cruelty to Children—Not Guilty

Count 38
First Degree Cruelty to Children—Not Guilty
Count 39
Aggravated Battery—Not Guilty
Count 40
First Degree Cruelty to Children—Not Guilty
Count 41
Aggravated Battery—Not Guilty
Count 42
First Degree Cruelty to Children—Guilty
Count 43
Aggravated Battery—Guilty
Count 44
Aggravated Assault—Guilty
Count 45
First Degree Child Cruelty—Guilty
Count 46
Aggravated Assault—Guilty
Count 47
First Degree Child Cruelty—Guilty
Count 49
Second Degree Child Cruelty—Guilty

The jury began deliberations on a Monday morning but were forced to restart on Wednesday after a juror was replaced. The defense made several motions to declare a mistrial. All were denied by the judge.

The foster parents said she choked, but the autopsy tells a different story. Now this evidence can't be used during the trial.

Foster parents still insist toddler choked on chicken bone as case heads to Georgia Supreme Court.

Additional indictments were handed down. It was very sad to see them both taken away at the end of their sentencing, so young, so much life to live, but they will live out their lives in a small cell.

CHAPTER 9

Victoria Rose Smith murdered by Ariel Robinson,
January 14, 2021

It was January 14, 2021, the final day for little 3-year-old Victoria Rose Smith, a foster child of Ariel Robinson, age 30 and Jerry Robinson. The Simpsonville, South Carolina woman was a contestant on the Food Network reality television show, charged with homicide by child abuse of Victoria Rose Smith on January 19, 2021.

Ariel Robison was a teacher at Sanders Middle School and left her job in 2018/2019 school year. She was a contestant on the 20th season of the Food Network Worst Cooks in America in 2020.

The evidence presented during her bond hearing shows her husband Jerry, says she beat Victoria with a belt until she died. Victoria died from multiple blunt force injuries after being found unresponsive in a Sellwood Circle home on January 14, 2021

Her husband Jerry Robinson was also charged with homicide by child abuse. His trial was after Ariel's. Jerry pleaded guilty and confessed in April 2021.

Victoria was under the care of the State of South Carolina and had not yet been adopted by the Robinson's. The formal adoption was to take place just five days after her death.

Victoria suffered from multiple blunt force injuries to her body and died from internal bleeding. There was no credible, non-accidental way Victoria ended up with the injuries she had. Ariel said

Victoria was being defiant, not listening to her, and eating her food too slow. Ariel said she would put Victoria on a timer so she would eat her food in a timely manner.

In January 2021, Jerry called 911 to report that Victoria was unresponsive in their home. He told 911 his daughter drowned from drinking too much water. The dispatcher told them to lay Victoria on the floor and do CPR. Jerry ended up pleading guilty to homicide by child abuse/aiding and abetting.

Fire and EMS personnel were at the home when Simpsonville police officers arrived January 14, 2021. A fire marshal said that Victoria was in cardiac arrest and there was suspicious bruising on her. Body camera shows that Ariel started providing excuses when the authorities walked into their home. She told them Victoria's stomach injuries were from her because she started pushing on her stomach. She said as she did, food came out of her, so she kept pushing on her. She told them the bruises on her feet and legs were from her brother, saying she bruises really easily and has sensitive skin. Her brother hits her and kicks her because he has anger issues. He was seeing a therapist for it, she said.

Ariel told them they were fostering to adopt Victoria's two brothers, age 5 and 7, along with Victoria. She told them it seems like Victoria was trying to breathe so she yelled Victoria, Victoria can you hear me? She reported Victoria becoming sick and vomited repeatedly.

Victoria was still alive when they took her to the emergency room. A room full of staff was working to save her. However, little Victoria died a little before 9:00 pm the evening of January 14, 2021.

The police searched the home for belts and other items that could have caused the injuries on Victoria. They found some belts in the closet and one belt was found on the couch in the living room by a laundry basket.

Victoria's bruised body had bruises that were black and purple running up and down her body. There were masses of black and purple bruises along the right side of her body and up and down both legs. She also had a bruise on her back that was scaled with a ruler to show how large it was. Her abdomen was completely black and purple including the insides of her thighs. Austin Robinson said he was outside working when Ariel was disciplining Victoria. He came in the house and found Ariel standing over her with a belt beating her. Austin said he told Ariel she had gone too far. They put Victoria in a bath of Epson salt, and then laid her on the bed. Austin testified that the last thing little Victoria said to him was I love you.

According to Ariel, the 7-year-old sibling had caused the bruises in other places besides the stomach area. Authorities talked to the school principal about the sibling and was told while he was in kindergarten, he was involved with hitting, pinching a child in the stomach, and hitting a classmate.

The night before the beating, the Robinsons went to church and after church went for pizza. She said everything was fine other than Victoria was vomiting on her way to church. A woman at the church testified at trial that she was in another stall in the bathroom and heard Victoria say she was cold. She said Ariel answered her with, "Well, little girls that make themselves throw up deserve to be cold." The woman said she was surprised to hear her talk to Victoria in such a tone. There is video at the church that shows them leaving the church and as they walk outside, Ariel jerked Victoria by the arm and lifted her up into her arms, a very cruel move.

An ICU pediatric doctor testified that Victoria had repetitive bruising caused by blunt force trauma. She said it was the worst she had ever seen.

Another doctor testified that all the bruises were likely caused at the same time. He said the beating was so hard that it separated her leg muscles. He said this is not just a usual bruise. It's an injury that is tearing tissue from tissue and allowing blood to collect under the skin.

Going back in time, we find that the two little boys and Victoria Rose were with their mother since birth, until they were placed into Jerry and Ariel Robinson's home. She signed over her parental rights, she said, because she could not care for them properly. She claimed DCFS talked her into it, and she should never have signed her children over. Even though she had no rights concerning her children, she was pleading to the courts to let her have a say in Victoria's burial. She claims she was a good mother, just made bad decisions.

Ariel was found guilty of homicide by child abuse. Ariel Robinson 30 years old sentenced to life in prison.

Jerry Robinson pleads guilty for his wife's crime. Sentenced to 20 years.

Children are a wonderful gift. They have an extraordinary capacity to see into the heart of things and to expose sham and humbug for what they are.

—Desmond Tutu

CHAPTER 10

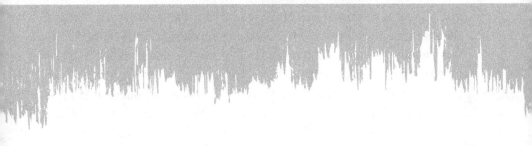

Mother Catherine Hoggle, son Jacob 2, daughter Sarah Age 3

Montgomery County, Maryland, 3 children spent the day with their father. The oldest son had his first soccer game that day, but that night, everything would change. His oldest son was born before they were married. Their second son was Jacob and daughter Sarah. That day was a beautiful Sunday in September. Troy said it was 80 degrees and just a perfect weather day. After the soccer game, they went to the park for a couple of hours and got snow cones. He said after that, he dropped the kids and Catherine off at her parent's house, and he went to work.

That evening when he got home, he saw that Catherine was sitting on the porch. She wanted him to take her to get a drink. They drove about three minutes from home and right back. He said the kids were sleeping (or so he thought). He didn't disturb them in fear of waking them. He had a long day and was very tired, so he went to bed.

The next morning when his oldest son woke him up, there was no one home other than his oldest son. He immediately thought something was wrong. He checked the place he kept his wallet and his wallet and keys were gone. He got his son ready for school and walked him to the school bus stop. While at the bus stop, he called 911 and reported Catherine missing. Just then, she pulled up. She was able to convince him she dropped the two kids off at a daycare. It's something they had never done before but had talked about.

She told him she wanted to let him sleep and took the kids there so they didn't wake him up. That afternoon when it was time to go pick up the children, Catherine claimed she couldn't remember where the daycare was. He asked her what street it was on, and she said she couldn't remember, and she told him she couldn't remember the name of the daycare. He called her mother and found out she was already calling all the daycares looking for her grandkids. Her mother knew something was up.

He began to panic, asking her what was going on. According to Catherine's mother, she battled mental illness, something no one told him until after their first son was born. He started to notice she was doing some very strange things, like when they were driving, she had him pull over and cover her mouth while she talked to him. There were certain rules they had to put in place and her parents agreed. She was not to drive with the children by herself, and really not supposed to be alone with the kids.

After leading him on a wild goose chase, he told her he was going to call the police. She told him to hold on; she would take him to where they were. She asked him to first stop by Chick-filet because she had taken her medicine and she needed to eat something. So, he stopped to get her something to eat. While inside, she went into the bathroom and called a cab. She went back out to the car then said she wanted to refill her drink. She went in one door and out another and disappeared. Police called and her mother came also. He learned that his two-year-old Jacob was not home the night before. Sometime during the day before, when she was at her parent's house, she asked her dad if she could borrow his car. She left with Jacob and when she returned three hours later, she did not have Jacob with her. She told his parents he was at a sleep-over. Side not here, two-year-olds do not go to sleep overs. Troy now knows that when he came home on Sunday night, his son was not home. When Catherine and her dad arrived at their house, Jacob was not with them. Their oldest son was able to tell them Jacob was not home that night, but he knew his mother was home.

So where did Catherine go, and was she playing games with him? By that Monday evening, there was a massive search for them.

No one knows for sure when Sarah went missing. They do know Catherine lied about taking them to a daycare.

Of course, police knew if they found Catherine, they would find the children. The entire county was searching for them. There was panic in the area.

Suddenly, new surveillance video showed Catherine wearing the same clothes going in and out of a federal building. She was about one third of a mile from the Chick-Filet. At 4:30 am, she was going in and out of that building. Catherine is alone though and that was very concerning. Three days after, police came to him and told him they were going to announce it was a homicide investigation. Five very tiring days, and they got a break. Someone recognized her from the poster that was posted everywhere. When they found her, she did not have Sarah or Jacob with her. Even though the police were considering it a homicide investigation, Troy was holding out that Catherine would lead him to the children.

Troy got a call from the police station and when he went to see Catherine, he begged her to tell him where their kids were. She was very well aware of everything, but she would not tell him where Jacob and Sarah were. She was acting and talking normal and told Troy and police the kids are safe. When Troy got to the police station, she asked him what he was doing there.

Police believed that when she asked her dad to use his car, she took Jacob with her and killed him and dumped his body somewhere. Then after Troy was asleep that night or the next morning, they feel she did the same to Sarah.

Police believe she had not planned to stop there. They believe when she came to the bus stop that morning, her plans were to do the same to their oldest. The first day Catherine came back, Troy had taken the 5-year-old to his mother-in-law and Catherine freaked out. Troy agreed she was going to kill their 5-year-old.

When she was hiding out, she tried to change her looks. She cut her hair so maybe people wouldn't recognize her. However, it's almost impossible for two small children to just disappear. The mystery around her actions gets worse.

Initially, she was only charged with misdemeanors. She was sent for a mental evaluation. The process took about one week and she was committed. Her mother said Catherine called her and wanted to tell them what had happened to the kids. However, the judge would not allow the District Attorney to go question her. The doctors deemed Catherine not competent to stand trial. Troy said she's faking her mental illness and so does her mother. She said she just doesn't want to go to jail.

On the third anniversary of the children's disappearance, Troy found out that Catherine's attorney could have gotten the misfeasor charges dropped. They can only have those charges follow them for three years. Then they have to fall off. So, the authorities are now charging her with murder, but those charges will only hold for five years.

For three and a half years, people of Montgomery County have searched and waited to find out what happened to Jacob and Sarah. They believe the murders were premeditated because she would have murdered them at two different times. A private investigator that was hired by Troy believes they are in water. He is using an underwater drone to look for the children.

Catherine's mother dropped a bombshell. She says the children are alive and they are safe with whoever they are with.

Police believe Catherine murdered her children and if they do not find them within five years, she can walk free. In the meantime, Troy will continue to look for the children.

Update: November 30 after 8 years a judge dismisses all charges against Catherine and ruled she is unable to stand trial. She may be a free person, however she will never be free of killing her sweet children.

If you want your children to improve, let them hear the nice things you say about them to others.

—Dr. Haim Ginott

CHAPTER 11

The Story of Adrian Jones 7 years old

Murdered by his father Michael Jones and stepmother Heather Jones

The little boy that was fed to the pigs

I had not heard anything about Adrian Jones, 7 years old, and his murder, until I started doing research for this book. If you haven't heard about this case, then prepare yourself. This is horrific. I know I say that about all these cases, and all of them are horrific. It just surprises me what people will do, and especially to the children they are supposed to love and protect.

I heard a District Attorney state in a court proceeding one time that A child is safe in the arms of his father. Or at least he should be but not Adrian Jones. Barely 7 years old, innocent, little boy that tried to rise above what was going on at home. The last few months of his life left him a little bag of bones. His life was a living hell as he was chained to a table, lived behind a plywood door in a shower, and was made to stand in dirty skum water up to his neck for hours at a time.

Adrian had six sisters, but he was the one his stepmother hated and before long, his dad picked up the abusive habits along with the stepmother almost as if it became a game. The discus they felt for that little boy was awful, and no human should have to live under the abuse that was so obvious. So why did the authorities allow it to get this far? As a little time went by his father became a worse abuser than his stepmother. They chose Adrian to be the one in the family that they could make his life nothing but torture and have fun with it. My opinion this is the lowest form of a human.

This story is just another story were the Department of Children and Family Services failed the child. When they fail a child, the child usually ends up dead. Usually brutal, torture, horrible death. We must find a way to help these agencies protect these children. These people I believe are over-loaded with cases to the point they cannot properly give each case the attention it needs. Let's face it, they can only work so many hours and have so many children on their caseloads. We need to realize how many children in the United States are in harm's way. We need to go to our law makers or whomever is in charge of these things through our government and insist they allow more money to be allotted for these agencies to hire more people.

This case shows the horrible way this little boy was abused and the horrible way the system that is in place to protect children, let him down. All that can be said is the system totally failed him. Adrian lived with his father Michael Jones and his stepmother Heather Jones in Missouri. Someone called and reported to the DCFS (Department of Children and Family Services) there was abuse going on in the home. When DCFS went to the home Michael and Heather refused to deal with them at all in fact refused to cooperate with them. They move to Kansas City but not realizing those are cross-over states for such agencies as DCFS.

In other words, there's a line in the sand. "Imagine you and another adult agreed to draw a line in the sand. You both agree that as long as you both are on your side; you have to leave the other person alone. The other adult turns out to be an abusive person who beats children. You can clearly see the child being abused, but you agreed not to cross the line. You decide that you at least have to call someone so you can clear your conscience and show that you made someone aware. It doesn't matter that the someone you made aware is just as incompetent as you are." Dr. Jamie Schwandt

His own father and stepmother disliked him so much they brutally tortured him and in the end he was starved to death. They brutally beat him every day until his little body could not take it any longer and he died. They allowed his body to lay in the shower until the smell was too much for them to deal with so they took his body to the barn. Who knows whose idea it was but the father went and bought some feeder pigs? He then starved the pigs for a few days so they would be extra hungry then fed parts of his son's body to them at a time.

November 20, 2015, Thanksgiving Day, someone called the police and told them Adrian had not been seen for over a month. The police went to the house, and because of the smell found parts of Adrian's body in the barn. Most of the rest of his body had already been fed to the pigs.

DCFS from both states faced accusations they had both failed little Adrian. They were supposed to be monitoring Adrian Jones, instead they allowed him to be tortured to death.

A Missouri case worker had made the statement they had made Kansas state aware that Adrian had disclosed by his father, Michael Jones and stepmother, Heather Jones during an interview held in Missouri. They went on to say it had also been reported that the children were home schooled and not seen by family on a regular basis. Which definitely raised their concern for the other children in the home.

Kansas DCFS stated in a report they had last had contact with the family in 2012. When they could get information about Adrian they did share what they learned with Missouri. However, the way the family moved back and forth between the states and the fact the family did not want to cooperate with them, made it more difficult to keep track of Adrian. Let's face it if someone wants to hide from an agency such as this, it's not real too hard to do.

Even Adrian's biological grandmother called and reported the abuse to DCFS. I literally had to go back and reread my notes, this story was so close to others I was involved in writing. It just boggles my mind. Adrian's grandmother reported she had seen with her own eyes the abuse that was taking place. She begged them to please help Adrian before it was too late. She could tell by the way Adrian looked that the end was near. However, she could not get anyone to intercede.

Yet DCFS maintained their offices thoroughly investigated each call that came to their offices.

In 2012 when Adrian was just two-years-old DCFS took Adrian from his biological mother and given to his father, Michael Jones which made no sense at all. When a social worker and a policeman went to the Jone's house they had a chance to talk with Adrian. He told them that his daddy kicks him and keeps kicking him in the head and keeps hitting him in the stomach and that his mom keeps pulling his ears and it really hurts really bad. At that time little Adrian was only 5-years-old. He went on to say he was often chained to a table and he was locked in his room and had to sleep without a pillow or a blanket.

When authorities talked to Michael and Heather they told them Adrian hoarded food, wet the bed often, picked at sores, and if they didn't watch he would light fires.

From the time Adrian was only a few months old until he was 5-years-old there was around 15 calls made about his neglect and abuse. Out of 14 of those calls the agency only found anything with one of those reports and that was one the police had made. After Adrian was removed from his mother and given to his father the reports continued and the caller reported there were guns laying all over the house, and Heather was high on drugs. It was also reported at this time, Adrian had visible injuries over his body. They were told Michael was choking Adrian and beating him until he bled. Michael and Heather continued to deny all accusations and DCFS never followed through with the accusations.

In 2014 Adrian was put into a residence house. After being there only 6 months he was given back to his father. Even though his father told them he could not take care of Adrian, they left him anyway. After that time there were ten calls that came to the agency claiming there was extreme abuse happening to Adrian. If you can imagine at one point Michael Jones asked DCFS if they would take Adrian, he didn't want him anymore. The agency refused and after that Michael stopped all communication with DCFS. DCFS did nothing further to protect or save Adrian.

On Facebook Heather Jones describes Adrian as a "Psychopath, saying he chased her around the house with a butcher knife and that he dumped her baby out of the bassinet" and "kills everything he comes in contact with." she said "pain compliance does not work," talked about using "leather belts," and said Adrian "has to be restrained 95% of the time." She posted that she "can't shoot him unfortunately" but she can "make him work until she feels better." She also posted about restraining him with handcuffs, ace bandages and a splint. In the warrant it states that Heather stated she had "no problem" with having the boy "look at flowers" the quote was from the tv show "The Walking Dead" in which a woman fatally shoots a troubled child after telling her to "look at the Flowers".

Very sad is Facebook exchanges between Michael and Heather shows pictures of Adrian strapped an inversion table and naked in a shower with a mouth wound that Heather Jones said came from him trying to remove the shower door. They also exchanged messages with pictures of Adrian in a straitjacket, a restraint bed, and "full body enclosure" one policeman reported.

In 2013 Missouri state welfare officials stated they could not ensure Adrian's safety at home after Adrian told them that his dad kicked him in the head and a "little bone came out."

When 7-year-old Adrian could no longer sustain his life, his parents left his little body in the shower until the stench was too much. He went and bought six feeder pigs and starved them for a few days. He dismembered Adrian's body and fed parts of him at a time to the pigs. He stored the rest of the body in the barn. The most unimaginable way to die and be laid to rest.

Most likely it was the grandmother who made the final call. Whoever it was had to be the only reason they found the parts of Adrian's body they did find. Had she not been persistent it could have been the case of the perfect murder and no one would have ever known that the sweet little child ever existed.

At one point an officer suggested the state needed to provide more resources for the family. Watching Michael during the trial it is amazing how there was no true emotion or guilt coming from the man for what he had done.

A jury found Michael and Heather guilty. Before the judge sentenced Michael Jones, his daughter, Kiki Doctor, spoke directly to her father. As she looked at him, she said, "When I was little and lived with you, I was terrified of you. My mother was terrified of you. She was always depressed, and you were abusive to her. You destroyed her self-esteem. I thank God every day that she was not hurt. I wanted so badly to believe my siblings would be safe with you. You are deserving of eternity in prison with no chance of parole. You took an innocent life and my family's emotional health."

Adrian's mother Dianna Pearce also spoke and said, "Adrian was in your care and you took his life from him and tormented him with cruelty. You killed him in the most gruesome, hideous manner. You failed him as a father. You were supposed to protect him, love him, kiss away his hurts, and show him how to be a great man. But you chose to murder your own flesh and blood."

Detective Stuart Littlefield spoke and made mention of the emotional effect that was suffered by the police that worked on the case. He said, "The abuse and torture were only compounded by the fact that Mike and Heather had systematically documented it."

He went on to say, "Nothing affected me more than when Mike told me that Heather would chastise Adrian for 15-20 seconds at a time." He stayed quiet so the court could realize how long 20 seconds is. He said, "Imagine the screams of that little boy." He talked about how we can remember the murderers but how many people remember the names of those that were murdered. He said, "In 25 years, when Michael Jones is eligible for parole, will people remember Adrian Jones.? He was 7 years old, he was tortured, shackled, and beaten to death. And when his killers could no longer stand the stench of his body, he was fed to pigs." Michael Jones told authorities he purchased the swine after keeping the body inside the house for nearly two weeks. One of the other children told he heard Adrian screaming, "I'm going to die" through the vent and his stepmother, Heather Jones, telling him to "suck it up."

Both Michael and Heather Jones pleaded guilty and were sentenced to life.

Michael Jones was sentenced to life in prison for the torture and murder of his son Adrian Jones. His wife, Heather Jones, was sentenced in prison with no chance of parole for 25 years. The judge's words as she was getting ready to sentence Michael Jones were, "This is the most heinous crime I have ever prosecuted."

The Jones landlady was asked by Heather Jones if she would go into her computer and make some pictures of her children for her. She gave her the password and the landlady was happy to help her. But Heather Jones did not prepare her for what she would find. There were pictures of the tortured little boy on the computer. It was horrifying for the landlady who was not sure what to do with them. She put the pictures on a DVD and gave them to the grandmother, who in turn gave them to the authorities.

So, what happens when everyone around a child fails them? When their voice is trying to be heard but no one is listening? How can we be that voice for Adrian? By telling his story, by doing our part with the DCFS agencies in our state, and make our voices heard. Justice for Adrian is what we should seek. Save a child so another one doesn't have to live in abuse. Be a good foster parent if you are able and give someone a kind, loving home. These children need us. They deserve to be loved like anyone else.

Daily Mail has a very large number of pictures, the ones that were on Heather Jones' computer.

Something **was** done to honor Adrian. May 2021 Governor Laura Kelly signed a bill unanimously passed by the Kansas Legislature that recognized the torture and murder of the late Adrian Jones by mandating that investigations of child abuse and neglect include a visual observation of alleged victims.

The measure featured Adrian's Law in remembrance of Jones, who was 7 when starved to death by his father and stepmother near Kansas City, Kansas, after years of physical and emotional torture that had been reported to officials in Missouri and Kansas. The child died in fall 2015 and his father fed the boy's body to newly purchased pigs. His remains were found later that year.

"It was horrible, horrible," said Sen. David Haley, a Democrat from Kansas City, Kansas. "Law enforcement was called out to look at the welfare of a child and did not physically see the child.

Woven into House Bill 2158, Adrian's Law mandates children alleged to be victims of abuse or neglect to be visually observed by an employee of the Kansas Department for Children and Families or a representative of the law enforcement agency investigating the report. To help prevent children from falling through the cracks, both DCFS and law enforcement must interact with the child during joint investigations.

Children are the keys to paradise.

-Eric Hoffer

CHAPTER 12

Hannah Wesche 3 years old, murdered by babysitter,
Lindsay Partin

Hannah was a bouncy, lively, beautiful little girl with huge brown eyes and dark brown hair.

It was a beautiful day in Ohio on January 11, 2015, if for no other reason because Hannah was born that day. Unfortunately, the beautiful baby was born a severely addicted meth baby. Her mother was also addicted to meth and of course, passed the addiction on to her unborn baby. The addiction was so severe that she remained in intensive care for three months. She was weaned off the meth by giving heroin in decreasing amounts until she was well. Thank goodness for hospitals such as the Cincinnati Children's Hospital where there seemed to be bountiful supply of really specialized and good doctors, I believe she got the best of care.

Her father Jason Wesche was awarded full custody of Hannah, and seems it was vitally important to him to care for Hanna's needs and love her unconditionally. It was hard times for Jason though. He lost his job and did not have a place to live or any money. His brother and sister-in-law though were kind enough to treat Hannah like their own and kept Hannah safe and well fed. Jason is the kind of man that did not want to impose on his brother and although he allowed Hannah to stay in their home, he slept in his car.

Finally, Jason landed a well-paying job and was able to rent a house from his landlord. As luck seemed to be on his side finally, his boss's wife did babysitting and said she would watch Hannah for a very fair price. This allowed Jason to work the required twelve-hour days his job required. Little did he know then that it was a fatal mistake to take his little Hannah to Lindsay Partin.

Doing the best he could, he trusted Lindsay. After all, she had two little girls of her own. One of them Hannah's age, plus she babysat another little girl. They lived just next door. Jason had no idea what lay ahead.

I have always feared leaving my children or grandchildren in an in-home daycare. There is no way to tell if the person you are trusting to care for your most valuable relationship is receiving good care or abuse that may start small and graduate into something horrific. This story is one of those that turned horrific. One that the father had no idea was happening. This sweet little 3-year-old baby girl loved and trusted her caregiver. Children are amazing because they have the ability to love unconditionally, even their abuser.

March 6, 7, and 8 of 2015 seems to be when the visible abuse began. No one has any way of knowing if neglect preceded the abuse. We don't know if during those days she made Hannah lay in bed most of the day or sit in a chair most of the day. Did she feed her properly, give her as much water that she needed? One can only hope she did. However, I find it odd the abuse just started on March 6, 2015. In court, Lindsay testified she thought it was alright to slap Hannah across the face, to give her "upper cuts" to the chin, to yank her ears, to spank her. I'm quite sure if you were to ask Jason how he felt about those things, he would tell you he most definitely did not want her or anyone to do any of those things to his daughter. It is totally ludicrous that anyone would think they had a right to lay hands on a three-year-old child.

On March 6 and 7, 2015, Lindsay started what seemed to be a string of abusive acts. When she got "mad" as she put it, she would punch Hannah, slap her across the face, and poke her hard in the chest and stomach area. She also would squeeze Hannah in the mid-section of her body, evidently hard as she had bruises that the coroner said were from being squeezed hard.

For two days at least, Hannah, a small, barely three-year-old little girl, was tortured and punished for things most normal 3-year-olds do. The morning of March 8, 2015 was pretty much a typical day for Hannah starting out. Jason her father testified in court, they got up, Hannah had breakfast, he brushed her teeth, she got dressed, and they left for Lindsay's house. In the trial, the defense made a huge deal over the timeline. Evidence showed Jason texted Lindsay at 6:52 a.m. as he always did, saying we are leaving now to come over. He said he put a blanket over her head because it was cold, picked her up, and headed to the car. He drove the approximately 300 feet to Lindsay's house. He says he left his car running and ran Hannah inside. He says he was inside maybe a minute because that morning, little Hannah wanted extra kisses and hugs. He gave her kisses, and she kept asking for more. Did this baby girl feel something was going to happen or was it because there was a twelve-hour day ahead that she thought she would be spending with an abusive babysitter—someone she loved and trusted?

Lindsay's house had an attached garage and it was heated. They had subdivided it off for a sort of family room, game room, and a place the children could ride their toys. Jason would come through that door to drop Hannah off. As he left, he said he saw Lindsay and Hannah going through the garage door into the house.

He drove to the end of the street where his place of employment was. He testified he got out of his car, leaving it running, and started his work truck. He said it was very cold that morning and his work truck was a diesel, so he had to let it warm up and got back into his car to let the truck warm up. He noticed that at 7:02, there was a call from Lindsay. He tried calling her back but there was no answer. He waited for a couple of minutes and tried again. This time, she answered, and she told him to come back to her house saying Hannah had collapsed. He was in his car, so he testified he immediately took off for her house.

When he got back to Lindsay's, Hannah was lying on the kitchen floor. She was gasping for air and unconscious. He yelled for Lindsay to call 911, not sure why she had not already done that. Jason picked her up and laid her on the couch in the garage. Lindsay testified that after she called Jason to come back, she went and got dressed. She was on the phone with 911 until the paramedics got there. When the 911 call was played in court, you could hear

Hannah in the background gasping. You could hear Jason calling out to Hannah to wake up. You could hear the fear in his voice as he talked to Hannah and begged her to wake up.

When the paramedics arrived, they immediately saw the situation as a crisis and wasted no time; one of them scooped her up and got her out of the house. They could not stabilize her so they left right away to take her to the hospital. Under oath, one of the paramedics said when they came in and assessed the situation, it seemed very toxic, and he just wanted to get Hannah out of there. When asked what he meant by that, he described all the bruises on Hannah's face and immediately felt there was abuse involved. At the emergency room, the doctor was taking a history of the patient. He testified in the trial that the father told him she ate a good dinner the night before, put her to bed, and got up that morning and everything seemed fine. He left her at the babysitter, and she almost immediately collapsed. He told the doctor she had been complaining of a headache for the past three weeks but they seemed mild and it did not change her activity so he didn't worry about it. Jason was convinced Hannah had a brain aneurysm because he was told the brain was bleeding. He still did not expect abuse by Lindsay.

At the emergency room, the doctor stated she had no movement in one eye and very slow in the other. He noted the bruises on her body and the head injury. He did a CAT scan and other x-rays. A decision was made to transfer her to Cincinnati Children's Hospital where they were better equipped to take care of her severe injuries.

Hannah was air-lifted to Cincinnati where she underwent emergency brain surgery. The doctors at both Hamilton Hospital and Cincinnati Children's hospital told Jason there was abuse that caused Hannah's injuries. After her brain surgery, she was admitted to the ICU and put on life support.

Several doctors and experts in the field testified and all of them agreed Hannah had been abused. Lindsay had excuses for all her bruises. She fell, she fell, she fell. Yet the professionals testified the injuries Hannah had were mostly in naturally protected areas of the body. The child had many bruises on all parts of her body from her head all the way down her legs. They also testified the bruises were not from regular fall of a 3-year-old child but those of great force.

After a few days, the doctors came to Jason and let him know Hannah was brain dead and there was no hope of her waking up. After ten days, Hannah succumbed to her injuries. Jason donated her organs so Hannah lives on.

CRIMINAL APPEAL FROM BUTLER COUNTY COURT OF COMMON PLEAS

Case No. CR2018-03-0462

Lindsay Partin appeals her convictions in the Butler County Common Pleas Court for endangering children involuntary manslaughter and murder. For the reasons described below, this court affirms Partin's convictions.

This case involves the death of Hannah Wesche, who was hospitalized with a traumatic brain injury on March 8, 2018, never recovered, and passed away ten days later. Hannah was 3 years and 2 months old at the time of her passing.

Partin had been Hannah's babysitter. On the morning of March 8, 2018, Hannah's father, Jason Wesche, dropped Hannah off with Partin and left to go to work. Minutes later, Partin called Jason and told him that something was wrong with Hannah. Jason raced back. Hannah was struggling to breath and unresponsive. Emergency responders rushed Hannah to the hospital.

Hannah had multiple bruises over her body, hemorrhages in both eyes, and a CT scan revealed a large subdural hemorrhage. Given her injuries, doctors and investigators suspected that Hannah's injuries were nonaccidental.

Detectives interviewed Partin that day. Partin denied any knowledge of what happened to Hannah, claimed that she seemed fine, and stated that Hannah just collapsed upon walking into Partin's home. Detectives interviewed Partin again the following day during which she made multiple inculpatory statements admitting to excessively disciplining Hannah earlier that week and shaking Hannah on the morning of March 8, 2015.

Following Hannah's death, a Butler County grand jury indicted Partin on six counts charged Partin with acts occurring on March

8, 2018, constituting felony endangering children (counts three and five), involuntary manslaughter (count four), and murder (count six). Counts three and five served as the predicate, underlying offenses for counts four and six respectively.

The matter proceeded to a jury that in April 2019, the state played Partin's call to 9-1-1, in which she relayed that Hannah had just "passed out." Partin told the dispatcher that Hannah "was fine," that she "walked into the house and just passed out," and that she "went limp." Twice during the call, Partin mentioned that Hannah "fell really bad yesterday." Partin also mentioned a bruise under Hannah's chin.

Evan Reedy, an EMT, responded to the 9-1-1 call at Partin's residence, located at 4050 Shank Road, Hanover Township. EMT Reedy testified that when he arrived, Hannah was laid on the couch. Her breathing was like a "sniffing," shallow and irregular. Her eyes were moving, but without purpose. Reedy noticed some bruising on various parts of Hannah's body, including the chest and eyes, which appeared sunken. Partin told him, another EMT, and a deputy on scene, that Hannah had fallen after standing on a toy a day earlier. Reedy and the other EMT secured Hannah for travel and then transported her to Fort Hamilton Hospital.

Deputy Damon Mayer testified that he was on road patrol for the Butler County Sheriff's Office that morning and responded to the 9-1-1 call. He noted bruising on Hannah's left eye and chin. Partin told him that Hannah had walked through the garage, walked up the steps, asked Partin for a donut and to sit on the couch, and then "passed out," falling forward onto the carpeted floor. Partin also said that on the previous day, at 4:00 p.m., Hannah had been playing in the garage, fell, and hit her head on concrete. Partin said she had informed Jason about this accident.

Dr. Ahn Quan Nguyen, an emergency room physician at Fort Hamilton Hospital, treated Hannah upon her arrival. Hannah was unresponsive and not able to breathe on her own. Dr. Nguyen intubated Hannah and placed her on a ventilator. He observed multiple bruises on Hannah's body, and further observed that her pupils were not reacting appropriately, and that there was blood behind her eyes. Dr. Nguyen ordered a CT scan of Hannah's head, neck, and face. Dr. Nguyen ordered that Hannah be transported by air care to Cincinnati Children's Hospital for further treatment. Hannah left on an air care flight approximately one hour after arriving at Fort Hamilton Hospital.

Dr. Marguerite M. Care is the staff neuroradiologist at Cincinnati Children's Hospital and testified for the state as an expert in pediatric radiology. On March 8, 2018, Dr. Care reviewed Hannah's CT scans taken at Fort Hamilton Hospital. Hannah had a large subdural hemorrhage that was causing the mid-line of her brain to shift over to one side of her skull. Dr. Care explained that this shifting would have caused brain injuries and significant brain abnormalities.

Dr. Care noted that the most likely cause of the subdural hemorrhage was trauma. Furthermore, Dr. Care opined that the subdural hemorrhage seen in Hannah's case was not consistent with everyday accidents, like a fall, but instead was consistent with "abusive head trauma." With Hannah's injuries, Dr. Care would not have expected her to be walking, or able to breathe on her own, and she would have been unconscious. Furthermore, Dr. Care opined that these symptoms would have started within seconds of the injury.

Based on Hannah's CT scans, Dr. Care determined that Hannah required immediate medical intervention. She shared her findings with a neurosurgeon who then removed part of Hannah's skull in order to drain the hemorrhage. The surgery was successful in draining the hemorrhage. However, because Hannah's brain had swollen from the injury, it began to swell out of the area where the surgeon removed the portion of the skull.

Dr. Michael Yang is a board-certified ophthalmologist at Cincinnati Children's Hospital and testified for the state as an expert witness in pediatric ophthalmology. Dr. Yang examined Hannah's eyes and found them to be extensively hemorrhaged. Hemorrhages were present in all three layers of the eye. Dr. Yang opined that Hannah's eye condition was most consistent with nonaccidental abusive head trauma and severe brain injury.

Dr. Ranjit Chima testified that he was one of the physicians in the pediatric ICU responsible for Hannah's care following her emergency surgery. While in the ICU, Hannah never regained consciousness and her neurological condition deteriorated after three days, Dr. Chima determined that Hannah was progressing toward brain death. On March 18, 2018, after meeting the criteria for brain death, doctors pronounced Hannah deceased.

Dr. Dorothy Dean is a forensic pathologist and performed Hannah's autopsy. She testified for the state as an expert witness in forensic pathology. Dr. Dean noted that Hannah weighed 32 pounds and was 38.5 inches long. After shaving Hannah's hair, Dr. Dean located bruises on the back and right side of Hannah's head and located two additional bruises. Dr. Dean further located a bruise in the deep muscle of the neck.

Dr. Dean noted that Hannah had "tremendous" brain swelling and a shearing injury to the brain. Dr. Dean opined that Hannah's cause of death was a traumatic brain injury due to a blunt, tremendous force that went through her brain. A fall from ground level would not cause the injuries observed. Hannah would not have been walking, talking, or behaving in a normal fashion after receiving the injury and would have been neurologically abnormal and unresponsive "within moments." Dr. Dean opined that Hannah's manner of death was homicide.

Dr. Kathi Makoroff, Associate Professor of Pediatrics at the Mayerson Center of Cincinnati Children's Hospital, testified for the state as an expert in child abuse pediatrics. At trial, she reviewed a series of medical file photographs, which were introduced into evidence, depicting the injuries observed on Hannah when she arrived at Children's Hospital. She noted multiple bruises that she found concerning child abuse, including those bruises around Hannah's eyes, left ear, under her chin, her flanks, upper arms, and buttocks. Given Hannah's overall medical condition, Dr. Makoroff opined that Hannah's injuries were nonaccidental with a diagnoses of child physical abuse and abusive head trauma.

Dr. Makoroff further opined that Hannah's injuries were not caused by a fall or multiple falls and that much greater force was involved in causing the injuries. Shaking alone could have caused the injuries that resulted in Hannah's death. Furthermore, Hannah would have been unresponsive after the injury.

On cross-examination, defense counsel asked Dr. Makoroff if her opinion testimony about bruises was "about the location and pattern of bruises on Hannah's body." Dr. Makoroff agreed that she testified in that manner as to some of the bruises. Defense counsel then questioned Dr. Makoroff as to whether she had offered an opinion about patterns and location of bruises in her expert opinion letter, which was provided in advance of trial to the defense. The state objected to this line of questioning and a sidebar ensued. The court ultimately found that Dr. Makoroff's opinion testimony that related to the patterns and locations of bruises was within the scope of the opinion letter.

Detective Jane Lambert testified that investigators first questioned Partin in a formal interview on March 8, 2018, in which the interview was video-recorded and admitted into evidence. In the recording, a detective initially read Partin her Miranda rights. Partin indicated she understood her rights and executed a Miranda rights waiver form.

As the interview began, a detective told Partin that Hannah had died, which was not true at the time. Partin denied any knowledge of what caused Hannah to become unresponsive. She stated that Jason had carried Hannah into the garage that morning. She examined Hannah's face and told Jason that "her face looks good" and "her bruise looks better." Hannah asked Jason for another hug and double kisses before Jason left. Hannah was acting "completely normal," was not acting different, and only acted a little tired. Hannah told Partin that she wanted "couch and donut" and then fell face forward onto the carpet. It happened within 30 seconds. Partin called Jason first before calling 9-1-1.

Later, detectives paused their questioning and left Partin alone in the interview room. During this time, Partin announced aloud, "I am going to prison for the rest of my life." When the interview resumed, Partin told detectives she had seen bruises sometimes on the back of Hannah's head and on her arms. Hannah had also fallen on some gravel on Tuesday, March 6. The next day, Partin had been "trying to make her chin look better by using vapor rub."

Lead Detective Dan Turner testified concerning a second interview with Partin, which he and another detective conducted in March 9, 2018. The second interview was video-recorded and admitted into evidence. Again, Partin was informed of her Miranda rights and again waived them in writing.

During the interview, Detective Turner produced photographs taken at the hospital of the various external bruising found on Hannah. While reviewing the photographs, Partin reiterated her earlier claims that certain bruises were the result of falling on gravel on Tuesday, March 6, 2018, or falling off a toy in Partin's garage on Wednesday, March 7, 2018. Partin again denied any knowledge of what caused Hannah to collapse in her home on the morning of March 8, 2018.

Approximately 50 minutes into the interview, Partin admitted for the first time that something had happened to Hannah in Partin's home on Thursday morning. Hannah had slipped at the entry door between the house and garage and hit her head on a concrete step. Partin said that after the fall, she picked Hannah up and then Hannah said, "I want donut and couch." And then Hannah collapsed.

Detectives told Partin that the fall she had just described would not have caused Hannah's injuries based on what Hannah's physicians were relaying to them and encouraged her to tell the truth. Partin then changed her story. She now stated that "when I opened the door, I dropped her, and I slipped and fell." Partin said she slipped on Hannah's blanket, they both fell, and Hannah hit her head on the metal part of the concrete step. Hannah hit "really hard." Partin sowed the detectives a bruise on her hand, which allegedly resulted from the fall.

The detectives continued to question Partin and informed her that a fall would not cause the severe injuries suffered by Hannah. Partin then admitted that she "probably shook Hannah hard" after the fall for one minute. Hannah's head was "snapping around." Partin was panicked. She also "probably" dropped Hannah.

Partin later modified her story once more and admitted that she shook Hannah before the alleged fall. Partin explained that Hannah had been whining because she did not want her father to go to work. Partin shook her, picked her up, squeezed her, then they fell. She shook Hannah again after they fell.

Partin admitted that she was frustrated. Hannah had been whining after her father every morning. Partin demonstrated violently shaking Hannah and yelling "stop doing this already!" Partin admitted that she shook Hannah until she stopped whining.

With respect to some of the bruising around Hannah's head, Partin explained that earlier in the week, she "slapped" Hannah "upside the head" because Hannah took ketchup and squirted it into the toilet. With regard to the bruise under Hannah's chin, Partin admitted that she twice struck Hannah under the chin. She demonstrated the double-strike with an uppercut-like motion using a martial arts-style clawed fist.

With regard to the bruises observed on Hannah's chest, which Partin had earlier claimed were from when Hannah fell on gravel or rocks, Partin confessed that the bruises were from physical discipline. Partin demonstrated aggressively poking Hannah while yelling "Hanna! You know better!" Partin also demonstrated how she squeezed Hannah around the middle of her body to discipline her. When asked why she would do these things to Hannah, Partin explained that it was because Hannah was mischievous and because Partin was frustrated with personal problems.

James Wesche testified that he and Hannah lived at 4004 Shank Road, which was about 300 feet from Partin's residence. Partin babysat Hannah during the day, babysat other children, and took care of her own children. The week of March 4, 2018, he had conversations with Partin about some injuries observed on Hannah. Hannah had bruises all over her chest and a "pretty bad" scrape on the chin. Partin told him that these occurred because Hannah had fallen on rocks in the driveway. On another day, Partin told him that Hannah stepped on top of a toy on wheels and it "kicked from underneath her. And she fell on the handlebar." Hannah had bruising around her eye from this incident.

On the morning of March 8, 2018, Jason helped Hannah put on her coat and shoes and at 6:52 a.m., Jason sent Partin a text indicating that they were "getting ready to head over" as he and Hannah left 4004 Shank Road. Partin texted hm back "ok."

Jason testified that he and Hannah left the home and went to his car. That morning, Hannah wanted to lay in the backseat for the drive over. They drove to Partin's residence. Jason estimated that he would have arrived at Partin's residence three minutes after sending the text or 6:55 a.m.

Jason carried Hannah, who was wrapped in a blanket, into Partin's garage and gave Hannah hugs and kisses. That morning was different because Hannah kept asking for more kisses. Then Partin took Hannah and he walked away. He did not see them enter the hone, but they were headed that way.

Jason got into his car and then drove down to his work truck located at a business down at the end of Shank Road. He got out of his vehicle, got into his work truck, and started it, then got back into his vehicle. He then saw that he had missed a call from Partin. He returned the call and Partin told him there was something wrong with Hannah. Jason then raced back to Partin's residence.

Jason also testified about the activities on Wednesday, March 7, 2018. That evening, he picked up Hannah from Partin's home at 7:00 p.m. A friend of his, Chris Davis, had stayed at 4004 Shank Road that day. After picking up Hannah, Jason and Hannah drove Chris to Chris' residence in Fairfield, Ohio. Then they returned to 4004 Shank Road and he and Hannah lay on the couch and went to sleep.

Jason admitted that at the start of the investigation, he told detectives that he had gone to Walmart on the evening of March 7 to get milk for Hannah and that he had not mentioned Chris or traveling to Fairfield. He remembered what had actually occurred after talking to Chris before he was going to testify. He told Detective Turner about this recollection the day before his testimony.

The state introduced Partin's cellphone records, which revealed that Jason texted "getting ready to head over" at 6:52:17 a.m. Partin responded "Ok" at 6:52:55 a.m. Partin then called Jason at 7:00:47 a.m., in which the call was not answered. Jason returned the call at 7:01:24 a.m. Partin called 9-1-1 at 7:02:51 a.m, which call lasted 13 minutes until emergency responders arrived.

On March 7, at 8:48 a.m., Partin used her phone to Google app to search "how to get rid of a bruise." This search was found to have been deleted from the phone. The same day, at 2:56 p.m., Partin searched "what essential oil is good for bruises" and "is vapor rub good for bruises." These two searches were not deleted. On March 8, at 9:13 p.m., Partin again searched "how to get rid of a bruise." This search was deleted.

Partin took the stand in her defense case. She denied causing any harm to Hannah between March 6 and March 8, 2018. She told detectives what she did in the second interview because she wanted to "protect everybody." This was because the detectives were asking about whether Partin's husband or Jason could have harmed Hannah and she did not want anyone to be in trouble.

Partin estimated that it took Jason 7-8 minutes to arrive after he sent his text at 6:52 a.m. Jason walked in with Hannah wrapped in a blanket. Partin and Jason "chit-chatted" about the snow and vapor rub. She looked at Hannah for "a second" and then told Jason that it looked like the vapor rub "worked." He said "yeah." Hannah stood up, grabbed Partin's hand, and the two walked into the residence. Partin then asked Hannah if she wanted to go to the couch or go to sleep because Hannah seemed tired. Hannah responded "donut and couch." She then collapsed. Partin said she then had Hannah for ten seconds before she collapsed.

Partin said she saw bruising below Hannah's chin on Wednesday morning and put vapor rub and essential oils on it. She assumed it was from when Hannah fell on gravel the day before. Partin admitted that her story about Hannah putting ketchup in the toilet was a lie.

On cross-examination, Partin stated that she did not think she would get in trouble for telling detectives she had hurt Hannah because Jason would "back me up." She confirmed that she did not feel she would be in trouble for poking Hannah in the chest, squeezing her in the middle, hitting her with a closed fist multiple times under the chin, and shaking her. Partin also confirmed that the story about her falling with Hannah was a lie and she also lied about getting a bruise in her hand from that fall. She told detectives the lie about the bruise on her hand because it "seemed logical at the time."

The jury convicted Partin on all six counts. During sentencing, the court informed Partin of her duty to register as a violent offender under Sierah's Law. Partin appeals raising seven assignments of error.

Assignment of Error #1

1. THE TRIAL COURT ABUSED ITS DISCRETION AND PREJUDICED THE DEFENDANT WHEN IT ALLOWED AN EXPERT WITNESS FOR THE STATE TO TESTIFY BEYOND THE SCOPE OF THE EXPERT'S REPORT IN VIOLATION OF CRIM R 16 (K)

Partin contends that the trial court abused its discretion by failing to exclude Dr. Makoroff's expert opinion that the "pattern and location" of bruises on Hannah's body indicated child abuse. Partin complains that Dr. Makoroff's opinion prejudiced her defense because she had no ability to contradict Dr. Makoroff's opinion was a new theory of the evidence and had not been disclosed in a written report as required by Crim. R. 16 (K). Partin argues the state's failure to disclose Dr. Makoroff's opinion was determined within a reasonable degree of medical certainty. Partin claims additional prejudice because the state highlighted Dr. Makoroff's opinion during closing argument.

Dr. Makoroff's opinion letter was dated December 14, 2018, and there is no dispute that it was provided to the defense in a timely manner. The letter indicated that Dr. Makoroff had examined Hannah and observed multiple bruises on her face, ear, head, chest, bilateral flanks, back buttock, bilateral upper extremities, and bilateral lower extremities. Dr. Makoroff further noted hemorrhages in both eyes, as well as subdural bleeding in the brain, shifting of one part of the brain to the other, and brain swelling. The letter indicated that Hannah's presentation was inconsistent with a fall or even multiple falls and that the severity of her indicated that she would not have been acting normally and would have become symptomatic and nonresponsive shortly after receiving the injury. Ultimately, Dr. Makoroff offered her diagnosis of physical abuse, including abusive head injury.

At trial during direct testimony, Dr. Makoroff reviewed the medical file photographs taken of Hannah that depicted bruising over various parts of her body. Dr. Makoroff indicated those bruises which were of concern to her, including the bruises on the upper and lower eyelids, the bruising underneath the chin, a left ear bruise, and bruises on the chest, on the flanks, arms, and buttock. Dr. Makoroff noticed that the extent of some of the bruises made them appear less accidental, and that the bruises that had occurred on "multiple planes" of Hannah's body was also very concerning for child abuse and that a couple's areas of buttock bruising appeared to have "some pattern to it." Ultimately, in conjunction with the other medical evidence including the injuries to Hannah's eyes and brain, and Hannah's autopsy report, Dr. Makoroff opined, within a reasonable degree of medical certainty, that Hannah's injuries were nonaccidental and her diagnoses were child physical abuse and abusive head trauma.

On cross-examination, defense counsel asked Dr. Makoroff if she agreed that her opinion testimony on direct included opinions "about the location and pattern of bruises on Hannah's body." Dr. Makoroff confirmed she had testified in that manner with respect to some of the bruises. Upon further questioning, Dr. Makoroff confirmed that her testimony concerning bruises "was very detailed." Defense counsel then confronted Dr. Makoroff with her opinion letter and asked whether she discussed "patterns of bruises" or "locations of bruises" in her letter. Dr. Makoroff confirmed that she had not used those words but argued that they were encompassed within her opinion letter.

During this questioning, the state objected, and a side-bar discussion ensued. Defense counsel moved to strike Dr. Makoroff's testimony, arguing that it was a new opinion outside of the opinion letter. After hearing argument from both sides, the court indicated that it did not agree that Dr. Makoroff's testimony constituted a new opinion, that Dr. Makoroff had not deviated from her ultimate opinion, and therefore, the court would not strike her testimony.

This is about half of this document, but the most important half. Lindsay's appeal was denied. If you would like to see the rest of this document, it can be searched on google.

Lindsey was found guilty and is serving life sentence in prison.

> Do not erase the designs the child makes in the soft wax of inner life.

> —Maria Montessori

CHAPTER 13

Murdered: Lucia Krim (Lulu) age 6, brother Leo Krim age 3

October 25, 2012

Murdered by their nanny, Yoselin Ortega

Manhattan, New York

Their mother had no idea when she left her Upper West Side apartment with her 3-year-old-daughter Nassie what she would come home to—the gut-wrenching horror that would be waiting for her—a horror that was just a few hours away and in her own home.

Kevin, her husband, was coming home that afternoon from work in San Francisco. In fact, when the horror took place, he was blissfully unaware of what was taking place at his home. His family was his everything—Miranda, Lulu, Nassie, and Leo. However, as Kevin's plane landed at JFK, there was an announcement over the speaker saying the NYPD needed to get him from the plane. His phone started to ping constantly with messages from people wanting to know what was going on. The horror was waiting for him, as the police took him to St. Luke's Hospital with very little information as to what was wrong. His family had now been reduced to two instead of four.

Marina and Kevin Krim were hardworking, law-abiding citizens with a beautiful family—Lulu 6, Nessie 3, Leo just turned 2. Their lives were for their children. They taught them to be upstanding, good people, using their talents to help others through life, the kind of people we all want as neighbors or family.

Kevin was away for work in San Francisco, so Marina employed their nanny to help her. The nanny was Yoselyn Ortega, a 50- year-old immigrant. Marina couldn't employ her full-time but she needed some help, and someone had referred Yoselin to the Krims as being a really good nanny. Marina followed up on references, not knowing at the time the references were family members and Yoselin had never been a nanny. They soon would find out not only was Yoselyn a liar and scammer but so was most of her family.

On October 25, the nanny was to pick Lulu up from school and take her to dance, allowing 2-year-old Leo to nap in his stroller, while Marina took 3-year-old Nessie to her swim lessons at a different time. Marina was supposed to meet Lulu and the nanny at the dance studio. This allowed for 3-year-old Nessie to take her nap before they had to be at swim classes by 4. This was not unusual; in fact, it was a regular weekly event.

Joselyn waited nearby with the children until she knew Marina was out of the apartment. As she walked into the apartment building, she asked the doorman if Mrs. Krim had left. He informed her, yes, he saw her leave. She then took the elevator and went to the apartment. Once inside, she gathered knives from the kitchen. She took the children to the bathroom in the back of the apartment.

As Marina got to the dance studio to meet Joselyn, she was upset to find out they had never made it to dance class. Very distraught, Miranda immediately knew something was wrong. She tried calling Joselyn. However, the call went to voicemail. She had no idea Joselyn intentionally left her cellphone at home. She knew Miranda would be looking for her and she didn't want her to find her by phone. She wanted Miranda to come to the apartment. She waited for Miranda to come and find her and experience the slaughter on her own. She wanted that image to be burned into the brain of Miranda Krim, and it is, forever a scene she will never be able to forget.

Around 4:30 that afternoon after Joselyn shut that bathroom door, she took little Leo and slit his throat cutting his main artery. He was just barely 2, so it was easy. However, when it was Lulu's turn, at age 6, she was strong and fought back, not nearly as easy as Leo. She fought with everything she had, but in the end, lost that battle. She was stabbed about 30 times and her throat was also slit and had many defense wounds on her hands and arms. Leo had 5 stab wounds.

After Miranda found out the children and Joselyn had not been to the dance, she started home as fast as she could go. There was a sickening feeling in the pit of her stomach, but she kept telling herself there must be a logical explanation for this and once she got home, she would relax. Everything would be ok; everything has to be ok.

She walked into the apartment holding the hand of Nassie. They walked room to room calling out the three names, Leo? Lulu? Josie? No one answered her. No one was in any of the rooms they went into. The last room was the bathroom, and the door was shut. As Miranda opened the door, she called out Joselyn's name. When she opened the door, she saw the most gruesome and horrible scene she could ever imagine. Her two babies were lying in the tub, eyes open, eyes fixed, she immediately knew they were dead. Almost simultaneously, Joselyn was in her face with a large knife. Miranda screamed the most blood-curdling scream that could be heard throughout the building. She took Nassie's hand and went running out of the apartment.

Joselyn took the knife and plunged it into her neck two times, damaging her spine and severing arteries.

The manager of the building came running when he heard Miranda in the hallway screaming and crying the most awful scream he had ever heard. Whatever had happened must be really bad because he had never heard anyone scream like that before. He ran into the apartment and when he came upon the horrible scene, he ran out and barred the door. He called 9-1-1.

When the police arrived, the scene was almost more than they could stomach. Both children were laying in the bathtub, so the blood was draining down the tub. Although they were obviously dead, they started CPR on them anyway, in the slim chance they could save them.

They lifted both of the children out of the tub and put them both on one trauma board, putting them in one ambulance. Miranda was taken in another ambulance to follow them to the hospital. My heart hurts to think of this woman and her baby girl in that ambulance and what she must have felt. Nothing could be more horrible than what she was going through. She must have thought how much she needed Kevin right now, how much she needed to wake up from this horrible nightmare she was living in this moment.

The paramedics also took Joselyn to a different hospital where she clung to life. When she woke up, a police guard was standing by. He testified that upon waking, she did not ask about the children, show remorse, or make excuses. She started to complain about the way she was treated by Miranda, how she had been worked so hard.

In court, the paramedics and police officers that came to the scene testified that it was a hard scene to work, the most horrible and bloody they had ever witnessed.

Testifying to autopsy results was Dr. Susan Ely. She said Leo was stabbed 6 times, all to the neck. It looked like she stood behind him to slit his throat. The knife was sunk 1 1/2" deep which hit the spine. He had no blood left in his body. He did not die immediately. It takes minutes, and not all of the knife wounds were fatal. It was a very painful death. He suffered before he died. Lucia had over 30 wounds in her head, neck, arms, torso, and hands. She fought hard against her attacker. Dr. Ely testified Lucia suffered over 30 wounds and she most likely twisted her body as the knife was plunged into her. The injuries on her arms and hands prove there was quite a lot of movement and struggle to get away from this knife. Lucia had her hands up at some point while she was being stabbed, she testified. In some way, they got between the knife and her body during the course of the violence, the doctor added. It's unclear which of the children died first, but by the time the paramedics arrived on the scene, it was clear they were both gone.

The cause of death was bleeding to death, and it takes several minutes for that to happen. The manner of death was homicide. Dr. Ely said both children suffered horribly before dying.

One of the detectives on the scene said she knew they were dead because they were white as a sheet and both children were laying in a pool of blood with their eyes wide open and said they were just staring at each other. She said their eyes were wide open and it looked as if nothing was in there.

When Miranda walked into the apartment, Joselyn was standing with a bloody knife in her hand and stabbed herself in the neck.

The detective said the mother was convulsing and had to be taken to the hospital and sedated.

Sometime during this time when the horror had settled some, I keep thinking how Kevin and Miranda must have thought back about how they could have been so wrong about this person they had in their home. The pain had to be great as they thought back. They were not to blame themselves, they were deceived, not by just one person but by several. How would you beat yourself up though and how would you wonder how this person who was supposed to love your children, who took care of them for over two years, could do something so awful, so inhumane, so horrible? It's beyond an evil act.

In May of 2018 Joselyn Ortega found guilty on all counts of murder. She was sentenced to life in prison without the possibility of parole.

While we teach our children about life, our children teach us what life is all about.

—Angela Schwindt

CHAPTER 14

Emani Moss, 9 years old,

Murdered by father Eman Moss and stepmother Tiffany Moss

Lawrenceville, Georgia

It was July 2, 2012 when police were dispatched to an apartment complex, Coventry Apartments, because of a runaway child. They went to the complex managers office where the child was there with the manager. The police questioned the child stating her name was Emani Moss, 9 years old. She told the police she had run away because of abuse in the home. When the officer questioned her further, she said her stepmother had tied her to a chair with belts. When the officer asked her if she had bruises, she told him, "No, the belts weren't tight enough to bruise me." She had a mark on her arm and when the officer asked her where she got the mark, she said she got it cooking.

He took her up to the apartment and talked with her stepmother, Tiffany Moss. She told the officer that Emani kept running away. He ended up leaving the apartment and left Emani with her stepmother.

On July 25th, 2012, the police were dispatched to the same apartment complex for a runaway child. When they arrived at the apartment, they met with Tiffany Moss. She told them Emani opened the front door and just took off running. She said she went after her and looked around the grounds of the apartment complex but could not find her. The police questioned her as to why she waited for two hours to call them. She said the child had done this before and she came back.

Later that evening, while police were searching for her, one of the neighbors found her sleeping in bushes. They went back to the apartment and the officer was questioning Emani, but she would not answer any of his questions. He cited her, and she had to appear before a judge in juvenile court. The parent signed a release, and she was released back into her custody. It is usual custom to write a citation in this instance, in hopes the judge can get more out of the child.

Emani's teacher was questioned about her behavior at school. The teacher said she had never had any disrespect or problems from Emani. In fact, she was such a blessing to have in class. The only thing she could say negative is that sometimes, Emani did not have her homework done on a consistent basis. The children had behavior sheets that were filled out every day and they would go home to the parents. The teacher had written about her failed ability to always have her homework done and Armani started to cry and got very upset. She begged the teacher not to send that home to her parents. The teacher decided not to send it home. The teacher said Emani got along with all the children. She was so kind to everyone, even a bully that would cause trouble for many of the children. Emani even tried to get along with that child. Again, she said she was just a precious child.

The teacher had commented that Emani was very little and small for her age. She passed the fourth grade and was promoted to the fifth grade but was deceased before school started in the 2013/2014 school year. The teacher stated that Emani loved pink, and she loved her long hair. She had long hair that she wore in braids. Before the end of the school year, her hair has been cut short.

Emani's aunt, her dad's sister, loved spending time with Emani. She said that there was an instance where Emani had been taken from her dad and was given to her paternal grandmother. There was a time when you could see visible cuts and bruises on Emani. After a time, she said her brother was given back custody.

The aunt used to have Emani over for sleepovers and weekends. She said she had never any problems with her, she never had to discipline her, and her children loved Emani. As time went on, however, she had Emani over less and less. Once Eman got remarried, she only saw Emani 3-4 times per year. She commented on the last time she saw Emani was on Mother's Day, 2013. Several people in the family came by her house. She said Emani had really changed. Her hair had been cut short, and she didn't seem happy and bubbly. She wasn't like a child anymore. She seemed very frail and quiet, not happy. She said Emani was timid, very different than she had been before. She said she asked her brother why they cut Emani's hair and he replied his wife had it cut. She said that was the last time she saw her niece. Her and her brother would text each other occasionally. She was not close with Tiffany Moss and never texted or called her.

The aunt said that she was talking on the phone with her brother one day and he told her that Tiffany was going to take Emani out of school and homeschool her. She said that was a red flag for her. She knew Tiffany had two other small children and after what she saw on Mother's Day, something was just not right. So, she called Department of Children and Family Services because she felt in her spirit something was very wrong. One interesting note, the desk where Emani did her schoolwork had a sign on the wall just above where she sat. It was the four rules of school. 1. Try your best! 2. Smile 3. Stay motivated 4. HAVE FUN. How could that poor child do any of those? Who was she trying to impress?

On November 2, 2013, police were dispatched to the Coventry Apartments. Eman Moss had called 911 to report a possible suicide. After police arrived, Eman's story changed. He then said there seemed to be a body, or a ten-year-old child had drunk a chemical or something, and there was a dead body. One of the officers walked up to Eman and asked him where his ten- year-old daughter was. He stated he wanted to make sure she was alright.

Eman then pointed across the street to a silver garbage can. He told the officers that his daughter had drank some chemicals and she was dead and he didn't know what else to do with her so he put her body in the garbage can and burned her.

The officer said he turned and looked at the can and couldn't believe what he heard. He walked across the parking lot to the silver can and opened the lid. He saw a foot sticking up. He looked closer in the can and he said he saw a very small body of a child that had been partially burned. He walked back to Eman and told him they needed to do a sweep of the apartment. A sweep is to thoroughly check each room of the house and make sure no one is in there that could be hurt or dead. They saw two baby cribs. There wasn't a lot in the apartment. No one else was in there.

He said they questioned Eman as to who lived in the apartment, and he told them his wife Tiffany and their two small children, that Tiffany had left just before the police got there with the two children in a silver Blazer. She was headed to her mother's house.

The officers handcuffed Eman and put him in the back of the squad car. He was under arrest.

The crime scene was secured with the yellow tape and so was the apartment.

After having enough officers at the crime scene, some of the officers went to Tiffany's mother. The SUV was at the house, but Tiffany was not there. Tiffany told her mother that she was leaving the two kids with her. She changed clothes and left, telling her mother she didn't want to go to jail. The officer said she had not been there long when Tiffany's sister showed up saying she had just left work, but she actually had taken her sister and dropped her off somewhere. She didn't know where she was and got lost coming back home. She did not know anything about what happened. He told them to stay away from the clothes and called more investigators. They also kept the mother and the sister separated from each other.

Tiffany's mother told the police that before she left her house that morning, she told her mother that Emani was dead. The mother knew something didn't sound good because back in 2010, her daughter was arrested for beating Emani. She had to go to court but never told her mother any of the circumstances around that. Emani was taken from her dad's home and put with her maternal grandmother for a time.

Tiffany's mother also told the police that she knew Emani was being homeschooled by her daughter. When Tiffany came to her home that morning, she woke everyone up. They were all sick and it was very early morning, and everyone in the house was sleeping. She made her sister Brittany get up and take her somewhere. Before she left, she told her mother not to let the police take her children.

Tiffany had her sister Brittany drop her off and later that afternoon, a policeman was patrolling in the area with his partner. It was very strange that someone would be walking out in nowhere the way she was. She had identification and some cash in her pocket. She did tell the police that her husband had been arrested because of his daughter. The officer asked him if there were any other children that might need help.

The officers ran her name and there were no warrants for her. However, one of the officers did see on the news on his laptop about the story of what was happening, and they were looking for Tiffany. The officers called the next county over which was Wilmette county, and they did want to speak with her. The police held her in their call until the Wilmette county police arrived to pick her up.

The trial started in May of 2019. It was interesting that Tiffany Moss represented herself instead of having her own team of attorneys.

Eman Moss, 35 years old, took the stand for the state. He was in shackles and told the court he was serving a life sentence without parole. He had taken a plea in 2015 to avoid the death penalty.

Tiffany and Eman went to the same church and that is where he and Tiffany met. He said Tiffany was in school still at the time. He testified that he has no idea where Emani's mother is at, he was given sole custody of Emani. The mother has never tried to have contact with Emani.

After 7-8 months of dating, Eman and Tiffany got married in July of 2009. When they first got married, they lived with his good friend Rudy and his daughter. In 2010, they got their own place. He worked at a warehouse, and she worked as a pre-K teacher. Things were going very well. In November 2011, they moved in with Tiffany's mother because money was tight. Tiffany was not working. They moved into their own apartment again after a few months. When the apartment lease was up, they moved back in with her mother-in-law again. In September of 2013, they once again moved out to their own apartment.

One day in 2010, he got a call from the police that he needed to come to the police station. When they got there, he was told Tiffany had abused Emani. She was arrested and ended up on probation. Eman stated that after that time, she never disciplined her again. They had to take parenting classes after that. He said he didn't know until then there were other forms of discipline besides spanking.

After the parenting classes, and Tiffany had to take anger management classes, the Department of Children and Family services allowed Eman and Tiffany to take Emani back into their home.

When they moved into their last apartment, Arman had to work two jobs. The day job he had needed him to be there by 6:00 a.m. which meant he had to leave home by 5:00 a.m. He would get home around 4:30 in the afternoon, then had to leave for his evening job around 5:30 p.m. to be at work by 6:00 p.m. He got off from that job around 1:00-1:30 a.m. He was only home for around 3 hours a day. On the weekend, he stated that it was Tiffany's time to get a break so she would go out with friends or over to her mother's house.

At his job, he was not supposed to have his cellphone with him, but he kept it with him anyway. He would get messages from Tiffany. Usually, he said the messages were about Emani. One time, it was about Emani pooping and wiping it on the walls. Another time, the message said Emani pooped again and put it in the oatmeal. Another time, Emani tried to run away. He said he didn't do anything about it. He said he believed Tiffany but didn't do anything about it.

The week of October 24, 2013, he said he knew Emani was sick. He said he thought she was going through a growth spurt, getting taller, so she looked thinner. He said during the week, it was Tiffany's job to feed her, and, on the weekend, it was his job to feed her. He said on the weekend, she would eat so much it was like she would gorge herself.

On Mother's Day 2013, his mother told Eman that Emani looked thin, and she needed to come live with her. He said his pride wanted to prove his mother wrong so he told her no, although deep inside, he knew that would have been the best thing for her.

He was told by Tiffany that Emani cut her own hair. He asked Emani about it and she said, "Yeah, I did it." He said he didn't totally believe Emani cut her own hair. His sister called him about it, and she was very unhappy.

On October 24, 2013, he came home from his first job and Emani was in the bathtub, shaking like she was having a seizure. He said he would call 911, but Tiffany told him she couldn't take her to the hospital. A few days before that, Emani had a large burn on her stomach. Tiffany said Emani was cooking and spilled the water on her.

When he found her in the tub, he picked her up and carried her into her bedroom. He laid her on a mattress on the floor. She was so thin that she could not get out of the bed. He said he tried to feed her, and it was beyond help. She would try to speak but she couldn't. He admitted he did not take her to the doctor. He said he was "trying to fix something that was beyond repair." Tiffany kept telling him they could not call 911 and they could not go to the doctor. She said she was on probation, and she would go to jail.

On October 28, 2013, Tiffany called him at work and told him Emani had passed away. He did not leave work until regular time in the afternoon. Tiffany kept telling him they had to get rid of the body. When he got home, Tiffany was watching television. They talked about making it look like Emani had run away. He was asked why he would agree to that. He said he could not explain. Tiffany came up with the idea of hiding the body. She was on the floor wrapped in a blanket. He went on to work at his second job. When he got off work from his second job, he went home and Emani was still on the floor in the blanket. Tiffany was in the back room sleeping with the two younger children. He said he went into the room with her for a while then went to sleep in the living room.

The day after she died, he picked her up in the blanket and moved her to the computer room. He had worked both jobs that day. He said every time he would come home, he would go into the room where she would just sit with her.

Eman said Tiffany told him they needed to use their criminal minds and do something. She wanted him to get rid of the body.

On October 30, after he got off work at his second job, he went to Walmart and bought a garbage can, charcoal, and lawn bags. He said he purchased those items so he could cremate the body. He said Tiffany wanted to bury the body, but he did not want to do that.

On October 31, 2013, Eman went to work as usual. Tiffany sent him pictures of the little ones in their Halloween costumes. When he came home, Tiffany started to push him to get rid of the body. He went into Emani's room, took her body out of the blanket, and said goodbye to her. He said her body was so stiff he couldn't hardly bend her body to get it in the garbage bag. He said he and Tiffany had to force her leg to bend and they had to force her arms beside her arm. They took duct tape and wrapped it around her to hold her arms down. They ended up bending the body over and wrapped it in duct tape. He talked about the cracking sounds that her body made as they bent it over. He got her in the trash bag and tied it up. Tiffany took the blankets and comforter from Emani's bed and put them in the trash bags. Tiffany cleaned the mattress and put Emani's clothes in one.

Eman said he loaded everything in the Blazer and Tiffany and the two little children went to Bethesda Park. Tiffany kept saying just find a spot. He ended up at Satellite Blvd. He said he was really just driving because he didn't want to dump her.

He pulled up a dirt road and got out of the car. He popped the back of the Blazer. Tiffany got out of the passenger side. He said he opened the bag of charcoal and Tiffany helped him put Emani in the garbage can head up. He said she was at an angle. He sprinkled lighter fluid on the charcoal and the body and lit a flame. He said the flame was big. He and Tiffany were standing there. He said he turned his back because he couldn't stand to watch it. He said after about five minutes, he put the fire out because it didn't work. The body was still there intact. They waited for the can to cool and put the can in the back seat of the Blazer.

By this time, it was 4:00 a.m. Tiffany wanted him to bury it, but he said he couldn't. He took Tiffany back to the apartment. He got ready for work, and the can with Emani was in the back of his car. After his shift, he went home to get ready for the second job. He said Tiffany was watching television and doing normal things.

He called his friend Rudy and told him he needed to talk with him. He said they met at a QT. Rudy got into the Blazer and he started telling him that Emani was dead and in the back of the Blazer. Rudy said "Let me out of here. You've got to call 911." Rudy got out of the Blazer and Eman drove home and told Tiffany they had to call 911. She started yelling no no you can't do that. She started to get the kids dressed and put them in the Blazer and took the garbage can out of the back and the two garbage bags and left for her mother's house. Eman called 911 at that point.

A crime scene specialist testified that on November 2, 2013 she was called out to the home of Eman and Tiffany Moss. She arrived around 7:00 a.m. After being briefed by a detective, she did an initial walk through. She said there was a Primary scene and a secondary scene. The primary crime scene was the trash can and the bags, the secondary crime scene was the third floor apartment that Eman and Tiffany lived in. As she was going about the secondary crime scene, she comes across a cabinet under the sink that had garbage bags stored there. As she went through each bag she found a bag with duct tape in one of them. There were overall pictures taken of the apartment. When you first walk into the apartment you walk into the living room. Off of the living room was a hallway, down the hallway was bedrooms. The first bedroom you came to had cribs in it and also seemed to be the bedroom for the two younger children. Next was Emani's bedroom. There was a bed, and there were no sheets on the bed. There was a comforter partially pulled back on the bed. On the carpet there were stains of yellow and brown. Upon opening the door there was an overwhelming smell of urine. The mattress was flipped over and on the underside of the mattress was almost completely covered with yellow and brown stains and possible blood. There was a strong odor on the mattress.

The medical examiner talked about the autopsy. She said Emani came to her in the trash can. The feet were sticking up and she could see the body had been burned some. There was a garbage bag around her and part of it was melted to her. She removed the body from the can. She had on pink socks and white underwear. She had duct tape wrapped around her to keep her feet up next to the body. X-rays were done, and there were no acute or healing fractures. She was looking for post mortem changes. There was fixed avidity. and she was starting to turn red and green. That shows it had been at least two days since she had passed.

She was 50" in length. That was in the 5th percentile. Meaning at least 95% of girls her age was taller. She weighed 32lbs. which was less than the 5th percentile. Her hands and feet and right side of body was burned which was done after death. She had some skin slippage. She had an area on her left buttock where the skin was worn away. It resembled a bed sore. She had a burn on her stomach that was in the healing stage. There were no other injuries that would have caused her death. Each organ was removed and weighed. The heart was normal size, the lungs were normal size and weight. The gastro tract had non-specific fluid in her stomach. Her liver weighed 340 grams. It should had weighed between 700-900 grams. Her kidneys were small, the spleen was very small. She had no muscle; she was virtually skin and bones. Her brain weight was somewhat small. When asked why her liver was so small the medical examiner said it's a sign of starvation. The spleen was small because of starvation also. The brain size is preserved but all other organs will be smaller. Since the brain was normal size it shows, the brain was trying to keep itself as the way it should have been.

Her feet were burned from where she had been set on fire. This charring was because that is where the lighter fluid had been put to start the fire. The Medical Examiner said she received all of those injuries after death. She had been put head first down in the garbage can.

She was tested for drugs, alcohol, and everything was negative. Anti-freeze was negative. The fluid that is in the eyes. The nitrogen in her body was very high caused from dehydration, and kidney failure.

The Medical Examiner said that Emani was gaunt and her eyes were sunk back in her head. She said she was literally skin stretched over skull. The Medical Examiner talked about the features of starvation and the sequence of starvation. The first is loss of wellbeing, cravings and hunger pains. 2nd is apathy, fatigue and weight-loss. Pigmentation changes in the skin. A skin over skull look to the person. Hyperthermia, extreme liturgy and mental retardation. An immune suppression, diarrhea, and death.

The burn that Emani had on her stomach actually covered her whole front almost. It was 8" by 8". It was a 3rd degree burn. The doctor testified that at one point it had been very painful.

Emani had a lot of duct tape on her skin. Since she was decomposing, and there was skin slippage, it was very hard to get all of it off.

During the entire testimony of the Medical Examiner, Tiffany Moss sat looking down, she would not look at the horrific pictures.

This little girl could not walk any longer. She was allowed to go to the bathroom where she laid, did not feed her, did not address any of her needs. Treated her worse than an animal. Most of us would not treat our animals even close to that cruel.

In the trial Tiffany Moss would not allow a public defender to take her case. She wanted to try her case herself. The judge offered several times for her to get an attorney, but in the end he said it was her right if she wanted to defend herself.

Emani was severely neglected. A malice murder with the sentence of death is what the state was asking for. The victim must be tortured, depravity of mind. The age and physical characteristics

Conclusion for autopsy was cause of death: Starvation Manner of death: Homicide

After the conclusion of the Medical Examiner's testimony, the State rested its case. It was now the defense case. Tiffany stood and said the defense rested its case.

In America our judicial system is built on the punishment should fit the crime. If you don't believe in the death penalty you have to ask yourself what about Emani. She paid with her life for something she didn't do. She was innocent of any crime, of any wrong doing. It takes 50-70 days for a person to starve to death, and what a terrible death it is. To balance what she did, I believe Tiffany should receive the death penalty.

Tiffany Nicole Moss was found guilty on all seven accounts and was given the Death Penalty for the murder of Emami Moss, the defendant's step-daughter.

CHAPTER 15

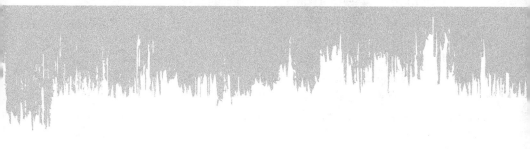

Murdered Kinsley Kinner age 2

Murdered by: Bradley Young, boyfriend of mother, and Rebekah Kinner, mother.

Middletown, Ohio Madison Twp. Died:

December 3, 2015. Kinsley's father is Scott Senft

Kinsley woke up the night before her death, screaming. It wasn't unusual for Kinsley to have a nightmare so her mother's boyfriend took her into the living room to watch cartoons. The mother said when she dozed back off to sleep, she left Brad and Kinsley on the couch and she went back to bed. Rebekah said the next thing she knew, the lights came on in the bedroom and Brad was standing there holding Kinsley. She said Kinsley had her eyes open just staring, and was not blinking. She said Kinsley was breathing but very slowly, and she knew something was wrong.

Brad said Kinsley woke up screaming again, less than 48 hours later, Kinsley would be dead. Rebekah has stated she felt Brad disciplined Kinsley a bit too harshly, but she was also afraid of him. She said he had hurt her too.

When Brad went to trial, Rebekah testified for the state. However, they threw her testimony out and the jury was ordered to disregard what she had to say because she was ruled incompetent.

They stated she may have been intoxicated by her medications. We all know you cannot un-ring a bell or unhear something.

Rebekah testified in his trial that he abused her as well. One time she said when she was pregnant, he hit her in the back so hard to the extent that it caused her to have bloody discharge and she was put on bedrest. She said he also punched her in the legs and pulled her around by her hair. Rebekah said he also had a thing with biting her. She said she could be just sitting and he would reach over and bite her face or bite her on the arm. Rebekah stated he made her feel trapped and she never called the police. He would tell her there was no place she could go that he couldn't find her. He said I was trained to kill in the military and I can make it look like an accident, Rebekah said she didn't think of it as abuse but she was scared of him. She said she kept telling herself things would change or maybe I was doing things to cause him to act this way. If she could just figure out what made him made then she could change and he would apologize and buy her something or take her out to eat.

Rebekah stated the night she called 911, Brad first took the phone from her and wouldn't let her call. She said the operator tried to guide her through CPR but she was freaking out so bad she couldn't do it. Kinsley's lips were already blue. She said Brad tried to perform CPR. At one point Brad's roommate said "What the hell did you do to her Brad?"

Kinsley was declared dead after her mother and Bradley Young were arrested. She was declared brain dead on December 3.at Children's Hospital in Cincinnatti, Ohio. Her family chose for her to become an organ donor .

When Rebekah was charged with Kinsley's murder, she was pregnant. She was visibly pregnant at her arraignment and gave birth on February 1 to a boy, Wyatt Matthew Kinner. Wyatt was given to his biological father when he was 6 weeks old. Jason White, Wyatt's biological father was a family friend of the Kinner's. Rebekah's attorney stated he seems very level headed. He has 2 children from a previous marriage, and he works. Rebekah was ending her relationship with Senft when she started a relationship with White. Two judges and a prosecutor removed themselves from the trial of Bradley Young.

In April Young's attorney tried to have the charges against him dismissed, saying his rights were violated when two deputies heard a partial phone conversation between Young and his attorneys. The defense team wrote that Young made the phone call outside of the usual place it should have been made. None of the phone calls that were in question were preceded by the usual warning stating that the telephone call was being recorded, except for privileged communications between client and attorney, Both the prosecutor and assistant prosecutor gave written affidavit's stating they had no idea what the conversations were about.

Kinsley's organs were donated and saved the lives of at least two children. One child, Wyatt, was born with a congenital heart defect transposition of the great arteries, which leaves a shortage of oxygen in blood. Wyatt received Kinsley's lungs one day after she died.

Kinsley's father said he knew one other organ was donated, but he was unsure of which and to whom.

"My daughter passed, but she's like passing on through everybody in the world," Senft said. "I had people from literally overseas try to contact me to help me out with everything."

Wyatt's surgery was a success, his family said in a Facebook post.

During the trial the jury toured the house where Kinsley was abused. It's not common for juries to tour the hone of a deceased victim, but the prosecution and defense teams agreed early in the case that the jury in Bradley Young's case should see the Madison Township home where Young, and Rebekah Kinner and Kinsley lived until Kinsley's death December 2, 2015.

The defense attrneys requested that the jury physically visit the scene rather than rely on photos taken by investigators. The defense team argued the jurors need to see for themselves the proximity of the rooms in the house as well as the garage.

At a hearing in March, prosecutors didn't object to the request, and Butler

County Common Pleas Judge granted the motion.

IN THE COURT OF APPEALS
TWELVTH APPELATE DISTRICT OF OHIO

BUTLER COUNTY
CRIMINAL APPEAL FROM BUTLER COUNTY COURT OF
COMMON PLEAS CASE NO. CR2015-12-1818

1. The defendant appellant. Bradley Young, appeals his murder conviction in the Butler County Court of Commom Pleas. For the reasons detailed below, we affirm.

2. On December 2, 2015k at approximately 6 a.m., Rebekah K. Called 911 for emergency assistance with regard to her two-year-old daughter, KK, who was not breathing Deputy Greg Turner and several other law enforcement officials arrived at Young's residence where Young was attempting to give CPR to K.K. until EMT squad arrived.

3. While life-saving efforts were ongoing, authorities made contact with Young and Rebekah. In describing the events leading to the 911 call, neither Young nor Rebekah reported that K.K. had been beaten or abused. Young, however, mentioned that he and K.K. had been in a recent car accident. Young also claimed that K.K. had recently fallen from a chair in the kitchen and that K.K. had a bump and cut on the back of her head from the faucet.

4. There were, however, conflicting stories about wot was with K.K. immediately prior to the 911 call. Subsequent investigations revealed that Young and Rebekah had been communicating through text messages. Shortly after 7:00 a.m., Young and Rebekah sent the follow8ing messages to each other.
   - Young: There (sic) going to try and make us look like bad parents babe not sure how they got three different stories either Chuck never said anything this is stupid.

*Young: I love you and stay strong will be with her (sic) soon.

*Rebekah: I know babe I love you to (sic)

*Young: Just telling them she was laying with both of us in the living in the couch (sic) they don't try and turn it around on you or me.

5. K.K. was transported to Atrium hospital, arriving in a state of cardio pulmonary arrest. While at Atrium, emergency personnel were able to restart K.K.'s heart and staff performed a CT scan on K.K.'s brain. Because of the seriousness of her injuries K.K. was transported to Cincinnati Children's Hospital.

6. Following transporting to Cincinnati Children's Hospital, medical staff performed a second CT scan of K,K,'s brain. However, efforts to revive K.K. were unsuccessful and she was pronounced dead on December 4, 2016.

7. Detectives interviewed Young and Rebekah while K.K. was still in the hospital. Young maintained that he had never harmed K.K. and insisted that both he and Rebekah were with the child on the couch when she suddenly cried out and began having problems breathing. Young continued, however, to tell law enforcement about various "accidents" that had happened to K.K. Young maintained that K.K. had previously fallen off a chair, had been involved in the previously mentioned car accident, and K.K. had recently struck her head on a faucet.

8. On December 10, 2016, Young was indicted for involuntary manslaughter, endangering children, permitting child abuse, and murder.

Voir Dire

9. On September 26, 2016, Young's case proceeded to a multiple-day jury trial.During voir dire, Juror 883 disclosed that, 41 years ago, he had been convicted of a felony drug offense in Indiana. Juror 883 indicated that he had been incarcerated for the offense for five months in the "youth center." Juror 883 continued to explain that he was released and subsequently earned an engineering degree.

10. Young moved to strike Juror 883 for cause under R.C. 2313.17 and R.C. 2945.25 on the basis of the former felony conviction. The state disagreed and argued that Juror 993 was eligible to serve. Following the exchange the trial court denied Young's request to strike Juror 883 for cause. Thereafter, Young used two preemptory challenges on two other jurors, but waived any use of his remaining preemptory challenges. Therefore, Juror 883 was empaneled on the jury.

TRIAL

11. The state introduced the testimonies of various medical experts and law enforcement personnel. Deputy Turner testified about his communication with Young and Rebekah after EMT's arrived. Deputy Turner testified that he spoke with Rebekah and Young because he was concerned about bruising, he saw in K.K.

12. Deputy Turner described Rebekah as emotional and distressed. Rebekah told Deputy Turner that K.K. had experienced a nightmare and eventually stopped breathing. Young reported the same general information to Deputy Turner.

13. The state called Bradley Peters a fire lieutenant and EMT for Madison Township. EMT Peters spoke with Young and

Rebekah to find out what had happened to K.K. EMT
Peters stated"

14. (Young) stated that he was asleep alone with the child.
(K.K.) was face down on

15. his chest. At some point the child had woken up screaming,
crying hysterically.

16. Young stated that he originally thought that she possibly
had had a nightmare.

17. He got up to go into a different part of the household to get
the child's mother.

18. at that point, * * * (K.K.) started breathing ineffectively and
they contacted 911

19. to have us dispatched.

20. The state aks called Sergeant Jam;y Chaney with the Trenton
Police Department. Sergeant Chaney spoke with Rebekah,
who is described as "nervous, upset, concerned." Rebekah
stated that K.K. had been screaming and crying, keeping
her and Young awake all night. Rebekah indicated that
they were holding K.K. when she went limp and stopped
breathing.

21. Sergeant Chaney then asked Young if he knew what had
happened and Young replied that K.K. had fallen from a
chair in the kitchen and hit the back of her head causing a
bump on a cut. Young also stated that he and K,K, had been
"in a minor, like, fender bender car accident several days
before."

22. Deputy 'Brian Romans from the Butler County Sheriff's
Office described Rebekah as upset, "emotionally shaken,"

and stuttering her words. Rebekah told Deputy Roman's that K.K. had two "night terrors" that night, the first occurring approximately two hours before the last one. During the second night terror, Rebekah stated that K.K. was screaming loudly and "gasping for air." Young was holding K.K. when she stopped breathing and Young then told Rebekah to call 911.

23. Deputy Romans then spoke to Young. Deputy Romans testified:

24. (Young) went on to explain to me that they were located on the couch. He

25. was lying in the couch with K.K. on his chest Rebekah was in the bedroom. He

26. stated that during that time, ***(K.K.), had experienced a night terror that

27. Rebekah claimed that they were having and he woke her up. He stood up,

28. she started crying, gasping for air, and at one point she went limp.
   He stated that he walked to the bedroom to get Rebekah. He summons her to call 911 and that is when they begin CPR.

29. Detective Joe Ventre of the Butler County Sheriff's Office testified and authenticated several photographs of Young's hands, which were visibly cut and bruised.

30. On the fourth day of trial, the state called Rebekah to the stand. Rebekah testified on direct examination, and Young's counsel conducted a lengthy cross-examination. Near the end of the day, young's counsel indicated that it still had

several hours of additional cross-examination to perform and the matter was adjourned until the following day,

31. The next day, Young's counsel asked the trial court to hold a competency hearing for Rebekah. Rebekah was questioned by the state, Young's counsel and the trial court. Following questioning, Young's counsel moved to strike Rebekah's testimony due to incompetence. Alternatively, Young's counsel moved to mistrial.

32. The trial court determined that Rebekah was "incapable of relating just impressions of the facts truthfully" and found her incompetent to testify. The trial court then struck Rebekah's testimony and Young withdrew the request for a mistrial. The trial court then instructed the jury.

Ladies and gentlemen, I'm instructing you and I'm ordering you to disregard the testimony of (Rebekah). Now, I appreciate that that's a difficult concept to disregard something that you've actually heard. The Court cannot instruct you to delete something from your mind of what you've actually heard. What I'm actually instructing you to do is, if somehow you should remember anything that (Rebekah) testified to you're instructed to disregard it.

For example, say to yourself, I cannot consider or be influenced by that in any way or for any purpose. Obviously that testimony must not be mentioned or otherwise be made part of your deliberations. Understood? Everybody is shaking their heads in a vertical fashion.

33. Following the conclusion of the state's case-in-chief, Young requested that the trial court dismiss the indictment because the state allegedly called Rebekah to the stand "knowing her mental state and understanding fully that she would take the stand and give false testimony." The trial court denied Young's request for a dismissal of the indictment.

34. Prior to the conclusion of its case-in-chief, the state also presented the testimony of numerous medical experts. A neuroradiologist at Cincinnati Children's Hospital testified about CT images of K.K.'s brain. The neuroradiologist at Cincinnati Children's Hospital showed that K.K.'s had suffered deep bleeding on her brain and brain stem and that the images showed that K,K.'s had suffered epidural and subdural hemorrhages.

35. According to the neuroradiologist the injuries that K.K. suffered could not be caused by a normal fall. Rather, the injuries that K.K. suffered were consistent with injuries that may be found on "a child hit by a car" or was involved in a "significant motor vehicle collision." Furthermore, based on the severity of bleeding, and its progression, K,K.'s condition could not have been a delayed response. In other words, the results of K.K.'s CT scan indicated that K.K. suffered a very significant inflicted injury that could have occurred close to the time that she arrived at the hospital.

36. The state then presented the testimony of a pediatric ophthalmologist at Cincinnati Children's Hospital. The doctor examined K.K.'s eyes while she was being treated and discovered that K.K. had a large preretinal hemorrhage that obscured K.K.'s central vision. The doctor also found hemorrhages in the periphery of K.K.'s retina and in all layers of the retina.

37. The state then presented the testimony of a pediatrician and clinical fellow in child abuse pediatrics at the Mayerson Center at the Cincinnati Children's Hospital. The pediatrician aad examined K,K,'s medical and radiologic records and had also examined K.K. prior to her death. The pediatrician testified that K.K. had suffered from non-accidental injuries caused by abusive head trauma. The two CT scans taken approximately two and one-half hours apart, revealed "significant brain swelling or cerebral edema." The

pediatrician opined that K.K. suffered her injuries in close proximity to the time she arrived at the hospital.

38. The chief deputy coroner at the Hamilton County Coroner's Office presented thr results of the autopsy and declared the manner of death a homicide.

39. The coroner testified that K.K. had bruises on the right and left sides of her face, as well as additional bruising on the right side if her neck. The coroner also explained that she did a internal examination of K.K.'s body and discovered internal bruising on K.K.'s brain and noted that K.K. suffered a subdural hemorrhage on the right side of her brain and a subarachnoid hemorrhage that covered the entire surface of the brain. The coroner explained K.K.'s brain swelled and caused herniation, which kills brain tissue and creates bleeding. As to the cause of K.K.'s brain injuries, the coroner testified:

There was an initial injury, trauma to the head. I don't know specifically what it is, if it was multiple blows to the head or if it was shaking, but what happened is it caused swelling in the brain. It caused that hemorrhage on the right hemisphere of the brain as well as- which is called the subdural hemorrhage -it caused *** the subarachnoid hemorrhage over the entire surface of the brain. The important thing here is that the brain swelled, because it was injured from the initial injury. Whether it was blows to the head or rotational injury which can occur if the child is shaken, twisted, turned- a child's brain can't handle that. And like any injury- like if you fracture your forearm, you're going to get swelling and pain. And the brain, if the brain is injured from this blow or this rotational force, this twisting, the brain swelled. That is the lethal injury un her head. It swelled enough that caused her to stop breathing and her heart to stop beating and she went to the hospital.

40. The coroner went on to explain K.K.'s injury "occurred around the time she went unresponsive and when her heart stopped beating. The coroner stated: The injury we're seeing here is something that was acute. She was injured. She went unresponsive and her heart stopped beating. It's not something that happened three or four days ago and took three or four days for her brain to get injured, her brain swelled, she died. This is -this is within minutes. This is not from three or four days ago. The coroner testified that, to a reasonable degree of medical certainty, the cause of K.K.'s death was "complications of non-accidental (sic) trauma to the head."

VERDICT

41. Following the close of evidence, the matter submitted to the jury for deliberation. Young was found guilty on all counts and the trial court imposed 15-year-to-life prison term for his murder conviction in violation of R.C. 2903.02 (B). Young now appeals his conviction, raising four assignments of error for review.

42. Assignment of Error Number 1:

43. THE TRIAL COURT ERRED BY OVERRULING YOUNG'S CHALLENGE TO JUROR 883 FOR CAUSE.

44. In his first assignment of error, Young argues that the trial court erred by overruling his challenge to dismiss Juror 883 for cause. We find Young's argument to be without merit.

45. Young argues that Juror 883 was a convicted felon who had not been pardoned, and thus was incompetent to serve as a juror. As a matter of state law, the Ohio Supreme Court has "recognized that where the defense exhausts its peremptory challenges before the full jury is seated, the erroneous denial of a challenge for cause in a criminal case may be prejudicial."

"However, (a) defendant in a criminal case cannot complain of prejudicial erroring the overruling of a challenge for cause if such ruling does not force him to exhaust his peremptory challenges." As a result, the Ohio Supreme Court has held that "(i)f the trial court erroneously overrules a challenge for cause, the error is prejudicial only if the accused eliminates the challenged venireman with a peremptory challenge and exhausts his peremptory challenges before the full jury is sealed.

46. We find Young's argument to be without merit because he failed to exhaust his peremptory challenges, but left the remaining two unused. Young could have excluded Juror 883 through his own volition. Because he did not, Young "acquiesced in the jury" that was ultimately selected. Young's first assignment of error is without merit and hereby overruled.

47. Assignment of Error No. 2:

48. REBEKAH'S TESTIMONY WAS INADMISSIBLE UNDER EVID. R. 601(A), R.C. 2317.01, AND DUE PROCESS BECAUSE SHE WAS UNCAPABLE OF RELATING TRUTHFUL FACTS.

49. In his second assignment of error. Young argues that Rebekah's testimony was inadmissible because she was incapable of relating truthful facts. We find Young's argument is without merit.

50. Evid R. 601(A) states that every person is competent to be a witness except "(t)hose of unsound mind, and children under ten years if age, who appear incapable of receiving just impressions of the facts and transaction respecting which they are examined, or of relating them truly." As related by the Ohio Supreme Court: A plain reading of Evid R. 601(A) leads to the conclusion that the competency of individuals

ten years or older is presumed, while the competency of those under ten must be established. *** The rule favors competency, conferring it even on those who do not benefit from the presumption, such as children under the age of ten, if they are shown to be capable of receiving just impressions of the facts and transactions respecting which they are examined and capable of relating them truly.*** As a result, absent some articulable concern otherwise, an individual who is at least ten years of age is per se competent to testify.

51. In the present case, Rebekah told two conflicting stories. To first responders, Rebekah did not disclose any abuse and told a story that mostly corroborated Young's account if the incident, i,e,, that K.K. had suddenly fallen unto the unresponsive state without any physical abuse. However, Rebekah told a different story while on the stand. In her testimony, Rebekah disclosed that Young had been abusing K.K. by spanking her, smacking her, holding her mouth shut, shaking her, and punching her. On the night K.K. became unresponsive, Rebekah testified that Young had shaken and punched K.K. multiple times because she was crying,

52. Young complains that Rebekah's testimony was inadmissible because she was incapable of relating truthful facts. The trial court agreed that Rebekah was unable to relate truthful facts and her testimony was stricken from the record. The trial court struck Rebekah's testimony following concerns Rebekah may have been under the influence of drugs at the time of trial. Furthermore, there were concerns Rebekah was relaying untruthful testimony in the hopes of "getting it over with." On cross-examination, Rebekah gave several inconsistent answers. When asked to explain her inconsistent answers, Rebekah admitted that some of her answers were not true, that she was anxious and stressed, and that sometimes she "just want(s) to hurry up and get it

done, so I just hurry up and answer the questions." The trial court also had the following exchange with Rebekah:

THE COURT: (Rebekah), when the jury is sitting there looking at you and I'm looking at you and all the lawyers are looking at you and all those people in the back row are looking at you, you told me you just answer the question just to get through it?

(REBEKAH): Yes.

THE COURT: And when you answer a question truthfully, do you know that it's not the truth?

(REBEKAH): No.

THE COURT: You just throw out an answer and you don't know whether it's truthful or untruthful, you just respond?

(REBEKAH) Yes

THE COURT: How do you pick how to respond, yes, or no, for example? How do you pick?

(REBEKAH): I – I don't—I just try to answer what they want me to answer.

THE COURT: SO, When (the prosecutor) is asking you questions and (the assistant prosecutor) (is) asking you questions, you'll say what you think they want to hear?

(REBEKAH): No

THE COURT: When (Defense Counsel 1) (is) asking you questions or (Defense Counsel 2) is asking you questions, then you just say what you think what (sic) they want ti hear.

(REBEKAH): Yes

THE COURT: Why is that?

(REBEKAH): Because I'm nervous and I don't like being yelled at and everybody in here just makes me really nervous.

THE COURT: So you told me that you don't care to give the answers-you're mot trying to give answers that you think the prosecution wants to hear but you want to give answers that you think the defense wants to hear?

(REBEKAH): Yes

(REBEKAH): I've told the prosecutors the truth about my story so I know that they already know.

THE COURT: So, since they already know the truth you don't care if you tell the truth to them today?

(REBEKAH): Yeah I do

THE COURT: Well, that's not what you told me a minute ago. A minute ago you said, you're not trying to please them and maybe that's not true.

So, we got on this question of whether or not you're trying to please the Prosecutors and you're saying I'm not trying to please the Prosecutors but you're trying-then you said you're trying to please the Defense attorneys?

(REBEKAH): Yes

THE COURT: Can I ask? Why are you trying to please the Defense attorneys?

(REBEKAH): Because the Prosecutors already know what happened. I told them everything so I don't feel like I have to please them and (Defense Counsel), he doesn't know the whole story, he doesn't know my side and I just feel like when he's coming at me I just have to agree with him.

53. As previously noted, the trial court found Rebekah incapable of relating just impressions of the facts truthfully and stuck prior testimony. Following It's decision, the trial court instructed the jury:

Ladies and gentleman, I'm instructing you and I'm ordering you to disregard the testimony of (Rebekah). Now, I appreciate that that's a difficult concept to disregard something that you've actually heard. The Court cannot instruct you to delete something from your mind of what you've actually heard. What I'm ordering you to do is, if somehow you should remember anything that (Rebekah) testified to, you're instructed to disregard it.

For example, say to yourself, I cannot consider or be influenced by that in any way or for any purpose. Obviously that testimony must not be mentioned or otherwise be made part og your deliberations. Understand? Everybody is shaking their head in a vertical fashion.

54. We find no error in the trial court's handling of Rebekah's testimony. Initially, Young complains that he was deprived of due process because the state put Rebekah on the stand as a witness. Young complains that the state "knew about Rebekah's potential for lying when she told responders, officers, detectives, and the trial judge that she had no idea who abused (K.K.)". As a result, when Rebekah testified at trial that Young had been KK.'s abuser "the prosecutor assumed the risk of what eventually materialized -Rebekah was deemed incompetent and infected the jury with inadmissible and incompetent testimony. The prosecutor's failure to safeguard against this manifest risk violated due process."

55. However, contrary to Young's arguments there was no violation of due process. It is well established that the touchstone if due process analysis is the fairness of the trial, and not any perceived culpability of a prosecutor. While Rebekah's testimony was stricken based on her strange and conflicting answers, "(t)here can be no such thing as an error-free, perfect trial, and ***the Constitution does not guarantee such a trial."

56. There is no dispute that Rebekah was a poor witness. The record reflects that on cross-examination Rebekah was timid and evasive in her responses. Though Rebekah never recanted her testimony that Young had abused K.K., she testified that she had agreed to certain statements made by defense counsel "to hurry up and get it done." Rebekah informed the trial court that she did so because the state already knew "the truth" and that the defense counsel didn't have the "whole story" so she felt compelled to agree with defense counsel.

57. While Rebekah was a poor witness and the trial court struck her testimony based on her unreliability. Young has failed to show that he was deprived of due process. Furthermore, though Young claims otherwise, there is no evidence to suggest that the state knew or should have known that Rebekah was incompetent or would provide incompetent testimony. As a result, we find Young was not deprived of due process, even though Rebekah's testimony was deemed incompetent and struck from the record.

58. Furthermore, the trial court sufficiently remedied any prejudice suffered from Rebekah's testimony. As this court has previously stated "©urative instructions are presumed to be an effective way to remedy errors that occur during trial." "A jury is presumed to follow instructions given by the trial court."

59. The trial court's curative instruction in this instance was appropriate and plainly instructed the jury not to consider Rebekah's testimony or be influenced by it in any way or for any purpose. Young asserts, however, that Rebekah's testimony was so prejudicial, that the trial court's minimal instruction could not "un-ring" the effect on the jury. Young's position, however, assumes that the limiting instruction was ineffective and that the risk of prejudice was too high for the instruction to negate it. However, we decline to make this assumption. As discussed in more detail below, there was enough circumstellar evidence to prove that Young was K.K.'s abuser. As a result, we overrule Young's second assignment of error

60. Assignment of Error Number 3

61. THE TRIAL COURT ERRED IN FAILING TO STRIKE REBEKAH'S STATEMENTS TO RESPONDERS AND OFFICERS AT THE SCENE.

62. In his third assignment of error, Young argues the trial court erred by admitting and not striking Rebekah's statements made to responders and officers at the scene following the 911 phone call. We find Young's argument to be without merit.

63. Young did not object to the statements at trial and he has therefore waived all but plain error on appeal. Pursuant to Crim.R 52(B), plain error exists where there is an obvious deviation from a legal rule that affected the defendant's substantial rights or influenced the outcome of the proceedings. As this court has stated previously "(n)otice of plain error must be taken with utmost caution, under exceptional circumstances, and only to prevent a manifest miscarriage of justice." An error does not rise to the level of plain error unless, but for the error, the outcome of the trial would have been different,

64. "Hearsay" is a statement, other than one made by the declarant while testifying at the trial or hearing, offered in evidence to prove the truth of the matter asserted." Generally, hearsay testimony is inadmissible unless the testimony falls within one of the recognized exceptions to the hearsay rule.

65. Young does not dispute the admissibility of Rebekah's statements under the aoolicable hearsay rules, but instead argues that her statements should have been stricken regardless. Young claims that the trial court should have stricken Rebekah's statements made to first responders when Rebekah was deemed incompetent to testify at trial. As previously noted, Rebekah initially denied that Young had abused K.K., but there were conflicting stories as to whether Young was alone with K.K. immediately before she became unresponsive. According to Young. "Rebekah's statements to responders and officers impacted the verdict because they established (Young's) presence with (K.K.) when (K.K.) fatal symptoms arose." Those statements then

"helped the jury to infer" that Young alone recklessly abused K.K. and proximately caused her death.

66. However, following a thorough review of the record, we find no error, let alone plain error, to sustain young's argument. Though Rebekah was deemed incompetent at trial, there is no evidence that Rebekah was incompetent when she made the statements to first responders. Furthermore, there was additional evidence tbat Young committed the abusive acts. Detective Romans and EMT Peters both testified that Young told them that he was with the child immediately before the abusive trauma occurred. In addition, there is evidence that Young sent a text message to Rebekah to get their stories straight that K.K. "was laying with both of us in the living on the couch(sic)so they don't try and turn it around on you or me." That evidence, coupled with the photographs of Young's cut and bruised knuckles, is circumstantial evidence that Young abused K.K. and inflicted the fatal blows. Asa result, we overrule Young's third assignment of error.

67. Assignment of Error Number 4

68. THE DEFENDANT'S FELONY MURDER AND PREDICATE CHILD-ENDANGERING CONVICTIONS WERE AGAINST THE MANIFEST WEIGHT OF THE EVIDENCE AND THERE WAS SUFFICIENT EVIDENCE TO PROVE THAT HE RECKLESSLY ABUSED (K.K.) AND PROXIMATELY CAUSED HER DEATH.

69. In his fourth assignment of error, Young argues the verdict is against the manifest weight of the evidence and there was insufficient evidence to sustain a conviction. We disagree.

70. The concepts of sufficiency of the evidence and weight of the evidence are legally distinct. Nonetheless, as this court has observed, a finding that a conviction is supported by

the manifest weight of the evidence is also dispositive of the Issue of sufficiency, "Because sufficiency is required to take a case to the jury, a finding that a conviction is supported by the weight of the evidence must necessarily include a finding of sufficiency,"

71. A manifest weight challenge scrutinizes the predictivity of the greater amount if credible evidence, offered at a trial, to support one side of the issue over another. In assessing whether a conviction is against the manifest weight of the evidence, a reviewing court examines the entire record, weighs the evidence an all-reasonable inference, considers the credibility of the witnesses and determines whether, in resolving conflicts in the evidence, the trier of fact clearly lost its way and created such a manifest miscarriage of justice that the conviction must be reversed and a new trial ordered.

72. It is well-established that both circumstantial and direct evidence have the same probative value. In fact, in some instances, certain facts can be established only by circumstantial evidence. Circumstantial evidence is proof of certain facts and circumstances in a given case, from which the jury may infer other, connected facts, which usually and reasonably follow according to the common experience if mankind. A conviction based on purely circumstantial evidence is no less sound than a conviction based on direct evidence,

73. Pursuant to R.C.2903.02(B) "(n)o person shall cause the death of another as a proximate result of the offender's committing or attempting to commit an offense of violence that is a felony of the first or second degree and that is not a violation of (R.C.) 2903.03 or 2903.04" child endangering is committed when one abuses a child under 18 years of age.

74. Child endangering in violation of R.C. 2919.22(B)(1) is a second-degree felony and is defined as an "offense of violence" and may therefore serve as a predicate offense for felony murder.

75. Young concedes that the state proved that some abusive act proximately caused K.K.'s fatal brain swelling and herniations. Young also concedes that the state proved that his roommate, Rebekah, and himself were present when the abusive acts occurred. However, Young maintains that the state failed to prove that he committed the abusive act in the relevant timeframe.

76. Following a thorough review of the record, we find Young's argument is without merit. In the present case, and as Young concedes, the state proved that K.K. died from an abusive act that caused horrific internal brain injury. Though Young remained steadfast during police interrogation that he had not harmed K.K. and that Rebekah was with him immediately prior to K.K.'s final scream, there is conflicting evidence in the record to rebut his prior statements.

77. The state presented evidence that Young and Rebekah had conflicting stories about who was with K.K. immediately prior to becoming unresponsive. As previously noted, both Detective Romans and EMT Peters testified that Young told them that he was with the child alone while Rebekah was in the back bedroom i.e., Young was alone with the child immediately before the abusive trauma occurred. Furthermore, Young's text message to Rebekah tat e was (j)ust telling them she was laying with "both of us" so that "they don't try and turn it around on you or me." could be considered evidence of deception. While a two-year-old child was unconscious on the floor, Young had the mindset to text Rebekah to get their stories straight about who was with the child and when. These prior statements along with

the pictures of Youngs battered and cracked knuckles could lead a jury to infer that Young was the responsible party.

78. The state's evidence was sufficient to support a guilty finding and the jury's decision was not against the manifest weight of the evidence. Acting as trier of fact, the jury was in the best position to resolve factual questions and evaluate witness credibility. The testimony and evidence introduced at trial supports a finding that Young so abused K.K. as to cause her injuries and ultimate death. As a result, we find Young's fourth and final assignment of error to be meritless, and it is hereby overruled.

79. Judgement affirmed.
S.POWELL, P.J. AND PIPER, J., conR=cur

Bradley Young was convicted of murder and in October of 2016 was sentenced to life without parole for 15 years. My opinion he totally lucked out. Very small sentence for what he did. Bradley appealed his conviction and it was denied.

Rebekah Kenner: Rebekah pleaded guilty to involuntary manslaughter in 2016. Her attorney asked for leniency for Rebekah saying she was a good mother. The Judge sentenced Rebekah to 11 years in prison.

9 781960 546975